Views from the Other Shore

Essays on Herzen, Chekhov, and Bakhtin

AILEEN M. KELLY

Yale University Press   New Haven and London

Grateful acknowledgment is made to the following editors and publishers for permission
to make use of earlier versions of some chapters in this book:
"Herzen and Francis Bacon" was first published in the *Journal of the History of Ideas*
(October 1980) and is reprinted with the permission of the
Johns Hopkins University Press.
" 'Dealing in Pluses': The Thought of Anton Chekhov" is reprinted with the permission of
the *New York Review of Books*. Copyright © 1997. NYREV, Inc.
"Herzen, Schiller, and the Aesthetic Ideal of Man" was first published in *Forschungen zur
osteuropäischen Geschichte* 44 (1990) and is reprinted with the permission of the editor.
"Herzen and Proudhon" is reprinted from *Common Knowledge* 1, no. 2 (1992), with the
permission of Oxford University Press.
The remaining chapters are published here for the first time.

Designed by Sonia L. Scanlon.
Set in Minion type by Rainsford Type, Danbury, Connecticut.
Printed in the United States of America by Vail-Ballou Press, Binghamton, New York.

Library of Congress Cataloging-in-Publication Data
Kelly, Aileen.
Views from the other shore : essays on Herzen, Chekhov, and
Bakhtin / Aileen M. Kelly.
p.   cm.—(Russian literature and thought)
Includes index.
ISBN 0-300-07486-7 (c : alk. paper)
1. Herzen, Aleksandr, 1812–1870.   2. Chekhov, Anton Pavlovich,
1860–1904—Political and social views.   3. Bakhtin, M. M. (Mikhail
Mikhaǐlovich), 1895–1975.   4. Russia—Intellectual life—1801–1917.
I. Title.   II. Series.
DK209.6.H4K45   1999
947'.073'0922—dc21   98-52435
CIP

A catalogue record for this book is available from the British Library.

10 9 8 7 6 5 4 3 2 1

Я одержимый новатор... Одержимых новаторов очень редко понимают.
[I am an obsessed innovator. ... Obsessed innovators are very rarely understood.]

—M. M. Bakhtin

Не ищи решений в этой книге—их нет в ней, их вообще нет у современного человека.
[Do not look for solutions in this book—there are none. In general modern man has no solutions.]

—A. I. Herzen

Странно, что люди боятся свободы.
[It's odd how people fear freedom.]

—A. P. Chekhov

For O.B. again, in the hope that it was worth the effort

Contents

Acknowledgments

I am indebted to the British Academy for the award of a Research Readership from 1992 to 1994 which enabled me to pursue my interest in the "Russian Idea" that is the subject of this book.

Like its predecessor, *Toward Another Shore,* this book owes its existence to the persuasive activity of John Campbell, and to Robert Silvers of the *New York Review of Books,* who encouraged me to write on Chekhov and Bakhtin.

I was privileged to have the comments and the criticism of Sir Isaiah Berlin on earlier versions of the chapters on Herzen in this book. I have tried to develop them in a spirit that he would have appreciated.

Introduction:
Two Russian Ideas

In the last decades of Russian communism many Western observers of the Soviet scene pinned their hopes for the regime's liberalization (and ultimately, its fall) on what one American Sovietologist called "the slow-acting magnet of Western culture."[1] It was widely assumed that the imperative of economic modernization would lead sooner or later to the entrenchment of liberal values and attitudes in Russian government and society.

But this scenario did not allow for the pull of a competing magnet: the Russian Idea. As defined by one of its most assiduous promoters, the philosopher Nikolai Berdiaev, this is the conviction that Russia's native spiritual values and communitarian structures destine it to lead the world in establishing a New Jerusalem: a community bound by fraternal love and shared beliefs. According to Berdiaev this messianic longing permeated the entire Russian intellectual tradition: even Russian communism was a perverted expression of the Russian Idea. "All Russian ideologies," he wrote, "have always been totalitarian, whether theocratic or socialist. Russians are maximalists, and precisely whatever looks like a utopia is for Russians the most realistic."[2]

The intellectual ferment accompanying the dismantling of communism seemed to lend substance to Berdiaev's claim. While Russia's new leaders were proclaiming her "return to Europe," some of the most vocal sections of the intelligentsia seemed bent on emphasizing the incompatibility of Russian spiritual aspirations with Western culture. The militant and isolationist nationalism that had existed as a strong though muted strand of Soviet intellectual life was now unrestrainedly expressed in a gamut of monthly journals, newspapers, and pamphlets ranging from respectable organs which carried the debates of academic philosophers and literary critics to vehicles for vicious anti-Semitic ravings. Alliances were formed between neo-Stalinist communists and religious conservatives, crude xenophobes and sophisticated neonationalists, on the basis of a shared devotion to the Russian Idea. As A. V. Zotov commented in 1997, this is the common slogan of all those who seek to alert the Russian people to the threat from West and East alike: "They are against . . . the Americanization of Russia and its Europeanization, against its Germanization and its 'Judaization,' against Catholicism and Islam, against Western films and Eastern dreams, i.e., against all that is not fundamentally Russian. They want Russian spirituality and the Russian Soul to become a fortress that can withstand all attacks from outside and the destructive work of diversionaries and renegades from within."[3]

At a conference on the current state of Russian philosophy held in Moscow in March 1993 the Polish scholar Andrzej Walicki observed that adherents of the Russian Idea seemed determined to prove what some Russophobic academics in the West had long believed: that the horrors of Stalinism were rooted in the inalienable characteristics of Russian culture and that the country was fated to remain a prisoner of its past. He suggested that if Russians continued to emphasize the uniqueness of their intellectual tradition and its concerns, it would come to be seen in the West as a cultural curiosity of interest mainly to Slavists.[4]

Walicki's warning has a special resonance for those scholars who have long been seeking to persuade Western audiences that the perspectives of Russian thinkers can shed important light on universal moral problems. These critics have focused not on the utopian tendencies of Russian thought but on a minority countertradition opposed to all forms of political and religious messianism.[5] Thinkers in this category can be said to represent an alternative Russian Idea, equally rooted in Russian experience but rejecting eschatological thought on humanist grounds; open to all cultures and all currents of thought that can contribute to the greatest possible fulfillment of human beings in the here and now. In the Soviet period this strand of thought was almost ignored; for ideological reasons both Soviet and Western commentators chose to focus on the maximalist tendencies that had led to the communist utopia. The same preference now evident in attempts to reclaim the heri-, tage of Russian thought can result only in the impoverishment of both Russian and Western culture.

The chapters in this book on Herzen, Chekhov, and Bakhtin are intended not merely to demonstrate that Russia and the West can learn from each other's cultures, but also to illustrate the less obvious fact that the alternative Russian Idea can make a significant contribution to current discussions in Europe and North America on the problem of defining freedom and morality in a postfoundationalist culture. Herzen, Chekhov, and Bakhtin are at one and the same time towering figures on a world scale and representatives of the Russian countertradition whose insights into the delusions of dogmatic systems were shaped by contact and conflict with the dominant utopian strand of Russian thought. This relationship was complex. Both Herzen's and Bakhtin's thought has often been identified with aspects of the dominant tradition, while Chekhov's trenchant rejection of it has led to his being labeled as un-Russian. It will therefore be useful to preface these chapters on their thought with a survey of the history of the Russian Idea.

The origins of the eschatological quest that is so distinctive a feature of Russian thought can be traced back to the eleventh century, when the schism between the Eastern and Western churches detached Russia (which had received Christianity from Byzantium) from the culture of Western Christendom. The Mongol conquest of 1241 made its isolation complete. It knew nothing of the Renaissance, the Reformation, and the first flowering of secular thought in the West; during two centuries of Mongol rule the Orthodox Church was the single unifying factor sustaining the people's sense of nationhood. With the defeat of the Mongols and the fall of the Orthodox Byzantine Empire the national consciousness acquired a messianic component: Ivan IV, the ruler of Moscow, crowned as the first tsar of a unified Russian state, adopted the doctrine propounded by religious writers that Moscow, successor to Byzantium as protector of the true Christian faith, was the Third Rome—and the last. "There will be no fourth," ran the prophecy.

It has been claimed that the distinctive asceticism and theocratic utopianism of much nineteenth- and twentieth-century Russian thought derives from a yearning for the future transfiguration of the world that is central to Orthodox spirituality. Peter the Great's opening of Russia to the West began the diffusion of Western thought among the educated layers of society, but until Catherine II's flirtation with the ideas of the French Enlightenment, philosophical activity remained tied to the concerns of the theological academies (Moscow University, Russia's first, was founded only in 1755). By the eighteenth century, however, the Russian church's identification with the interests of the autocracy had alienated those members of the elite who were most critical of the status quo and most open to new ideas from the West. Equipped with the French Enlightenment's ideal of a rational and just society, they began to see themselves as the cultural and moral leaders of their backward country, a view reinforced by the persecution of advanced ideas that reached its height in the second quarter of the nineteenth century under tsar Nicholas I. Hence the passionate social commitment of most Russian thinkers, who have focused their attention on ethics, social theory, and the philosophy of history. (Academic philosophy was a latecomer on the Russian scene, and those who devoted themselves to questions of ontology and epistemology, such as the neo-Kantians at the end of the nineteenth century, were widely condemned for their failure to address the pressing social problems of their time.)

Acutely conscious of their country's humiliating backwardness with regard to her European neighbors and of the terrible injustice of serfdom, the dissident intelligentsia who emerged as a force in the 1840s were obsessed with solving the riddle of their place in the general movement of humanity. The tools for their investigation were the organicist visions of German idealism—a factor of crucial importance to the subsequent development of the Russian Idea. These doctrines taught the intelligentsia to see their rootlessness and frustration as part of a universal process of suffering and struggle whereby history was moving toward a transcendent goal: the overcoming of all conflict and division through the fusion of the real with the ideal. By providing unitary explanations of human history that resolved their moral and philosophical dilemmas, idealism offered alienated Russian intellectuals a foretaste of the millenarian ideal of integral wholeness. Their memoirs and letters reveal the importance they attached to the possession of an integral worldview (*tselnoe mirovozzrenie*), which allowed them to identify with higher forces that bestowed a sublime meaning and purpose on their isolated, finite lives. Some (the early Westernizers) found fulfillment in the belief that as proponents of liberal ideals they were participating in the universal march toward rational enlightenment as expounded in Hegel's system. The more rebelliously inclined were drawn to the revolutionary version of this doctrine, which, as preached by the Left Hegelians and, subsequently, Marx, would shape the Russian radical movement in its successive incarnations.

A nationalist countereschatology—the Russian Idea in its undiluted form—was developed in the 1840s by the Slavophiles, whose model of personal wholeness was inspired by a mixture of influences, including Friedrich Schelling's mystical idealism, Orthodox spirituality, and the romantic cult of national distinctiveness. They argued that an emphasis on individual autonomy had led to the spiritual bankruptcy of Western societies, which consisted of isolated individuals held together by external formalized bonds; in contrast, the underlying principle of Russian society, embodied in the peasant commune, was *sobornost*—the word launched by Aleksei Khomiakov to denote what he called the "free unity," or fellowship of believers united by faith in a transcendent truth and by unanimous adherence to a body of moral truths. As such, the commune was the seed of a universal Christian society toward which the Slavophiles hoped that Russia would lead the world.

Sobornost was both history's goal and the means to the goal. The Slavophiles argued that analytical reasoning could penetrate no further than the external relations of things: God's plan for the world was discoverable only through the efforts of the collective religious consciousness (*sobornost soznaniia*), whose insights were lodged in the customs and traditions of communities—family, commune, church, and nation. The Slavophile utopia had no place for dissenting individuals and no safeguards against the abuse of power; although they recognized that the authoritarianism of the existing Russian church and state was not consonant with their ideal of free unity, they believed that legal guarantees and formal brakes on power were symptoms of societies that had lost their spiritual cohesion. Their thought was expressed in foggy generalities which enabled them to avoid confronting this and other awkward issues, such as the contradiction between their professed universalism and their belief that a chosen people had the right to impose its principles on others.

The next generation of Russian nationalists was more clear-sighted about the contradictions between the goals of freedom and unity and opted for unity. In the 1870s ambivalent universalism was succeeded by aggressive nationalism and outright support for autocracy in the writings of the pan-Slavist Nikolai Danilevsky, who reinterpreted Russia's historical mission in biological terms as the creation of a new kind of civilization dominated by the Slavic "historico-cultural type." To attain this goal, Russia must liberate and unite her fellow Slavs by conquering Constantinople and establishing it as the capital of a new Slavic Empire under Russian leadership. Danilevsky considered the Slavophiles' ideal of a humanity united in universal love realizable only in the world to come; in this world, the realities of evolutionary struggle in competition with the West demanded "patriotic fanaticism" in the pursuit of an aggressive policy of imperial expansion.[6] Internally, in order to implement her Idea, Russia must become a monolithic state in which all particular interests were subordinated to the common good (identified with Russia's political and economic pre-eminence).

Pan-Slavist ideas fueled the paranoid nationalism of the later Dostoevsky and the ugly xenophobic chauvinism that made its appearance in the early 1900s, when nationalists began to argue that in order to enlighten the world in the future Russia must pursue a policy of rigid isolationism in the present, to cleanse itself of the corrupting Western influences that were the source of all the country's misfortunes. Such ideas led some nationalist intellectuals to justify the activities of the Black Hundreds, the extreme Right group whose thugs were responsible for the first pogroms in modern Europe.

That the Russian Idea maintained a modicum of respectability at that period was largely on account of the philosophy of Vladimir Solovyov, whose ideal of integral wholeness, or "All-Unity" (*vsetselostnost*), elaborated in the last quarter of the nineteenth century, would be a dominant influence on Russian thought in the next. He held that the ultimate purpose of the universe was the synthesis of the temporal with the divine. The path to this goal was the reintegration of knowledge. The pluralism of philosophical systems and the wars between science, religion, and philosophy were the result of the dissolution of the psyche's primitive spiritual unity, a spiritual crisis especially evident in the West, where the preeminence of rationalism had led to an extreme fragmentation of knowledge and of the inner life of individuals. The "integral knowledge" of the future would be the foundation of an "integral society," a free community founded on love (Solovyov's version of the Slavophiles' sobornost). This would be a theocracy, which would come about through a reconciliation of East and West and a unification of the Christian churches. Solovyov rejected all forms of nationalist exclusivism, deploring the degeneration of the Slavophile movement into "tooth-gnashing obscurantism";[7] but his universalism had a curious twist: he believed that the Russian people had a unique ability for empathizing with foreign cultures and on that ground were destined for a messianic role in the redemption of Europe. The Russian Empire would become the Third Rome, reconciling the principles of spiritual and temporal power that had inspired the first two.

Solovyov's ideal of a Russian theocracy as a model for Western Europe was subsequently taken up by many Russian philosophers as an answer to the utopias of the left. In the famous *Signposts* (*Vekhi*) symposium of 1909, which attacked the radicals' revolutionary mystique, the former Marxist and future priest Sergei Bulgakov called on intellectuals to reject the rationalist and materialist culture spawned by the "so-called 'Enlightenment'" and return to the Orthodox Church, under whose guidance they would come to perceive Russia's spiritual mission to the world. In the same volume Berdiaev, who in the 1920s would describe the new fascist corporative state as the "sole creative force in contemporary Europe", argued the need for a national religious philosophy which would satisfy the Russian people's yearning for an "organic union" of theory and practice, knowledge and faith.[8]

Berdiaev contended that "the thirst for an integral world view that would fuse theory with life" was one of the few positive qualities of the radical intelligentsia's outlook. In common with many other Russian religious thinkers, he and Bulgakov believed that the Russian Left was driven by an eschatological dream of the City of God on earth, a dream based on what Bulgakov called "an unconscious religious aversion to . . . 'the kingdom of this world' with its placid self-satisfaction."[9] Many Western commentators have pointed to the strength of eschatological faith in the Russian revolutionary tradition. Russian Marxists contrasted their allegedly scientific approach to social processes with the romantic utopianism of earlier Russian socialists, but their faith in the paradise that would be delivered by historical necessity had much less in common with the increasingly pragmatic Marxist parties of the West than with the visionary Marx of the early Paris manuscripts, who held communism to be "the true solution of the conflict between existence and essence, between objectification and self-affirmation, between freedom and necessity, between the individual and species. It is the solution of the riddle of history and knows itself to be this solution." It has been argued that Russian Bolshevism conforms to the standard definition of a millenarian movement: led by a charismatic figure, its adherents envisaged the coming of a heaven on earth via the radical reversal of the existing order.[10]

Since the early nineteenth century the main impetus of both religious and radical thought in Russia has been toward the future, as thinkers strained to discern the features of the "new human being" (a term common in radical parlance from the 1860s, with the addition of the adjective "Soviet" after 1917); the type who would one day be free from the cognitive and moral defects that had hitherto prevented the human race from realizing its potential. The nature of these flaws and the specifications of regenerated humanity were the subject of bitter disputes between rival movements. Even on the Left, models of the new human type varied widely, from the narrow rationalist who was the ideal of the radicals of the 1860s, to Bakunin's vision of the eternal rebel who would embody the spontaneous spirit of freedom in defiance of all established authorities and orders. In the early 1900s a group of Bolshevik philosophers inspired by Nietzsche's aesthetic immoralism proposed a collectivist version of the Nietzschean Superman as the ideal of socialism.[11] All these disparate models shared one common trait: their strength would be grounded in an integral worldview which would preclude hesitation and doubt, allowing them to devote their entire being—reason, emotions, and will—unreservedly to the pursuit of the ideal.

Some religious maximalists achieved an ideological accommodation with the 1917 Revolution by means of apocalyptic theories which first came into vogue in literary and philosophical circles as ways of resolving intractable political and moral dilemmas in the crisis-ridden years leading to the revolution of 1905. That event had spawned many mystical theories presenting it as the prelude to a final universal reconciliation of the flesh and the spirit, Christ and Dionysus; similarly after 1917, members of the émigré "Eurasian" movement found consolation in apocalyptic fantasies of a new light from the East shining on the ruins of European culture. Berdiaev began to argue that the Revolution had played a redeeming role: it was the Russian people's sublime mission to live through a terrible process of expiation and purification in order to prepare the world for a new era of the spiritual transfiguration of earthly existence.[12] His writings were secretly circulated in Russia, where his eschatological yearning for the end of history influenced the continuing development of the Russian Idea in the Soviet underground.

In the last years of the communist system, the émigré Russian historian Alexander Yanov sought to alert the West to the vitality

and destructive potential of the Russian Idea as the theoretical nu-
cleus of an ideology that united members of the dissident right with
neo-Stalinist elements in the Soviet establishment.[13] The revival of
nationalist messianism in the Soviet Union in the 1960s was led
both by dissident intellectuals who believed that Russian Marxism
and Western capitalism were equally spiritually bankrupt, and by
members of the Soviet establishment who held that the official ideology had lost its power to unite and mobilize the Russian nation.
Samizdat manifestos and establishment magazines such as *Molodaia
gvardiia* (The young guard) and *Ogonyok* (The spark) began to call
for a national rebirth, based on a return to Russian roots. The
Orthodox religion enjoyed a revival among the intelligentsia; the
underground group *VSKhSON* (the All-Russian Social Christian
Union for the Liberation of the People), whose main influence was
Berdiaev, preached a theocratic Russian path, in opposition both
to Marxist communism and Western capitalism. In the early 1970s
the idea of Russia's universal mission was revived by groups like
Veche (The assembly) in response to the perceived threat from
China: it was Russia's role, they argued, to succeed the spiritually
exhausted West in defending Aryan civilization against the barbarism of black and yellow races. Once again, the country's disasters
were blamed on the decadent values of Western culture and its
agents in Russia. The villains were Zionism, Americanization, the
bourgeois spirit of Western democracy, and cosmopolitanism—an
accusation leveled by the establishment Right against liberalizing
elements in the Soviet hierarchy. The new fashion for this sinister
word was coupled with an attempt to rehabilitate Stalin, whose
campaigns against cosmopolitan "wreckers" were now praised for
protecting the people from spiritual corruption from the West. As
Yanov points out, these intelligentsia movements sometimes fused
with a mass mood of chauvinism, isolationism, and a nostalgic
yearning for the iron hand of dictatorship, all fed by a central tenet
of the Russian Idea: that Russia would regain a lost paradise once
it cast off the yoke of foreign influences. From 1974 this longing
for a strong hand received powerful moral support from the newly
exiled Aleksandr Solzhenitsyn, commonly regarded as the con-

science of his people, who commented from abroad with relentless repetition on the political crises and spiritual confusion of Western democracies that had made an idol of political freedom and the multiparty system.

Those few Western Sovietologists who remarked on the growth of messianic nationalism in the Soviet period tended to welcome it as a force hostile to communism. This was a view common among liberals, as attested by the fawning reception given to Solzhenitsyn after his expulsion from Russia. Such people were taken by surprise when the breakup of the Soviet Union was followed by a wave of anti-Westernism, fueled in part by the Russian Idea as elaborated by philosophers like Solovyov, Berdiaev, and Bulgakov, whose works had been banned until the beginning of glasnost and thence-forward were issued in multiple and eagerly sought after editions. As Walicki noted at the conference in 1993 entitled "Russian Philosophy in Russia Today," the tables have been well and truly turned. At that conference not one paper on the philosophical heritage of nonreligious tendencies in Russian thought was presented. In response to the argument that secular Russian thinkers had received more than their share of attention in the Soviet period, Walicki pointed out that that tradition had been ideologically falsified by the Soviet policy of reinterpreting some thinkers as precursors of Marxism and ignoring others who could not be packaged in that way. Any reevaluation of Russian thought that aimed to deepen the nation's understanding of its culture, its relation to Western culture, and the causes of the recent national catastrophe could not afford to be similarly selective in its methods.[14]

Any such reassessment will have to give due attention to the alternative Russian Idea. Its history will be rather more difficult to track than that of Russian messianism. The countertradition founded no schools of thought and had no leaders, little cohesion, and a floating membership—Tolstoy, Dostoevsky, and the ideologists of radical populism, for instance, all launched devastating attacks on contemporary manifestations of the utopian mentality while continuing to write their own prescriptions for the attainment of a final state of universal harmony. But a small minority of thinkers sought to develop a consistent critique of teleological reasoning about history and society, perceiving their own revolt against the tyranny of dogma to be part of a much more general questioning of the view of the world as an ordered and purposive system—a vision that (in a variety of religious and rationalist forms) had shaped European thinking. Some of these Russians, for example, the liberal Pyotr Struve, were considered by their nationalist opponents to have been infected with the godlessness of Western post-Nietzschean thought. But while their boldness was less self-advertising than Nietzsche's, they often probed more deeply than he had done in their questioning of values and assumptions that had nourished two thousand years of European culture.[15]

The three subjects of the present book belong in this category. Herzen was not only a pioneer in the assault on the philosophies of rational progress which have dominated the nineteenth and much of the twentieth centuries; he also exposed the faintheartedness of pessimistic antirationalism as preached by Arthur Schopenhauer (and subsequently developed by Nietzsche).[16] It has been argued that Chekhov's unflinching portrayal of the realities of human existence in an unprogrammed world was so far ahead of its time that we are only now coming to comprehend its full subversiveness, while scholars in both Russia and the West are currently pointing to the significance of Bakhtin's approach to ethics as a third way between the prescriptivism of traditional ethical systems and the boundless relativism of much postmodern theory.

There is no need to seek the source of these prescient insights in the special virtues of the Russian national character. A more prosaic reason is closer to hand: the ability of these three men to make maximum creative use of the perspectives afforded by their marginal position in their society and on the boundaries of two cultures. All three were direct victims of the persecution that focused the minds of Russian intellectuals on the problem of freedom and on practical ethics. Herzen suffered prison followed by years of exile as punishment for harboring advanced opinions; he was later forced to emigrate in order to be able to express himself freely.

Chekhov, the grandson of serfs, was brought up in a milieu un-
acquainted with the notion of human dignity. Bakhtin's philosophical investigations led to arrest and exile by the new communist
state. But none of the three succumbed to the temptation of seeking
to escape from their isolation and frustrations into compensating
fantasies of an idealized nationhood or a socialist paradise. They
were all distinguished by a sober sense of reality which was rooted
in a culture of exceptional richness and depth. Herzen and Bakhtin
were accomplished linguists with an encyclopaedic knowledge of
European history, philosophy, and literature. The adolescent Chekhov educated himself through omnivorous reading in his town
library. Theirs was no undiscriminating Westernism, however. Each
had a profound and sympathetic understanding of his native culture: Herzen campaigned passionately to attract the attention of
European social theorists to the history and democratic potential
of the Russian peasant commune; Chekhov movingly portrayed the
inner lives of Russians from every social stratum; Bakhtin attained
his belated international celebrity through his work on the most
Russian of writers, Dostoevsky.

In their approach to the West all three availed themselves of what
Bakhtin would describe as the unique privileges of cultural "outsideness"—the ability of those situated outside a given culture to
uncover hidden meanings and potentials in it by exploiting their
external perspective, thereby enriching both the foreign culture and
their own. The dominant tradition of Russian thought tended to
approach Western ideas in a utilitarian spirit, as sources of support
for prior beliefs and systems. Herzen, Chekhov, and Bakhtin measured theories and ideals by their accumulated understanding of
what human experience in the most diverse situations and contexts
had shown to be possible and desirable. This gave their reflections
on the problem of freedom a distinctive contextual thickness even
when they were conducted with a very broad historical sweep, as
when Herzen explores the historical paths taken by the search of
the human mind to free itself from oppressive authorities and systems, or when Bakhtin traces the same phenomenon in literature
through the history of the novel form. The way in which our power

to maneuver in the world is circumscribed by chance and time was made palpable and visible by Chekhov in plays which revolutionized world theater.

From their perspective as outsiders who were victims of rigid systems one strand of Western thought stood out as being especially significant: those discoveries in the biological and physical sciences that from the early nineteenth century had been progressively chipping away at traditional views of processes in nature and history as linear movements toward predetermined goals, whether religious or rational. Echoing Freud, Stephen Jay Gould has observed that "our relationship with science must be paradoxical because we are forced to pay an almost intolerable price for each major gain in knowledge and power—the psychological cost of progressive dethronement from the center of things, and increasing marginality in an uncaring universe."[17] The hostile reaction to the publication of Darwin's *Origin of Species* in 1859 was compounded of anger, fear, and a sense of disorientation; but Herzen (who observed the furor in London) greeted the Darwinian revolution as a momentous step in the dismantling of the teleological systems that misrepresent the world and humans' place in it. Chekhov and Bakhtin both drew on the perspectivism of the biological and physical sciences in their battle with the orthodoxies of their time. All three called attention to the contrast between the increasing acceptance of the scientific evidence of the unpredictability of processes in nature and the continued reluctance of enlightened individuals to extend these insights to the study of human societies. They saw the doctrinaire determinism of Left and Right as evidence of a fundamental inconsistency in the human race's attitude to the world which was stunting its creativity and its moral growth.

Herzen, the chief subject of this book, probed more deeply than any other Russian thinker the subterfuges adopted by the human consciousness to evade the unwelcome truth of our precarious situation in unrepeatable space and time. A decade before Darwin published his treatise (and two before Nietzsche announced the death of God), he expressed the belief that humanity was moving toward "another shore," away from its traditional reliance on ab-

solutes and final truths, universal norms and fixed systems of rewards and punishments, toward a sober realism that would ac-
knowledge the impermanence of all ideals and goals, the absence
of all final certainties, and the responsibility of individuals to shape
their own selves as best they could with the contingent resources
of their time and place.[18] In the foreseeable future most would be
held back on the old shore by the fear of freedom, of setting sail
without compass or firm directions, and by a sentimental attachment to a familiar landscape with fixed and dependable coordi-
nates. Herzen points out that the few who had dared to describe
the view from the other shore had been misunderstood, when not
wholly ignored. This had been the fate of Francis Bacon's destruction of idols, Schiller's and John Stuart Mill's assault on the universalist assumptions of rationalist ethical systems, Proudhon's rejection of the socialist ideal of a perfected humanity; and finally,
Darwin's theories, which, Herzen observed, clerics and scientists
alike were busily attempting to reconcile with providentialist or
rationalist views of progress.

We shall see how Herzen's reflections on all these thinkers
helped shape his own original and inspiring view of human freedom in a world dominated by chance. But his understanding of all
five is also of considerable intrinsic interest. Focusing on their role
as intellectual liberators who were attempting to articulate new ways
of talking about the world and the human being, he makes judgments on them that are still novel and sometimes contentious, but
more faithful to how they saw their work than are many of the
standard commentaries. His insights into their significance are also
closely relevant to current debates about how ethics can be
grounded in a postfoundationalist era. Like Herzen himself, the
thinkers whom he admired were neither ethical absolutists nor relativists. Those who fear that rejection of prescriptive systems must
ultimately plunge our culture into a cynical nihilism could be re-
assured by Herzen's reminder that a rich tradition in Western
thought has already mapped out a coherent alternative to these two
extremes. Herzen believed that as cultural outsiders eager to benefit
from the most advanced thinking of the West without sharing its

filial devotion to hallowed traditions, the Russian intelligentsia were particularly well equipped to make the final transition to the other shore and proclaim the principles of the new sobriety to the world. This is the Russian Idea as first preached by Herzen. But he underestimated the drawing power of the alternative version, which satisfied the perennial human thirst for certainties. Herzen's Idea offered none: it was not an easy option. "Outside us everything changes, everything vacillates," he wrote. "We are standing on the edge of a precipice and we see it crumbling. Twilight descends and no guiding star appears in the sky. We shall find no haven but in ourselves":[19] this is the terrifying but liberating prospect offered by Herzen, Chekhov, and Bakhtin.

Herzen and Francis Bacon

C H A P T E R   O N E

Our road does not lie on a level, but ascends and descends; first ascending to axioms, then descending to works.
—Francis Bacon, *Novum Organum*

Real truth must reflect the influence of events, while remaining true to itself; otherwise it will be not *living* but eternal truth, which has retreated from the world's troubles into the deathly calm of sacred stagnation.
—A. I. Herzen, *Byloe i dumy*

Aleksandr Herzen's thought eludes all attempts at categorization. In the West he has been commonly labeled a utopian thinker, a product of the romantic age who went on to found a Russian offshoot of French utopian socialism. But nearly a century after his death Isaiah Berlin drew attention to the fact that he had been the author of astonishingly farsighted and profound critiques of utopian thought. He pointed to the vividness with which Herzen's writings convey the "inner feel" of political and social predicaments—a quality that Berlin attributed to a unique sense of reality, a grasp of the critical moral and political issues of his time that is far more concrete and specific than that of the philosophers who shaped social and political theory in Herzen's century.[1]

Although Berlin's interpretation is solidly anchored in Herzen's thought, the contrary image of Herzen continues to affect scholars' views of his work. While the influence of German romanticism and idealism on his early thought has been exhaustively examined, the intellectual sources of his realism remain largely unexplored. He is recognized as one of the foremost interpreters of Hegel in Russian thought, but little attention has been given to the fact that among Russian Hegelians he struck a dissonant note from the first, approaching Hegelian historicism, as he did all other "-isms," from the critical perspective of a different source of criteria and values: experimental science. Herzen's abiding passion for the natural sciences was to shape his view of historical method. It would lead him to make analogies between natural and historical processes that subverted teleological thinking in both domains, anticipating Darwin's theories in their emphasis on the influence of chance and unpredictable events on the course of nature, history, and human lives.

Although Herzen's view of liberty was much indebted to the German Left Hegelians (especially Ludwig Feuerbach's critique of religious self-alienation), it has a distinctive character. His defense of the autonomy of individuals against encroachments by all collective entities and his desacralization of such concepts as humanity and the state have been compared to Max Stirner's apotheosis of egoism in *The Ego and Its Own;* but Herzen was writing on this theme two years before the appearance of Stirner's book in 1845, and while Stirner, like Nietzsche, looked forward to the emergence of sovereign individuals, bound by no laws and absolute masters of their world, Herzen addressed the problem of freedom within the constraints of experienced historical reality.[2] The eschatology of the Left Hegelians and Karl Marx was alien to him. His resistance to the charms of utopian thought dates back to a powerful vaccine administered in his youth: the inductive method of Francis Bacon.

An abundance of references in Herzen's writings testifies to his interest in Bacon, but (perhaps because the majority of these occur in Herzen's commentaries on Hegel's philosophy) most of his biographers have bypassed them to focus instead on the influence of idealism on his thought.[3] But we shall see that Herzen used Bacon's ideas to support a critique of idealist positions. His letters and diaries reveal the intense intellectual excitement he experienced in reading Bacon along with his study of Hegel and throw doubt on the accepted view that gives Left Hegelianism the full honors for what has been called Herzen's "turn to reality"—his abandonment of idealist fantasies in order to address the political and social issues of his time.[4] By exploring Herzen's affinities with the great Renaissance philosopher of science I hope better to define the sense of reality that was his unique contribution to political theory.

All Bacon's writings were inspired by an eminently practical concern: to bring about a revolution in humanity's approach to knowledge that would lead to its dominion over nature and the improvement of all aspects of life on earth. In his *Novum Organum,* part of a great, uncompleted project to reform all knowledge, he attributes the stagnation of learning in his age to idols—tendencies of the human mind that give rise to false representations of the external world, which he divides into four categories. "Idols of the Tribe" are errors common to the human race, arising from the intellect's tendency to suppose more order and regularity in the world than exists in reality. "Idols of the Cave" are the personal preferences and predispositions that color our interpretations of new phenomena. "Idols of the Marketplace" are prejudices and superstitions reinforced by the language of everyday discourse. "Idols of the Theater" are the fictions enshrined in scientific and philosophical systems, which Bacon likens to stage plays, "representing worlds of their own creation after an unreal and scenic fashion." He urged that errors and distortions of reality be eliminated through experimental methods in which reason is allied with sense experience. Through his inductive method, based on close observation of the physical world, he hoped to unite two approaches to knowledge, each insufficient by itself; to establish a "true and lawful marriage between the empirical and the rational faculty, the unkind and ill-starred divorce and separation of which has thrown into confusion all the affairs of the human family."[5] In the history of science his iconoclastic method must share credit with Descartes' systematic doubt, but in his treatment of the causes of human error he was far ahead of his time.[6] When, two centuries after it appeared, his *Novum Organum* came into Herzen's hands, it could still produce the shock of novelty.

Born in 1812, the illegitimate but pampered son of a rich and cultivated nobleman, Herzen was typical of the intellectual elite of his generation in passing from an adolescent diet of romantic literature heavily emphasizing the poetry and dramas of Schiller to the idealism of Schelling, which gave the faculties so much prized by the romantics—feeling, imagination, intuition—primary importance as instruments in the uncovering of the secrets of the universe. He adopted Schelling's organic vision of the universe as a process of evolutionary becoming, a progression from unconscious to conscious forms at whose summit is humanity, through whose collective mind the absolute (the common ground of all being) finds its highest expression.

For Herzen's generation idealism filled a need that was at least as much emotional as intellectual. In the period of extreme reaction after the failure of the Decembrist revolt of 1825, which had sought to introduce into Russia a constitutional regime on a Western model, the most talented and sensitive members of the cultured elite became acutely conscious of the gulf separating them from the brutal regime on the one hand and from the backward masses on the other. Denied an outlet for their energies in political or social action, these alienated intellectuals focused their attention on their inner world and found in contemporary German philosophy a means of sublimating their need for a sense of dignity and purpose. The harsh facts of Russian reality could be seen as mere epiphenomena; true reality, they believed, was to be found in the inner world of the individual, the reflection of absolute mind. By means of contemplation and self-perfection one could reach an understanding of the transcendent meaning of the historical process and of one's own existence as a means to the realization of the purposes of the absolute in the world.

But although Herzen shared his contemporaries' absorption with the inner self, finding in idealism a refuge from the indignities of life under a despotic regime, he was from the first less indifferent to external reality than most in the Moscow intellectual circles of the 1830s. He relates in his memoirs how at the age of sixteen, in emulation of the Decembrists, he and his cousin Nikolai Ogaryov

took an oath to combat the despotism of tsar Nicholas I. Abstract
and romantic though his ideal of freedom then was (a conception
of wholeness or inner harmony derived from Schiller's aesthetic
ideal of the "beautiful soul"), it nevertheless led him to look to
philosophy for an indication of how such harmony might be attained in the individual's relations with the external world, and this
he could not find in Schelling. As he wrote to Ogaryov in 1833, for
all its impressive formal coherence, idealism was defective "on the
level of *application*," as illustrated by the fact that Schelling had
found refuge in a mystical Catholicism and Hegel had defended
despotism: Johann Fichte, though a lesser philosopher, had shown
more understanding of the "dignity of man." It was necessary,
therefore, to look beyond idealism for a new method, an approach
to reality that would avoid these contradictions.[7]

Herzen had already found a basis for that method in the natural
sciences. In 1829, at the age of seventeen, he was enrolled as a
student in the Faculty of Natural Sciences at Moscow University.
His choice of faculty was unusual for a budding leader of Russia's
intellectual elite in the romantic era. Most of the other luminaries
of his generation were products of the Faculty of Philology and
History. But before he entered the university, Herzen had developed a keen interest in the natural sciences under the influence of
a cousin known in the family as the Chemist, who had a laboratory
in his house. He had heated disputes with the Chemist, a convinced
materialist and an experimentalist who regarded all philosophy as
nonsense, but years later he acknowledged him to have been "right
in three quarters of everything I had objected to": "Without the
natural sciences there is no salvation for modern man. Without
that wholesome nourishment, without that strict training of the
mind by facts, without that closeness to the life surrounding us,
without humility before its independence, the monastic cell remains
hidden somewhere in the soul, and in it the drop of mysticism
which can flood the whole understanding with its dark waters."[8]
The training of the mind that would wean Herzen from the se-
ductions of idealist fantasies was a self-administered process which
began at the university. Although at that time Schelling's idealism

permeated all teaching in the sciences as well as in literature, aesthetics, and history, the range of Herzen's reading ensured that his approach to science was dominated by no single perspective. His university essays reveal both a thorough acquaintance with the history of the natural sciences and a familiarity with all the important scientific literature of his time, in particular the theories of Erasmus Darwin, grandfather and predecessor of Charles, and Georges Cuvier's defense of the immutability of species against the evolutionism of Geoffroy Saint-Hilaire, the anatomist Lorenz Oken, and the botanist Augustin de Candolle. Herzen had no difficulty in reconciling the new evolutionist theories with his Schellingian approach to the world as biological becoming, but Bacon's method sowed in him the first seeds of doubt about the validity of the idealist vision of the world.

Schelling's *Naturphilosophie*, expounded in Herzen's faculty by the celebrated Professor M. G. Pavlov, taught that as nature is a spiritual whole, the natural sciences are the cornerstone of all knowledge, but that the rationalist methods of the eighteenth-century materialists are inapplicable in this field—the cosmic organism is not governed by mechanical laws discoverable through analysis and dissection: its vital essence can be grasped only through intuition and imagination. In an essay of 1832 Herzen echoes this doctrine in a typical idealist tirade against the one-sidedness of materialism, which leads to "precise knowledge of the parts and a total ignorance of the whole," reducing nature to a "cold corpse": "The slogan of analysis is dissection, parts, but the soul, life, is to be found in the whole organism." But he follows this attack on materialism by pointing out that idealism is no less one-sided in its rejection of empirical methods in the investigation of reality. It is concerned only with the noumenal, but nature is the world of phenomena: thus Fichte "failed to perceive nature beyond his ego."

In attempting to interpret the self and the world, humanity had historically alternated between two approaches: the analytical and the synthetic, represented in the modern age by materialism and idealism, respectively. The destructive criticism of the eighteenth-century materialists had generated a new image of the human being, embodied in the principles of the French Revolution, but their determination to make reality conform to theory had led to the terrorism of 1793. Idealists, too, had no compunction in forcing the facts to fit a brilliant hypothesis: they "prefer to do violence to [nature] rather than to their own concepts." Synthetic and analytical systems alike had hitherto failed to provide adequate explanations of the world because of the incompleteness of their methods, based on a false division between "idea and form, the inner and the outer, spirit and body." These principles, indissolubly bound in the real world, had been artificially separated by the intellect: hence the tendency of seekers after truth to "drown in the ideal or be swallowed up in the real." In modern philosophy, Herzen explains, these two extremes are embodied in traditions rooted, respectively, in Descartes' speculative method and Bacon's empiricism, which many of Bacon's followers had transformed into a crude materialism. But Herzen stresses that this distortion of Bacon's ideas did not detract from the enormous importance of his discovery that neither an analytical nor a synthesizing approach to knowledge was complete in itself—they were "two moments of a *unitary* act of cognition." To comprehend both the object and the concepts that it represents, one must link "the rational method with the empirical." Bacon's insight, Herzen observed, had been a significant step toward the goal of all contemporary thought. In interpreting its world, humanity had passed back and forth between idealist and materialist extremes, often "flooding its path with blood" as a consequence; until at last, wearied by the inadequacies of all theories that excluded some dimension of experienced reality, it had come to demand that the warring principles of spirit and matter be brought into harmony.[9]

"Of course, this will not lead to the end of intellectual activity," Herzen wrote, "for the very process of uniting the two principles is surely an endless task?"[10] The harmony to which Herzen looked forward was not static but dynamic: a state of being in which, no longer constricted by one-sided systems and theories, people would be able to fulfill their intellectual, emotional, and aesthetic potential in their own way. In 1833 he found in the doctrines of the Saint-

Simonians a theory of history that buttressed these radical hopes: they taught that the potential of human nature, expressed only imperfectly in the pagan and Christian epochs of civilization, would be fully realized in a future organic age, when the principles of domination and subjection in social relations would be replaced by free association in accordance with an ethic that would represent the fulfillment of the Christian message. In a letter to Ogaryov, Herzen suggests that this regeneration will be attained through a synthesis of mystical and sensual approaches to knowledge—the first historically represented by Catholicism, the second by the empirical tradition in philosophy.[11]

Although couched in the visionary language of the French utopian socialists, Herzen's reflections on the development of thought were in advance of their time. Feuerbach would define his opposition to Hegel's philosophy of religion as follows: "Hegel opposes the finite to the infinite, the speculative to the empirical, whereas I ... find the infinite in the finite and the speculative in the empirical."[12] This passage was written in 1841, a decade after Herzen, inspired by Bacon's method, launched his attack on dualistic systems that divided all being into warring principles—matter and spirit, the real and the ideal.

In 1834 Herzen was arrested with others of his circle on suspicion of harboring seditious opinions; after a spell in prison he was exiled for five years, most of which he spent in a town close to the border of Siberia. In the shock of isolation he found comfort in the religious mysticism he had condemned in Schelling. But toward the end of his exile he resumed his attacks on idealist approaches to reality, writing to Ogaryov that it was time to dispense with "mystical fantasies" and to combine the study of science and philosophy with practical activity.[13] On returning to Moscow in 1839, he discovered that his former circle had embraced a conservative version of Hegel's doctrines, stressing the rationality and inevitability of existing reality: he found their philosophical jargon as irritatingly abstract and scholastic as the religious nationalism of the emerging Slavophile movement. In 1842 during a second, short spell of exile he was sent Feuerbach's *The Essence of Christianity*, published the previous year, and "leapt up with joy"[14] on reading Feuerbach's account of historical progress as the reappropriation by human beings of their essential humanity through the destruction of the authorities that they had set up over themselves—religious and philosophical illusions that prevented them from actualizing their full potential. The German Left Hegelians confidently believed that the transformation of consciousness through the critical destruction of inherited illusions would culminate in the revolutionary transformation of political practice: the emancipation of humanity from hierarchal authority. Herzen's contemporary Mikhail Bakunin, newly emigrated to Germany and an enthusiastic adherent of the movement, declared in 1842 that the destruction of repressive systems by the forces of negation would lead to a new world "in which all the discords of our time will be resolved in harmonious unity."[15] *Dilettantism in Science*, the cycle of essays that Herzen began writing in the same year, expresses a similar confidence that the new revolution in consciousness will be the prelude to historical change, but in language far more restrained than Bakunin's. Extreme vagueness on political questions was a necessary precaution in writing intended (as Herzen's then was) for publication in Russia, but that was not the reason for the absence of extravagant hopes and distant vistas in Herzen's essays. Much of their argument is explicitly directed against those—the dilettantes of the title—who use philosophy to buttress their cherished dreams and utopian fantasies. He presents the emancipation of consciousness as a process of suffering in which the joys of illusion are exchanged for "the heavy cross of sober knowledge," without which there can be no effective action.[16]

Herzen followed his own prescription, embarking on a program of reading in the natural sciences as well as attending lectures in anatomy and physiology. His friends in Moscow's philosophical circles, still immersed in metaphysical speculation, reacted with astonishment and derision. Herzen responded, "It's stupid to attack me for studying the natural sciences . . . in our time there can be no philosophy without physiology."[17]

In a sentence that encapsulates the philosophical project that would produce his most profound and original writings on the nature of history, Herzen wrote, "Now that the *Jenseits* (the world beyond) has vanished into nothingness, we need to define the foundations of the *Diesseits* (the real world)."[18] More acutely than any other thinker before Nietzsche, he perceived that a new anthropocentric philosophy would demand a fundamental rethinking of our relation to the contingent world with its transient and unrepeatable phenomena. He diagnosed both dilettantes and buddhists, his name for the Russian conservative Hegelians, as suffering from an attenuated sense of reality: the imaginary futures that they had constructed had more meaning and substance for them than the present in which they lived. But "the future is a possibility, not a reality: in fact, it doesn't exist." Doctrinaire Hegelians regarded the historical present as a mere means to the ultimate realization of the transcendent purposes of absolute spirit in the world, whereas each stage in history "has its end in itself, and hence its own satisfaction and reward." No truth or value was immune to the action of time and change: "However original and exhaustive some definitions may seem, they all melt in the fire of life." To comprehend the nature of the self and the external world, philosophy must "descend into the marketplace of life," forsaking the symmetry of abstraction for the messy details of the everyday world—the subject of the experimental science so disdained by Herzen's friends.[19]

Herzen's own return to science was part of the preparatory reading for his most important philosophical project of the 1840s, *Letters on the Study of Nature,* a work modeled on Hegel's history of philosophy, which traced the gradual movement of humanity away from ignorance and superstition toward rational understanding of itself and the world. In the course of his reading, Herzen returned to Bacon's works, which in the light of radical interpretations of Hegel seemed to him even more strikingly modern and relevant than before. He copied into his diary an aphorism summarizing the main theme of the *Novum Organum:* "all [idols] must be renounced and put away with a fixed and solemn determination, and the understanding thoroughly freed and cleansed; the entrance into the kingdom of man, founded on the sciences, being not much other than the entrance into the kingdom of heaven, whereinto none may enter except as a little child."[20]

Herzen observes that Bacon's method is "*certainly* not empiricism in the sense in which it has been understood by some French and English natural philosophers": Bacon had sought to establish the unifying principles of phenomena, although not in abstraction from their concrete manifestations. His language and ideas are thus "more comprehensible to us, and more contemporary" than those of Schelling.[21] As he continues his reading, new enthusiasms temporarily eclipse Bacon. He greets Spinoza as "the many-sided father of modern philosophy" and then pronounces Leibniz's monadology "incomparably higher" than the ideas of Descartes, Bacon, or Spinoza. But in the middle of 1845 he returns to a more detailed study of Bacon, and his enthusiasm revives. He comments that unlike "systematizers" such as Descartes, whose ideas can be thoroughly grasped on one reading, Bacon demands attentive study: "One finds quite unexpectedly, on almost every page, something strikingly new and perceptive."[22]

The first result of this new interest in Bacon was a short essay published in 1845, in which Herzen calls for more attention to the benefits offered by a study of the natural sciences: by purging the mind of prejudices and training it in the "humble acceptance of truth"—a readiness to come to terms with the consequences of one's reasoning, however unpalatable these may be—they enable even the young to contribute usefully to discussion of social questions. Herzen points out that only a handful of scientists had responded to Bacon's call to return to a direct observation of nature. The fruits of their study had remained within academic walls and had not provided "our dislocated understanding with that *orthopaedic* help for which one might have hoped." The natural sciences had played little part in the education of cultured Europeans:

> This has remained . . . an education in remembering rather
> than reasoning, in vocabulary rather than concepts, in
> style rather than thought, an education that relies on au-
> thority rather than independent activity: rhetoric and for-

malism continue as before to push nature aside. Such a
training nearly always leads to intellectual arrogance, to
contempt for everything that is natural and healthy and a
preference for everything that is exaggerated and over-
wrought. Thoughts and judgments continue to be injected
like vaccine when the spirit is immature; when a person
reaches consciousness he finds the trace of the wound on
his arm, finds himself with a collection of ready-made
truths, and sets out with them on his journey, good-
naturedly accepting both the wound and the truths as something over and done with. Against this education, which is
both false and pernicious through its one-sidedness, there
is no remedy more efficacious than the universal propaga-
tion of the natural sciences.[23]

Herzen's belief in the importance of Bacon's insights shaped the
Letters on the Study of Nature, which appeared in 1845–46 in the
journal *Notes of the Fatherland.* He would not have been pleased
by a later description of them as an "able popularization" of Hegel's
History of Philosophy: as he takes pains to point out, although he
followed Hegel's interpretation of ancient philosophy, he differed
from him in his view of the modern period, and he believed in
particular that he had something original and important to say
about Bacon, whose significance Hegel had greatly undervalued.[24]

While giving Bacon credit for spearheading the revolt against
medieval scholasticism, Hegel contends that the esteem in which
Bacon was held for this was "greater than can be ascribed directly
to his merit." The English mode of reasoning by proceeding from
facts and experience was common among cultivated men, and Bacon was no more than such a man, with clear perceptions but
without "the power of reasoning through thoughts and notions that
are universal."[25]

In Hegel's view, the English were notably deficient in this power;[26]
hence the modest role he accords Bacon in the world-historical
scheme: he is "leader and representative of that which in England
is called philosophy and beyond which the English have not yet

advanced, for they appear to constitute that people in Europe which, limited to the understanding of actuality, is destined, like the class of shopkeepers and workmen in the State, to live always immersed in matter and to have actuality but not reason as object."[27]

To Herzen it was clear that Hegel had not understood Bacon's importance as a "Columbus" who had opened up a new world in science by exposing the ways in which enshrined dogmas and systems clouded the mind, presenting it with a distorted view of nature. Fewer than a dozen pages of Hegel's four-volume *History of Philosophy* are concerned with Bacon. Herzen attempts to redress the balance by devoting to him the greater part of two chapters in his own much shorter work, to which he adds a lengthy appendix of his own translations of more than sixty extracts from Bacon's writings, assuring his readers that these are typical of the insights of "striking truth and breadth" to be found on every page of Bacon.[28]

The importance that Herzen attached to his interpretation of Bacon is evident from a comment to a friend on the first of the two chapters, "Descartes and Bacon," which he describes as the best in the work so far, adding that he is certain that its central idea can be found in no other contemporary history of philosophy. This idea, adumbrated in Herzen's essay of 1832, was that in its two dominant traditions, the speculative and empiricist (founded by Descartes and Bacon, respectively) modern philosophy reflected a polarization between the principles of mind and matter, the outcome of the dualism of medieval thought and the dialectical premiss of a future integral knowledge, when the two principles would be synthesized. But at the cost of detracting from the neatness of his schema, Herzen again emphasizes that while both Descartes' method and the empiricist tradition—which had led to the crude materialism of the eighteenth century—were one-sided, Bacon's own philosophy was not: his protest against scholasticism was inspired by "that disobedient element of life which looks smilingly on all manner of one-sidedness, and goes its own way."[29]

The second chapter, "Bacon and His School in England," is a

lucid, highly sympathetic assessment of Bacon's aims, his method, and his historical significance. Herzen defends him against the charge of crude empiricism leveled by Hegel with a degree of enthusiasm and personal commitment and a wealth of quotations not to be found in his treatment of any other philosopher. Much of this enthusiasm can be ascribed to the prominence in the *Novum Organum* of a theme of which Herzen was particularly fond—the comparison of two opposing and equally incomplete types of intellectual personality, and in the course of his discussion he paraphrases three relevant aphorisms from Bacon's work:

> There are some minds more able to observe, make experiments, study details, gradations: others on the contrary strive to penetrate to the most hidden resemblances, to draw general concepts from them. The first, lost in details, see only atoms: the second, floating in generalities, lose sight of everything particular, replacing it by phantoms. . . . neither atoms nor abstract matter, devoid of all determination, are real: what are real are *bodies, as they exist in nature.* . . . One must not be carried away in either direction: in order that consciousness may be deepened and broadened, each of these attitudes *must in its turn pass into the other.*[30]

This passage is strikingly close to Herzen's own assessment, in the same chapter, of the defects of idealism and materialism, respectively, and the form that a reconciliation between them should take: "Idealism . . . has recognized only the universal, the generic, essence, human reason abstracted from all that is human. Materialism, just as one-sided, set out to annihilate everything that was not matter: it denied the existence of universals, held thought to be a compartment of the brain, experience the only source of knowledge, and truth to be found only in particulars, in tangible and visible things. It accepted the existence of rational persons, but not of reason or humankind." The way to truth, he asserts, lies in overcoming these kinds of imbalances through an understanding of "the link, the transition from the outer to the inner, . . . the essential oneness of both."[31]

Herzen was impressed by the similarities between Bacon's approach and the Left Hegelians' critique of speculative philosophy: "[Bacon] regards philosophy that does not lead to action as *worthless:* for him knowledge and action are two facets of a single energy." (Herzen's work *Dilettantism in Science* contains a similar formulation: "Science is a moment, on both sides of which is life: on one side, life striving toward it, natural and immediate; on the other, life flowing from it, conscious and free.")[32] He remarks that if Cartesianism is, as Leibniz had called it, the gateway to truth, "we may be wholly justified in calling Bacon's empiricism its storehouse"—a curious observation in a work that elsewhere proclaims Hegel's dialectic to be the foundation of the harmonious knowledge of the future. But in Herzen's view Hegel had one cardinal defect not shared by Bacon—one-sidedness: he had subsumed the temporal and concrete in absolute spirit, and for all Herzen's admiration for the liberating philosophies of the Left Hegelians, he is closer to Bacon than to them in the often lyrical way he writes of the marvels hidden in the humblest natural phenomena, his insistence on the importance of close and detailed observation as the basis for all generalizations about our physical and historical environment: "Thought must become flesh . . . unfold with all the luxuriant beauty of transient existence." Only thinking that was riveted to the needs and hopes of the passing moment could result in "passionate action, quivering with vitality."[33] In defining his method as "speculative empiricism," Herzen is echoing Feuerbach. But it is Goethe's scientific writings that he cites as epitomizing the "profound realism" of such an approach, pointing to his startling ability to make the processes of emergence and evolution palpable through the minutely observed physical details of natural phenomena.[34]

Thus defined, speculative empiricism is none other than the approach that Herzen had recommended in 1832: proceeding from direct observation of reality to its unifying "forms" and thereby allowing one "to know both the empirical object and the idea which it represents." As set down in the *Letters,* Herzen's aim is Baconian rather than Hegelian: "To show (to the extent to which this can be done) that the antagonism between philosophy and the natural sciences is becoming daily more absurd . . . that it is based on mutual incomprehension."[35]

In the 1840s Herzen began to develop a theory of moral freedom consistent with a Baconian approach to knowledge, and here his reading of Bacon prepared the ground for a new appreciation of Schiller, whose aesthetic idealism he had recently rejected as a form of romantic escapism. In 1843 he read Schiller's treatise *On the Aesthetic Education of Man* and was deeply impressed with what he perceived to be a prophetic work.[36] His own reflections on freedom echo Schiller's view that the aim of moral education is to produce aesthetically modulated individuals whose conduct is governed not by adherence to fixed and universal precepts, but by freely adjusting the relations between their sensual and rational drives in order to respond sensitively and appropriately to the demands of specific situations. Here, transposed to the sphere of moral conduct, is that "lawful marriage between the empirical and the rational faculty" that Bacon's inductive method sought to achieve in the study of nature.

The passages appended to Herzen's study of Bacon show the degree to which the Left Hegelians' critique of self-alienation reactivated his interest in Bacon's method. His choice reflects an extensive reading of Bacon's works, but the themes he selects are all to be found in the *Novum Organum:* the practical aim of philosophy, the importance of grounding it in the data of the natural sciences and on an inductive method that did not separate forms (Bacon's word for the fundamental laws governing matter and physical processes) from their material manifestations, and the need to clear the way for this method by purging the mind of idols.

Herzen's selection from the aphorisms is significant in the light of the subsequent development of his political philosophy. He gives most prominence to Bacon's Idols of the Tribe, the innate human characteristics which distort our perception of reality, such as the longing for permanent and incontrovertible truths and the urge to discover ultimate ends and final causes. But he also cites Bacon on the influence of education in inculcating false beliefs and reverence for authorities, the role of language in the distortion of reality, and the stultifying effects of received systems and dogmas.

Undoubtedly, Left Hegelian notions of alienation kindled Herzen's interest in Bacon's discussion of the idols that obstruct the advancement of knowledge. But his reading of Bacon on this theme in turn crucially affected his approach to the phenomenon of self-estrangement, leading him to focus much more closely than other radical philosophers of his time on the intellectual and psychological predispositions that falsify our understanding of ourselves and the external world. This problem would become his central philosophical concern after he left Russia in 1847 in order to be able to write in freedom, and Bacon's influence would continue to be evident both on his diagnosis of the disease of idolatry and his prescriptions for its treatment.

Herzen arrived in Paris in time to witness the violence and the failure of the revolution of 1848 in France, an experience that profoundly affected him and inspired his most brilliant work, *From the Other Shore*. He introduces it as the "protest of an independent individual against an obsolete, slavish, and spurious set of ideas, against absurd idols, which belong to another age and which linger on meaninglessly among us, a nuisance to some, a terror to others." He defines this self-enslavement in Left Hegelian fashion, as "the transference of all that is most individual in a man on to an impersonal, generalized sphere independent of him,"[37] but he parts company with every radical movement of his age by including the concept of progress among those idols to which living individuals are sacrificed, and his reflections on the role of language and mental habits in sustaining fictions about the world are a direct echo of Bacon (to whom he pays tribute, in an early draft of the work, as one of only two great philosophers—the second being Bacon's admirer Hume—who had not sought to set themselves up as priests of the new secular religion of progress).[38]

Much of *From the Other Shore* is written in the form of dialogues with radical idealists who are in despair at the failure of the revolution to realize their dream of a just and rational society. Herzen argues that their disappointment is based on expectations unfounded in empirical experience. The belief that Bacon defined as the source of Idols of the Tribe—that "the sense of man is the measure of things"[39]—is for Herzen the root cause of the illusion that history is a linear advance to the goal of an ideal freedom. The fact that "ideals, theoretical constructions never materialize in the shape in which they float in our minds" never ceases to surprise and disappoint us. Preoccupied with final goals, ultimate results, always looking beyond the action to its end, the human understanding has "not yet become used to the ways of life." The play of chance in nature reveals that "life has its own embryogenesis that does not coincide with the dialectic of pure reason"; but while we accept the limitations imposed by physiology, heredity, and circumstance on our power to control natural processes, we like to think that we are free to mold history in accordance with our most cherished desires.

The misrepresentations to which Herzen attributes this error are a mixture of Bacon's Idols of the Theater and of the Marketplace: illusions inculcated by religious and philosophical systems and reinforced by the concepts of everyday discourse. Their common source, he argues, is the "insane dualism" that corrupts our simplest notions. The legacy of the philosophical and religious traditions of the West, dualism divides into supposed opposites (such as body and soul) what in reality is inseparable, instilling "contempt for the earth and the temporal, . . . adoration of heaven and the eternal," leading us to believe in the existence of abstract principles and absolutes independent of physical phenomena and creating "demands for some unattainable bliss." This dualism is now less crude, but it "still lingers unnoticed in our souls. Our language, our first notions, which become natural by force of habit, by repetition, prevent us from seeing the truth." Education "deceives us before we are in a condition to understand"; we "demand too much, sacrifice too much, scorn the possible, are indignant because what is impossible scorns us." We give up faith in a heavenly paradise only to adopt the secular religion of progress, which regards the present generation as mere material for the realization of the future utopia. Those who believe that humanity is marching to perfection are guilty of "contempt for facts." Instead of studying the masses in the villages and marketplaces, the French liberals of 1848 "constructed their people a priori, created it out of memories of things read, dressed it up in a Roman toga or a shepherd's cloak. No one thought about the real people. . . . Its lot remained unchanged, but the fictitious people became the idol of the new political religion." The people's worshipers were indignant when it did not fulfill their expectations, but they had never troubled to study the "physiology" of its social existence, the influences shaping the "dark instincts [and] unaccountable passions" that made it violent, fickle and capricious.[40] Sober observation would have taught the liberals too, that the mass of humanity neither understood nor valued individual freedom: they loved authority and were dazzled by the glitter of power: "In the present as in the past, I see knowledge, truth, moral strength, craving for independence, love of beauty, in a small group of men, antagonistic, unsympathetic to the majority, lost in their milieu. On the other side, I see the painful advance of the other strata of society, narrow ideas based on tradition, mean needs, petty efforts toward good, petty tendencies toward evil."[41]

In one of the book's dialogues these unpalatable truths are uttered by a doctor, whose interlocutor accuses him of being a "dreadful aristocrat." He retorts that he is merely a naturalist, trained to live in the world of facts and phenomena: "Yours is an a priori point of view and you are perhaps logically right in saying that man should aspire to independence. I look at the question as a pathologist and see that up to now slavery has been the permanent condition of social development. Therefore either it is indispensable or it does not arouse as much disgust as it might seem to."[42]

The doctor asserts that he is neither an optimist nor a pessimist about humanity's future; he is constantly adjusting his opinions to the facts. His idealist opponent interprets his refusal to make a priori moral demands of the human race as evidence of indifference to its suffering. He retorts, "I am merely—you must forgive me—more modest than you." He exhorts his companion to study the unique physiology of human societies. Instead of trying to change the world to fit a program, "learn what its course is; and you will abandon your moralistic point of view and gain strength." Elsewhere in the book Herzen recommends the experimental methods of the natural sciences as a means of exercising and sharpening the brain: "The naturalist is used to watching and waiting and not introducing anything of his own until the time comes to do so. He will not miss a single symptom, a single change; he seeks truth disinterestedly, without colouring it with either his love or his hate."[43]

From the Other Shore looked back to Bacon's method, but also forward to one of the greatest scientific revolutions of the modern age. What Herzen called his modest approach to the human and natural sciences, rejecting teleological assumptions in both domains and stressing the role of chance in the development of all species, foreshadowed that aspect of Darwin's theories which would be perceived as the greatest threat to both religious and rationalist representations of the world.[44] "Believe me, men are predestined to nothing": in the last essay of *From the Other Shore* Herzen points out that the contrary view has been an inexhaustible source of confusion and moral darkness throughout human history, leading to the veneration of abstractions and contempt for real individuals: "All those maxims like *Salus populi suprema lex, Pereat mundus et fiat justitia,* have about them a strong smell of burnt flesh, of blood, inquisition, torture, and in general the *triumph of order.*"[45]

In his discussion of idols Bacon observes, "Matter rather than forms should be the object of our attention, its configurations and changes of configuration . . . for forms are figments of the human mind."[46] In the last two decades of his life Herzen devoted much of his political journalism (as editor of the Free Russian Press he set up in London) to exposing contemporary manifestations of formalism—his term for the idolatry of political abstractions. He discovered to his chagrin that the disease was rampant in Russia when, on the eve of the emancipation of the serfs, the new tsar Alexander II began to permit some public discussion of political and economic issues. Herzen was deeply critical of the new orthodoxies emerging in the period of the Great Reforms of the 1860s, when liberal and radical intellectuals engaged in bitter ideological conflicts in the name of doctrines of progress borrowed from Western sources. Herzen accused them of a worship of political forms—whether "the arithmetical pantheism of universal suffrage" or "the exotic socialism of literature"—which diverted attention from the much more pressing matter of social content:

> Is it not ridiculous for a person in the second half of the nineteenth century who has borne on his shoulders or trampled underfoot so many forms of government, to fear some and idolize others? A form, as understood in the language of military regulations, is a "uniform," and it adapts willy-nilly to a living content . . . if it does not, that means that the content is feeble and without substance. . . . And you may be sure that there are neither any very good nor any absolutely bad uniforms. In our view a bourgeois chamber of popular deputies who do not represent the people is just as repugnant as a Governing Senate which governs nothing.[47]

Toward the end of his life, Herzen described the advances made by political formalism in his century in some fine pages of savage satire, constructed around an image borrowed from the writer whose critique of one-sidedness had so much influenced him in his youth. He introduced his theme with a paraphrase of the following passage from the *Novum Organum:* "Those who have handled sciences have been either men of experiment or men of dogmas. The men of experiment are like the ant; they only collect and use: the reasoners resemble spiders, who make cobwebs out of their own substance. But the bee takes a middle course; it gathers its material from the flowers of the garden and of the field but transforms and digests it by a power of its own."[48]

The first half of the nineteenth century, Herzen observed, was a poor time for bees; to gather honey one needed fields and groves, wings and a sociable disposition. The spinning of webs required only "a quiet corner, untroubled leisure, a great deal of dust, and indifference to everything but the inner process." Such conditions had existed between the battle of Waterloo and the European revolutions of 1848, a period of relative stability:

> Governments openly encouraged "true enlightenment" and quietly smothered the *false* variety: there was no great freedom, but there was also no great slavery: even the despots were benevolent. . . . Industry flourished, trade flourished even more, factories operated, a mass of books was written. It was a golden age for all the webs that were endlessly being woven in academic lecture halls and in scholars' studies.
>
> History, criminal and civil law, international law, and even religion—all were raised to the sphere of pure understanding and wafted down like the velvety lace of a spider's web. The spiders swung freely on their threads, never touching the ground—which was very sensible, because other insects were crawling around there, representing the great Idea of the State in its "moment of self-defense" and locking up spiders who were too bold in Spandau and other fortresses. But the doctrinaires understood all this immensely well *à vol d'araignée*. The progress of humanity was as well mapped out as the route of an emperor traveling incognito—from stage to stage, with horses waiting at each post station.[49]

The French revolution of 1848 produced flies too big for the webs of the system-builders, but they quickly adapted their strategy. Authorities were produced to show that a period of democracy must necessarily be followed by one of centralization: Catholic conservatives aspired to recreate the religious universalism of the Middle Ages, while radicals demanded a return to the principles of 1793. In academic auditoria doctrinaires of all persuasions demonstrated the rationality or the democratic tendency of the historical process. Meanwhile Austrians fought Frenchmen in Italy in battles that defied rationality and international law; American democrats waged a war in defense of slavery; English liberals ruled India by force and sought together with French republicans to impose their will on China by invading Peking. Such recent phenomena were beyond the competence of the "monks of science": "[They] know nothing of the world outside their monastery walls; they do not test their theories and solutions by events: while people are being killed by the eruption of a volcano, they take delight in beating time to the music of the heavenly spheres, marveling at its harmony."[50]

In "Robert Owen," a long essay published in 1861, Herzen developed the comparisons between historical and natural processes that had been a central theme of *From the Other Shore*. His argument can be summed up in an aphorism of Bacon's which he cites imperfectly from memory: "To the extent that a man knows nature, he can govern her."[51] By studying the workings of natural processes, humanity had achieved mastery of the sea and the land, but it did not have the same respect for the objective reality of the historical world. All theories of inevitable and predestined progress depended on the fantasy of "some historical *arrière-pensée*" which incarnates itself in peoples and kingdoms, wars and revolutions, in order to achieve its ends. Such explanations of the historical process had the effect of making the simplest things and the most everyday objects utterly incomprehensible:

> For example, can there be a fact more obvious to anyone than the observation that the longer a person lives, the more chance he has of making a fortune; the longer he looks at an object, the better he sees it, if nothing obstructs his view or he does not go blind? And yet out of that fact people have contrived to create the idol of *progress,* some sort of golden calf incessantly growing and promising to grow to infinity.
>
> Is it not easier to understand that a human being lives not to *fulfill a destiny,* not to embody an idea, not for the

sake of progress, but solely because he was born and he
was born *for* (however bad that word is) the present,
which in no way prevents him either receiving a heritage
from the past or bequeathing something to the future.[52]

Idealists believed that if human beings were denied a transcendent destiny they would become the mere playthings of chance; but
the role of chance in nature and history did not turn these into
random processes. The procedure of induction permits us to make
certain predictions about the future: "When we perform an induction we know what we are doing, basing ourselves on the permanence of certain laws and phenomena, but also allowing for the
possibility of their infringement."[53] When we use this method to
determine our actions and choices, we are expressing our sense of
responsibility and freedom.

On the question of the objective nature and limits of freedom,
the father of inductive science was Herzen's guide. He was fond of
quoting Bacon's term *"magnum ignotum* (the great Unknown)"
for the realm of ultimate causes: "Now there you have an honest
thinker—whereas others, as soon as they come up against something that they can't solve, invent a new force, such as a soul."[54]
In the mid-1860s, debating with his son, a physiologist, on the
question of the freedom of the will, he points out that while some
philosophers had deified the human will and others denied its
existence, few had given thought to the sole aspect of this
magnum ignotum that the human mind was competent to investigate:

We have yet to analyze the idea of liberty as a phenomenological necessity for the operation of human intelligence, as a psychological reality.

. . . .

Humans are bound by the *necessity of knowing themselves
to be free.*
How does one escape from this vicious circle?
One doesn't. The aim should be to comprehend it.[55]

Herzen's son adhered to the dogmatic materialism popularized by natural scientists like Ludwig Büchner and Karl Vogt; in the 1860s this became the dominant credo of the Russian radical youth. Their refusal to recognize anything that could not be justified by rational argument, their narrowly utilitarian criteria of progress, and their repudiation of traditional aesthetics as a socially useless pursuit led them to be called nihilists after the radical natural scientist Bazarov in Turgenev's novel *Fathers and Children*. Herzen strongly objected to the use of that term to denote intolerance and an adolescent desire to shock. Serious nihilists, among whom he counted himself, marched under the banner of "science and doubt, investigation in place of faith, understanding in place of obedience." If Bazarov had been a true scientist he would not have regarded others with contempt: "Even more than the Gospel, science teaches us humility. . . . She stops before the facts as an investigator, sometimes as a physician, never as an executioner, and still less with hostility and irony."[56]

In the political journalism of his last decade Herzen attempted, with little success, to convert the Russian radical youth to his Baconian vision of a genuinely scientific approach to history, emphasizing the importance of the dimension of time in historical processes, which develop by a complex process of embryology that does not coincide with the laws of logic.[57] His arguments are summed up in the essays addressed to an "old comrade" (Mikhail Bakunin), essays which can be seen as his political testament. Herzen's contemporary, Bakunin had made common cause with the most extreme groups among the young Russian émigrés who, undeterred by the apathy of the masses, were determined to force a revolution on Russia. Herzen urges him to adopt a more physiological approach. The slowness of history infuriates them both. They yearn to speed it up, to advance with one stride from the first month of pregnancy to the ninth; but processes of growth can be accelerated only within narrow limits without aborting precious new beginnings. Human consciousness must be accepted as a natural fact, the complex product of historical developments, deviations, and disasters: one cannot force new ideas on people in the way medicine is poured into the mouths of horses. Lack of development cannot be overcome by violence: terror destroys prejudices no more effectively than conquest destroys peoples. It shatters forms and structures but leaves their content untouched: "If the entire bourgeois world is blown up by gunpowder, once the dust has settled and the ruins are cleared, it will rise again, with a few alterations, as *some sort of bourgeois world*." Why?—because its hold on the human consciousness still exceeds that of the new values that Bakunin and his fellow-believers seek to impose.

"I . . . try to understand the *human pace* in the past and in the present," Herzen writes, "so as to learn how to go in step with it, not falling behind and not running so far ahead that people will not, cannot follow me."[58] A rare figure among the great iconoclasts of history, Herzen claimed no special status for his own ideal. He proposed the form of anarchism that he called "Russian Socialism" as a means both of avoiding the creation of a landless proletariat in Russia and of combining the values of individual liberty and social cohesion. But unlike Marx, who proclaimed communism "the solution of the riddle of history,"[59] Herzen denied that any theory of society, including those of socialism, could ever claim an absolute or universal validity. All would eventually prove too constricting for new, as yet unpredictable needs and aspirations, for which as yet unforeseen answers would have to be found. Such was "the eternal play of life."[60]

Bacon's method must take at least some credit for developing what Isaiah Berlin has defined as Herzen's most distinctive quality: an extraordinary sensibility to characteristics and processes in society "while they are still in embryo and invisible to the naked eye."[61] But there were other reasons, too, for the warmth and admiration with which Herzen always referred to the great Renaissance thinker: a resemblance both in their historical roles and in their temperaments.

In his *Letters on the Study of Nature* Herzen had greeted Bacon as a Columbus heralding a new age in the understanding of the world. In the aftermath of 1848 he began to hypothesize that historical circumstances might destine the Russian intelligentsia to play an analogous role in the field of social thought. He believed that attachment to religious and philosophical fetishes and authoritarian systems was so deeply ingrained in European culture that even the Left Hegelians had not grasped the full subversiveness of their critique of transcendent entities. Russians on the other hand, as latecomers to the feast of culture, did not share the Europeans' filial obedience to the past, while the brutality of their own regime was not conducive to respect for traditional authorities. The thinking Russian was thus singularly unencumbered by "all those inherited hindrances and obstructions, that historical ball and chain which holds back the Western mind."[62] What Bacon had striven to do for science Herzen hoped that his compatriots might accomplish in the field of political and social thought—dispel the illusions that barred the way to the realization of human potential.

True to his method, Herzen discarded this hope when confronted with hard empirical evidence to the contrary: the doctrinairism of the radical leaders of the 1860s convinced him that idolatry was thriving as well in Russia as anywhere else. But the generation that followed was more sympathetic to his ideas, and it is notable that the populist tradition he founded was the only one to consistently question the goals and values shared by nineteenth-century European liberals and radicals alike: quantification, industrialization, mechanization, mass democracies, and above all, progress, as an absolute aim to which individuals, and in some cases whole classes, might be sacrificed without compunction. Such criticism has long since become commonplace, but in his lifetime Herzen's attack on the idolatry of progress was almost universally misunderstood, and in this regard another analogy presents itself between his predicament and that of Bacon.

Bacon had pointed to the dual difficulty faced by those who sought not merely to replace old ideas with new ones, but to change fundamental categories and modes of thought: "For that knowledge which is new and foreign from opinions received, is to be delivered in another form than that that is agreeable and familiar. . . . For those whose conceits are seated in popular opinions, need only but to prove or dispute: but those whose conceits are beyond popular opinions, have a double labor: the one to make themselves conceived, and the other to prove and demonstrate." The second labor leads to something of a vicious circle: "This must be plainly avowed: no judgment can be rightly formed either of my method or of the discoveries to which it leads, by means of . . . the reasoning which is now in use; since I cannot be called on to abide by the sentence of a tribunal which is itself on its trial.

"Even to deliver and explain what I bring forward is no easy matter; for things in themselves new will yet be apprehended with reference to what is old."[63]

The truth of this last assertion is vividly illustrated by the isolation and frustrations of Herzen's political life. He too was deeply aware of the difficulty of his task: "There are not one, but two kinds of reason," he wrote—that of the old world and that of the future world of freedom—but while many guessed at the truths revealed by the new reason, "none dares come straight out with them, so little have we yet succeeded in delivering our intellect and our tongues from the thrall of various paper dragons and outworn sacred relics." People showed their incomprehension of his attacks on formalistic thinking by seeking to label him as the spokesman for a specific ideology. As he remarked toward the end of his life, he had been classified as a moderate, a socialist, a Jacobin, an anarchist, a governmentalist, a Hébertist, a Marquis Posa, a bloodthirsty terrorist, and a timid gradualist: "What is most offensive of all is that people seem to understand you, to agree with you; and yet your thoughts remain alien in their heads, without ever acquiring relevance to reality."[64]

The incomprehension continued after his death, with an ironical twist that he would have appreciated. During his lifetime Russian liberals and radicals, respectively, had identified him with the opposing camp; after his death each side sought to claim him as a precursor. He has been represented both as a great Russian liberal and as one of the patron saints of Russian communism.[65]

The intellectual personalities as well as the aims of the two thinkers had much in common. Both were men whose cast of mind was out of harmony with the intellectual climate of their age. In epochs dominated, respectively, by the dead weight of scholasticism and the vast abstractions of romantic idealism, Bacon and Herzen were distinguished by their acute powers of observation, their love of the immediacy and unrepeatability, the color and variety of contingent existence, and their ability to convey this in direct and vivid language: gifts which have led both of them to be frequently described as poets. Bacon vigorously opposed the tendency of his age to exclude things "which are mean and low" from the study of natural history: "The sun enters the sewer no less than the palace, yet takes no pollution." Similarly, Herzen devoted much energy to combating what he saw as the dangerous illusion that nature is no more than "corrupted Idea";[66] and his sensitivity to significant detail is reflected in the vividness of his style, in particular in the brilliantly observed vignettes of individual personalities in his memoirs, which stand among the great works of Russian literature.

Such qualities of observation lend themselves particularly well to the use of aphorisms as a method of capturing fundamental truths. Bacon affirms that delivery of knowledge by means of aphorisms

> has many excellent virtues whereto the methodical delivery does not attain. First it tries the writer, whether he be light and superficial in his knowledge, or solid. For aphorisms, not to be ridiculous, must be made out of the pith and heart of sciences. For illustration and excursion are cut off; variety of examples is cut off; so there is nothing left to make the aphorisms of but some good quantity of observation. . . . Secondly, methodical delivery is fit to win consent or belief, but of little use to give directions for practice; for it carries a kind of demonstration in circle, one part illuminating another, and therefore more satisfies the understanding; but as actions in common life are dispersed, and not arranged in order, dispersed directions do best for them. Lastly, aphorisms, representing only portions and as it were fragments of knowledge, invite others

to contribute and add something in their turn; whereas
methodical delivery, carrying the show of a total, makes
men careless, as if they were already at the end.[67]

Bacon's three points are richly illustrated in Herzen's writings, especially in *From the Other Shore*, Herzen's *Novum Organum* in its brilliant concentration of aphorisms. Based on acute observation of historical processes, these are deliberately provocative and often paradoxical, designed to startle the reader into reaction and, ultimately, action. Thus: "It is not enough not to consider *lèse-majesté* a crime, one must look on *salus populi* as being one"; "The truly free man *creates* his own morality"; "Faith in the human soul is either an individual matter or an epidemic." Herzen's philosophy is summed up in an aphorism on the first page of his book, where he warns the reader not to look for solutions in it: "In general, modern man has no solutions."[68]

Both men failed to realize the projects dearest to them. Bacon never completed his attempt to construct an outline for a system of integrated knowledge; Herzen's hopes for Russian Socialism were swept away by the dissolution of the peasant communes during Russia's industrialization. But both seem to have been aware that their greatest contribution to thought lay in their destruction of idols. Bacon wrote of the judgment which he supposed would be passed on him in future ages: "That I did no great things, but simply made less account of things that were accounted great."[69] Compare Herzen's description of his philosophy of history: "It is not a science, but an indictment; it is a scourge to be used against absurd theories and absurd liberal theoreticians, a fermenting agent and no more than that. But it engages people's attention, it stimulates and angers them; it makes them think."[70]

Herzen, Schiller,
and the Aesthetic Education of Man
CHAPTER TWO

No European thinker had so pervasive an effect as Friedrich Schiller on the development of Russian literature and thought in the first half of the nineteenth century.[1] But while Schiller's humanism is generally agreed to have fostered the spread of notions of justice and freedom in tsarist Russia, he has also been held responsible for strengthening the utopian tendencies in Russian radical thought, and the name most frequently mentioned in this regard is Aleksandr Herzen. In the words of Herzen's biographer, Martin Malia, Schiller's aesthetic ideal of the human being provided Herzen with "an education in revolutionary intransigence and the 'maximalist' utopia . . . which will settle for nothing short of the complete emancipation of the individual personality from all external constraint."[2]

Herzen's political philosophy has proved notoriously difficult to define. Undeniably the most original and profound of Russian radical thinkers, he is also the most elusive. He has been claimed as a precursor by Russian liberals and by Soviet communists, while some of his contemporaries refused to take him seriously as a theorist, regarding him as a brilliant and wayward literary gadfly. But most commentators agree on the importance of aesthetic criteria in his thinking; and they maintain that his aesthetic idealism was expressed in utopian politics.

The first of these points is self-evident to any reader of Herzen (contemporaries like Dostoevsky often described him as an artist or a poet);[3] however, I shall contest the second by showing that the aesthetic education which Herzen proposed as the means of regenerating society was, like Schiller's, based on a far-sighted op-

position to all varieties of political maximalism and utopian intransigence.

Studies of Schiller's influence on Herzen have tended to concentrate on Schiller's poetry and dramas.[4] This chapter will focus instead on his debate with Kant on the nature of moral freedom and
its reflection in his most mature philosophical work, *On the Aesthetic Education of Man;* I will then compare Schiller's and Herzen's
models of moral freedom and of its relation to political liberty.
Although, as argued below, their resemblance is as much a case of
parallelism as of direct influence, Schiller's treatise offers a useful
perspective from which to approach Herzen's political writings, as
well as a key to some of their more obscure passages. The critical
reception of the *Aesthetic Education,* which, until relatively recently,
was interpreted as preaching an ivory tower aestheticism, also sheds
light on the reasons for some misconceptions that persist in scholarship on Herzen. By comparing Schiller's and Herzen's ideals of
moral harmony, I aim to define more precisely than has hitherto
been done Herzen's aesthetic ideal of the human personality.

Published in 1795, *On the Aesthetic Education of Man* was warmly
received by Hegel, Kant, and Goethe, but most critics found the
work obscure, and it was soon almost forgotten, although its title
(often confused with that of an earlier work by Schiller) helped
reinforce the image of the author as an apolitical artist who with-
drew into aesthetic contemplation after the French Revolution
failed to realize his dream of absolute liberty. Only in the second
half of the twentieth century has the work begun to arouse general
interest among philosophers and political theorists, who have
pointed to passages that anticipate Hegel and Marx in their analysis
of the self-estrangement of modern human beings.[5] Attention has
focused especially on Schiller's formulation of the problem of preserving individuality in a modern state: he is now recognized as
one of the first thinkers to confront what is perhaps the greatest
dilemma of modern societies. As one critic has put it, all Schiller's
philosophical works are an attack on the same evil in myriad
form—"the evil of authoritarianism which arises when law, instead
of setting man free, tyrannises over him."[6]

This could equally well be a characterization of Herzen's work. I shall seek to show that these two philosophers of freedom understood the nature of the enemy in closely similar terms.

Schiller's treatise was the product of long reflection on the Kantian opposition between nature and freedom. While recognizing the importance of Kant's strict distinction between the beautiful and the good and acknowledging the primacy of the idea of duty in ethics, Schiller objected to the rigorous dualism of the Kantian model of moral life, which presupposed an inevitable conflict between duty and inclination and demanded the suppression of natural impulses and passions by the will in the name of imperatives furnished by reason. In a satirical poem he mocks the gracelessness and logical absurdity of equating moral freedom with successful self-coercion: in a philosophical discussion taking place in hell a disciple admits to his mentor that he is disposed by inclination to do good to others—where is the virtue in this? The reply is: "Endeavour to despise your neighbour, so that you may perform with revulsion what duty commands you to do."[7]

In his essay "On Grace and Dignity," Schiller offers a more serious challenge to the Kantian model of virtue. He agrees with the "moral rigorists" that the will must always obey law rather than impulse but claims that Kant's harsh presentation of the idea of duty could lead one to conclude that the only way to moral perfection lies in a somber asceticism. The fulfillment of duty should not have the degrading appearance of servitude to a law enforced by an alien authority but should be seen as a sublime expression of one's moral autonomy, a prescription that one freely imposes on oneself as a rational being. The source of this misconception was the opposition that philosophy had set up between the sensual and rational faculties: an analytical abstraction which did not correspond to the actual workings of the human psyche. Human beings are mixed natures; our destiny is surely not to cast off part of this nature as a useless burden. The full expression of our humanity demands that the sensuous drive be not "the oppressed partner in the moral order" but united with all the ardor of its sentiments to the will. Reason alone can define the moral good, but morality can be secure only when obedience to reason becomes the object of inclination, and we no longer run the risk of finding our instincts in discord with the decisions of our will: "The moral perfection of man cannot shine forth except from this participation of his inclination with his moral conduct. The destiny of man is not to perform isolated moral acts, but to be a moral being. What is prescribed to him are not virtues, but virtue, which is an inclination for duty."[8]

The rigidity and constraint demanded by the Kantian model of virtue were alien to beauty and thus required the sacrifice of aesthetic sentiment to moral duty; but in the *schöne Seele* (the "beautiful soul": the model of moral perfection proposed in Schiller's essay) beauty and virtue, reason and sense, would be reconciled. This "peaceful soul, in harmony with itself," would perform the most heroic sacrifices and the most painful duties with as great a facility as if prompted by instinct alone. It would never occur to such a being that any other way of acting might be possible. This disposition of the spirit would manifest itself externally in grace.

Schiller accepts, however, that this ideal harmony between spiritual demands and the world of sense is unattainable on earth, and with regard to the conflicts of human nature in the everyday world he takes a no less rigorous line than Kant: it is always the duty of will to make the demands of instinct give way to reason.[9] Nevertheless, inclination and aesthetic sentiment should not always be suspect, as in Kant's austere philosophy; for "it is surely not an advantage for moral truth to have against itself sentiments to which man can confess without shame."[10] The same person might exhibit moral grace and moral dignity—defined as the mastery of will over impulse—as appropriate responses to different situations: the ideal of the beautiful soul was less a goal than a guideline, a general orientation. One should strive toward it with constant vigilance, exercising moral dignity in its appropriate domain but seeking also to extend the domain of moral grace, through the transformation (rather than the repression) of primitive impulses and the cultivation of feeling as an ally of the will.

"On Grace and Dignity" is a complex work, reflecting a conflict in its author between belief in the organic unity of the human psyche and acceptance of the Kantian antithesis between nature and freedom. But, unfortunately for his reputation as a moralist, Schiller is best known not for his ambivalences, but for the static simplicity of the moral ideal presented in this essay.[11] The cult of the beautiful soul allowed young romantics to indulge in aesthetic fantasies of self-aggrandizement; but the agonized soul-searching of Russian idealists of the 1830s, as recorded in their memoirs and letters, testifies to the shortcomings of such visions as yardsticks for regulating conduct in the world of harsh reality. The defect of Schiller's ideal was not its utopian nature (a risk for all moral ideals). It was the inappropriateness of a model of static equilibrium as a guideline for a moral education which recognized the inevitability of moral conflict in the real and imperfect world and aimed to replace rigid adherence to fixed precepts by a flexible response to changing situations.

Preoccupied with the necessity for such a reeducation, Schiller was led to reconsider his unitary model of the psyche. In the *Aesthetic Education*, published five years after "On Grace and Dignity," the static harmony of the beautiful soul was replaced by a dynamic model of moral freedom, incorporating division and conflict.

Through this work, which grew out of his disenchantment with the course of the French Revolution, Schiller has come to be regarded as the father of the concept of alienation.[12] He saw the violence of the Terror as the result of the divorce of politics from morality, a symptom of the destructive effects on the psyche of the specialization of knowledge and function in modern societies. Valuing the individual citizen only for the functions he performs in the operation of the entire social body, the state encourages the disseverance of his intuitive and speculative faculties, and ultimately his dehumanization, a condition Schiller describes in terms that anticipate Marx: "Enjoyment was divorced from labour, the means from the end, the effort from the reward. Everlastingly chained to a single little fragment of the Whole, man himself develops into nothing but a fragment; everlastingly in his ear the monotonous sound of the wheel that he turns, he never develops the harmony of his being, and instead of putting the stamp of humanity upon his own nature, he becomes nothing more than the imprint of his occupation or of his specialised knowledge."[13]

Schiller contrasts the inner fragmentation of contemporary human beings with a model of psychic harmony which he held to be exemplified by the ancient Greeks. But while sharing the then common belief in the myth of Greek wholeness, he emphasized that the further development of culture was impossible without a greater differentiation of faculty and function and the increased role of reason in the regulation of human affairs. The central problem of the age was how to reconcile this progress with the development of individuals, how to preserve political liberty within a highly organized modern state. These issues, whose resolution, he asserts, will decide the fate of humanity, had been brought to a head by the French Revolution. It was the pressing duty of the philosopher, as citizen, to deal with them.

He argues that the Terror revealed not the bankruptcy of enlightened principles, but the failure of human beings to relate intellectual convictions to moral character. There must, it seemed, be "something in the disposition of men which stands in the way of the acceptance of truth, however brightly it may shine, and of the adoption of truth, however forcibly it may convince."[14]

Modern human beings could be at odds with themselves in one of two ways, according to which of their two basic drives, the sensual and the rational, dominated their psyche. Those ruled by sensation (savages) were bound to the realm of physical necessity by their crude and ungovernable instincts. The opposite type (barbarians) regulated existence by principle; but their intellectual enlightenment, unaccompanied by nobility of feeling, too often resulted in the support of heartlessness and brutality by precepts. The clash between the two types (epitomized, respectively, in the French revolutionary mobs and the ideologues of the Terror) was, Schiller contends, reflected in the character of the modern state, which, representing "that ideal and objective humanity which exists in the heart of each of its citizens," of necessity observed toward them the same relationship as they had toward themselves. Where in the character of a people blind impulse and rationality were habitually set against each other, the antagonism between the two was played out in an alternation between tyranny and insurrection, force being the ultimate arbiter of human affairs. Attempts at political reform would succeed only when humanity ceased to be at odds with itself: "Wholeness of character must . . . be present in any people capable, and worthy, of exchanging a State of compulsion for a State of freedom."[15]

This condition could not be attained by following the Kantian model of moral freedom, which in its letter if not its spirit postulated a primary and therefore necessary antagonism between humanity's two fundamental drives. Once this premiss is accepted, Schiller asserts, "there is, of course, no other means of maintaining unity in man than by unconditionally subordinating the sensuous drive to the rational. From this, however, only uniformity can result, never harmony, and man goes on forever being divided."[16]

The intellectual heirs of the Enlightenment needed no persuading of the pernicious effects on thought and action of an undue surrender to their sensual natures; but Schiller believed that modern human beings were insufficiently conscious of the threat to freedom posed by the preponderance of the rational drive. There are, he argues, two ways in which the state, as an ideal construct of universalizing reason, can relate to its individual human components: "either by the ideal man suppressing empirical man, and the State annulling individuals; or else by the individual himself becoming the State, and man in time being ennobled to the stature of man as Idea."[17]

A person who has formed his character by suppressing feeling will naturally incline toward the first of these two alternatives: "Armoured by principle against all natural feeling, [he will] be equally inaccessible to the claims of humanity from without as he is to those of humanity from within."[18] From a strictly moral standpoint, it did not matter whether or not the cultivation of reason in the individual psyche was achieved through the blunting of feeling; to the state, too, it was a matter of indifference whether the citizen's conformity to law was one of free acquiescence or servile submission:

> But in the complete anthropological view, where content
> counts no less than form, and living feeling too has a
> voice, the difference becomes all the more relevant. Rea-
> son does indeed demand unity; but Nature demands multi-
> plicity; and both these kinds of law make their claim upon
> man. . . . Hence it will always argue a still defective educa-
> tion if the moral character is able to assert itself only by
> sacrificing the natural. And a political constitution will
> still be very imperfect if it is able to achieve unity only by
> suppressing variety. The State should not only respect the
> objective and generic character in its individual subjects; it
> should also honour their subjective and specific character,
> and in extending the invisible realm of morals take care
> not to depopulate the sensible realm of appearance.[19]

In order to achieve such a balance, the citizen must be able to universalize his conduct without suppressing his individuality; but all human activities, by demanding the more or less separate exercise of one or other of our drives, seem designed to perpetuate the division between them. With one exception—the contemplation of beauty, which, as an instance of human beings' not needing to renounce their sensual impulses in order to express their spiritual nature, proved that the Kantian model of virtue was not the only possible one. In the aesthetic contemplation of abstraction in sensuous form, Schiller argues, the faculties separated in other activities are exercised simultaneously, activating a third, play drive. At once spontaneous and purposive, serious and frivolous, representing a momentary union between matter and form, passivity and freedom, this drive proves "the compatibility of our two natures, the practicability of the infinite being realised in the finite, hence the possibility of sublimest humanity."[20]

By freeing the psyche from the limitations induced by the sensual and rational drives when operating separately, the play drive makes us master simultaneously and to an equal degree of all our powers.

The contemplation of beauty releases us in a state of freedom by restoring to us the potentialities that we lose with every determinate state, whether of thought or feeling, that we enter. We emerge from such contemplation in a mood in which "we shall with equal ease turn to seriousness or to play, to repose or to movement, to compliance or to resistance, to the discursions of abstract thought or to the direct contemplation of phenomena."[21]

As a mediating agency between constraint and freedom, aesthetic contemplation can "enchain nature in the savage, and set it free in the barbarian." As form, beauty can lead from sensation to thought; as living image it unites concept with intuition, offering thereby the means of developing all our sensual and spiritual powers in the greatest possible harmony. In order not to be limited or defined by any of the goal-directed determinations of our psyche, Schiller claims, we must reactualize our potential by a recurrent retreat into a state of "active determinability" through the contemplation of beauty.[22]

Although maintaining that "it is only through Beauty that man makes his way to Freedom,"[23] Schiller insists on the importance of Kant's distinction between beauty and the good: the achievement of completeness through aesthetic culture is a necessary but not, he stresses, a sufficient condition of moral freedom. He does not argue that this psychic state can of itself provide a moral code of conduct; it can merely, by intensifying the power and depth of the personality, ensure that we respond to challenges with our full potential as integrated human beings.

Schiller never suggests that aesthetic freedom is an ideal to be pursued to the exclusion of all else or that its achievement will free us from the strains of moral choice. What he promises is (as one commentary on the *Aesthetic Education* puts it) "not freedom from passion, but freedom to do more than just passively suffer the brute impact of passion: not immunity from prejudice, aberration, even hallucination, but the possibility of not being blindly identified with any one of these our conditions."[24]

Unlike the beautiful soul, the aesthetically modulated individual is not immune from inner conflict. Some moral choices will demand struggle, renunciation, the sacrifice of personal harmony in the interests of something transcending the self. Schiller agreed with Kant that our moral dignity depends on a strict distinction between our sensual and rational drives—but added that our hope of "joy and blessedness" relies on their "due and proper reconciliation."[25] He conceived of personal wholeness as a reciprocal subordination of drives, whose relations would be shifted and balanced in appropriate and flexible responses to specific situations, neither rigidly adhering to principle nor blindly obeying the compulsion of instinct.

The aesthetic ideal of Schiller's treatise has been interpreted both as a call to retreat into the inner life of the spirit and as the vision of a society led by a priesthood of artists.[26] It is neither. Schiller emphasizes that his ideal cannot be achieved merely through the development of particular faculties: it is a modulation of the entire psyche. The aesthetically modulated individual (*der ästhetisch gestimmte Mensch*) is distinguished by the quality of his responses to his entire human and natural environment. Aesthetic education is not to be the perquisite of an elite of gifted individuals, a training in the contemplation or creation of works of art: Schiller sees it as the universal cultivation of a sense of relationships, a taste which will be reflected in all human pursuits, from the most trivial to the most esoteric, informing all our moral, intellectual, and physical activities. Manifested in the relations between individuals, the "aesthetic state,"[27] as Schiller calls it, will produce the discriminating insights on which the improvement of society depends.

If the belief that Schiller was a proponent of the divorce between art and politics stems largely from a misinterpretation of his use of the term *aesthetic*,[28] it was also supported by the image of Schiller as the romantic poet of an ideal freedom, who, when the French Revolution failed to realize his dream, turned his back on politics to preach the gospel of self-cultivation. But Schiller's position could hardly be less ambiguously stated in the treatise which he described as his profession of political faith:[29] the construction of true political freedom is "the most perfect of all the works to be achieved by the art of man."[30] His correspondence and essays, far from reflecting a progression from romantic radicalism to apolitical conservatism, reveal a consistent liberalism of the kind preached by his friend, the scholar and statesman Wilhelm von Humboldt: a belief that the rights of the individual are sacred and that the role of the state is to provide a secure framework for their protection and mutual regulation[31]—hence his comment in the *Aesthetic Education* on the imperfection of political constitutions which achieve unity by suppressing variety. Schiller had none of the romantics' hostility to analytical reason; he did not yearn for a prescientific golden age but sought to confront a modern challenge: to combine individuality with specialization, intensity of knowledge with breadth of experience. Contemporary states, constrained to impose servile conformity in order to govern unrestrained nature, maintained their stability through an "equilibrium of evils"; a state which fostered the integration of sense and reason in the characters of its citizens would, Schiller predicts, be "removed alike from uniformity and from confusion."[32]

The vagueness of such formulations has caused the accusation of otherworldliness to resurface in recent Schiller scholarship: he is accused, for example, of failing to translate his concept of totality "into terms of citizenship, institutional policy, common welfare, government responsibilities, jurisprudence."[33] But had he attempted to do so, he would have risked falling into contradiction with his aesthetic model of the personality, whose social relationships, if they were to respond flexibly to a rapidly changing world, could not be prescribed in advance, and whose moral freedom grew in inverse proportion to his need to regulate those relationships by "hardened, fixed rules."

Schiller never denied the connected charge that his ideal was unrealizable. He accepted that aesthetic enjoyment could never produce more than an approximation to total determinability. All he wished was that humanity should set out on the way toward wholeness, and he had none of the utopian's sanguine confidence in the speed of its progress—what he proposed was "a task for more than one century." This conservative estimate was based on an insight that ran counter to the political optimism of the age: in Schiller's view the greatest obstacle to political emancipation was not (as generally believed by enlightened persons) ignorance or external oppression, but people's inner resistance to freedom. History and psychology offered overwhelming evidence that human beings preferred the security afforded by subservience to external directives and precepts to the risks involved in assuming responsibility for their own inner development: "Since it costs effort to remain true to one's principles when feeling is easily stirred, we take the easier way out and try to make character secure by blunting feeling; for it is, of course, infinitely easier to have peace and quiet from an adversary you have disarmed than to master a spirited and active foe."[34]

While people remained in this state of inner bondage, no liberating movement could change their relation to the body politic: "The old principles will remain; but they will wear the dress of the century, and Philosophy now lend her name to a repression formerly authorised by the Church." The human race will continue to lurch convulsively between tyranny and revolt: "Fearful of freedom, which in its first tentative ventures always comes in the guise of an enemy, we shall either cast ourselves into the arms of an easy servitude or, driven to despair by a pedantic tutelage, escape into the wild libertinism of the natural state. Usurpation will invoke the weakness of human nature, insurrection its dignity; until finally blind force, that great imperatrice of human affairs, steps in and decides this pretended conflict of principles as though it were a common brawl."[35]

It was under a tyranny—the regime of tsar Nicholas I—that Russians turned to Schiller as the prophet of freedom: not the mature author of the *Aesthetic Education*, but the poet-playwright who was the spokesman of idealistic and rebellious youth. Schooled in a cult of feeling by sentimentalist and romantic literature, Herzen's generation of young gentry intellectuals was entranced by Schiller's ideal of the *schöne Seele*. As Martin Malia observes, "Schiller furnished the first ideological point of convergence for Herzen's youthful frustrations, and the most kindred articulation of his dreams."[36] Schiller's poetry and dramas helped Herzen compensate for a lack of liberty in the real world through an unfocused humanism expressed in hopes for the future free flowering of all personalities, and a cult of self-fulfillment through aesthetic contemplation and idealized friendship and love. His adolescent worship of Schiller was shared with his cousin and bosom friend Nikolai Ogaryov. In their fantasies the two boys became the titanic heroes of Schiller's dramas, superior beings in revolt against the mediocrity and moral ugliness of a philistine world. There followed for Herzen (as for most of his generation) an immersion in Schelling's idealism, counterbalanced in Herzen's case by his study of natural sciences at Moscow University and the influence of Bacon's inductive method, which persuaded him of the one-sidedness of idealist speculation and the importance of testing generalizations through experiment. Whereas his contemporaries were still looking to philosophy for a refuge from the external world, Herzen was beginning to demand, as the German Left Hegelians would do nearly a decade later, that philosophy not merely interpret the world, but change it. Yet although Bacon was a seminal influence on his thinking, he was conscious, as he notes in an early essay, that the Renaissance philosopher's insights represented only the beginning of a new phase in humanity's progression toward an approach to the external world in which reason would be harmonized with sense experience as a necessary premiss for effective action.[37]

Herzen points out that this transformed understanding of the world, whose beginnings were as yet only dimly perceived, could not by its very nature be enshrined in fixed and universal formulas. He therefore began to evolve his own definition of the new method, as he called it, by explaining what it was not, through a critique of various one-sided visions of the world. This led him first to repudiate the idol of his youth and then to rediscover him, as he perceived that he and Schiller were engaged in the same enterprise, preachers of a new humanism to be attained by means of an aesthetic education.

The isolation of the exile to which Herzen was sentenced in 1834 forced him back to an inward-looking idealism, but toward the end of his sentence he became preoccupied again with the reform of human societies, reacquainting himself with the ideas of the French utopian socialists which he had first encountered in 1833. He urged his friend Ogaryov to desist from his "theurgical" dreaming and address the problem of action in the real world: "We have no more time to waste." He tells him not to let his love for Schiller blind him to the fact that Schiller "understood life one-sidedly." He was obsessed with an ideal of perfection: "That is why it seemed to him '*und das Dort wird nimmer hier* (yonder will never be here)'—but it *is* 'hier'"—one must not neglect the possibilities of self-fulfillment in the here and now.[38] Herzen rejected the contemplative Hegelianism that was then the philosophical fashion in Moscow, along with all other forms of idealism which provided an escape route from the present through fantasies of future bliss. In a diary entry of 1842 he writes, "There is nothing in the world more foolish than despising the present for the sake of the future. The present is the true sphere of existence. One must grasp every moment, every pleasure. The soul must be constantly open to the surrounding world, absorbing it and suffusing it with its own being."[39] Inspired by the theories of the Left Hegelians, he had come to equate historical progress with the destruction of the religious and philosophical illusions that alienated humans from their nature, preventing them from actualizing their potential as rational, emotional, and volitional beings.

This new radical humanism seems worlds away from the inward-looking aestheticism of Herzen's adolescence. But it coincided with a revival of his early enthusiasm for Schiller. In a fragment published in 1840 he records the changes in his attitude to Schiller over the preceding decade. His adolescent worship of the "poet of youth" ended when the sentiments in Schiller's poetry and plays came to seem shallow to him in comparison with the sufferings of Shakespeare's Hamlet and Goethe's Faust: "But soon I came to my senses, blushed for my ingratitude, and with hot tears of repentance threw myself into Schiller's embrace."[40]

Herzen had come to see Schiller as a giant who with Goethe

transcended the limitations of the romantic and classical visions alike. While conceding that Schiller was closer to the romantics than Goethe, Herzen argues that his last and most mature works were "purely *humanist*." His outlook, like Goethe's, possessed an extraordinary breadth, depth, and humanity, "uniting opposing and conflicting tendencies . . . in an amazing fullness."[41]

Why this transformation in Herzen's view of Schiller? He is not explicit on this point, but I believe the answer lies in his reference to Schiller's mature works. Herzen's writings throughout the 1840s are centrally concerned with the question of moral freedom, and the resemblance between his formulation of the problem and Schiller's (in his later philosophical works) is so close as to suggest that Schiller's ideas had at least as great an influence on him in this respect as those of the Left Hegelians.

The parallels between the two thinkers are most striking in an essay of 1846 in which Herzen sets out, in typical Left Hegelian fashion, to attack the concept of duty as one of the hollow abstractions that humans have elevated above themselves: "There is no universal and true idea from which people will not weave a rope to bind their feet and, if possible, those of others. . . . Friendship, brotherhood, . . . the love of freedom itself, have served as inexhaustible sources of moral oppression and servitude."[42]

The body of Herzen's argument, however, recalls a much earlier critique of human self-alienation: Schiller's polemic with Kant in "On Grace and Dignity" and the *Aesthetic Education*. Herzen attacks those secular moralists who, as the church had done before them, present virtuous acts as acts of self-coercion in obedience to external imperatives. Remarking on the absurdity of the idea that people should force themselves to obey the commands of their own reason as though it were an alien authority, Herzen protests, as Schiller had done to Kant, "To regard oneself as stupid, . . . weak, deserving of contempt . . . and owing all one's significance to some external source—surely that isn't virtue?"[43] Herzen points out that animals are not held to have instincts contrary to the basic purposes of their existence; why then should this be true of human beings?

Moral acts are not a denial of human nature, but are rather the natural behavior of persons who have attained full consciousness of their human dignity.

This argument was consistent with the "rehabilitation of the flesh" proclaimed by the Left Hegelians and the French utopian socialists: but Herzen departed from them in his paradoxical presentation of this natural state of being as the result of an arduous process whereby human beings learn to overcome their fear of freedom—a fear which, like Schiller, Herzen attributes to moral laziness and a desire for order and security. Humanity's love of moral freedom is "purely platonic": it has contracted a marriage of convenience with moral servitude. It is easier to uphold a social morality that cripples human nature, outlawing egoism and condemning the passions, than to recognize the rights of these to expression as integral parts of the personality. For the first course there are clearly defined rules, sanctions, and rewards; the second "terrifies people with its endless vistas, the possibility of advancing in any direction whatsoever."[44]

It is on the question of responsibility for asserting one's personal autonomy that Herzen's moral philosophy most strikingly resembles Schiller's and, by the same token, diverges most sharply from those of his radical contemporaries—as is illustrated by his first essay on the subject, "Concerning a Certain Drama," written in 1842.

The theme of the essay was relations between the sexes, a topic that French utopian socialism and the novels of George Sand had placed high on the agenda of the contemporary European Left. Many radicals believed that by casting off the fetters of social convention and marital duty and following their instincts in sexual matters, men and women could strike a vital blow in the battle for human emancipation. Herzen's essay presents a much more complex view of that process. He begins by emphasizing the heavy responsibility that moral freedom entails. Problems previously resolved by appeals to traditional codes of behavior may appear insoluble to those who have discarded such codes: for example, the conflict between duty and passion, as epitomized by a contemporary French drama, whose plot (a marital triangle with a tragic outcome for the three participants) Herzen recounts in his essay. He argues that the cause of the tragedy was the characters' limited personalities. They had cut themselves off from the universal concerns of the time to devote themselves to their emotional lives; when their private world was shattered, they had nothing else to live for. But he rejects the solution of moral formalists—that passion be sacrificed to universal moral norms, in this case the duties imposed by the marriage bond: "The supreme form of such a marriage would be when husband and wife cannot stand one another and perform their marital functions ex officio."[45]

This remark recalls Schiller's satirical verses on Kant's concept of duty. Herzen knew them: in a later essay he quotes them against those moralists who confront the human spirit with "the terrible opposition between duty and inclination," presenting duty as a burden and seeing merit in its reluctant performance—a premiss, Herzen argues, that could logically lead only to the bizarre conclusion of Schiller's poem. A moral act should be seen as an act of self-fulfillment, through the blissful reconciliation of heart and mind, duty and passion.[46]

In "Concerning a Certain Drama" Herzen charts the relation of feeling to reason in a morally free act in a manner reminiscent of Schiller's polemic with Kant. Moral formalists, he observes, are always talking about the reconciliation of humanity's conflicting drives in a "higher unity," but in reality

> their aim is to crush all the natural side of the human being. . . . They want from it not a free sacrifice, but a slavish recognition of its own insignificance; *they don't take the trouble to direct the heart to rational goals,* but demand that it renounce itself because it is closer to nature. But the proud human heart does not recognize such demands . . . it knows how weak and uncompelling, once the flame of passionate attraction has been kindled, is the obligation to sacrifice oneself to formal duty. . . .
>
> One must not reject the impulses of the heart, not

deny one's individuality . . . but open up the egoistic heart
to all that suffers, universalize it through reason and in
turn enliven reason through its agency.[47]

Herzen's argument is identical with Schiller's: forcible subjugation of the passions to reason will lead either to their rebellion against all rational control or to their slavish submission: moral freedom can result only from the "free sacrifice" of the heart to the imperatives of reason. Herzen saw such freedom as much more than a joyous release from the oppressive authorities of the past. It was above all an acceptance of the terrifying responsibility for one's own moral development, through the mutual regulation of those "opposing and conflicting tendencies" which he believed to be so admirably united in Schiller.

Herzen's observations on the relations between the sexes were potentially as subversive of radical ideologies as they were of the status quo. The theme of a love triangle recurs in his semiautobiographical novel of 1847, *Who Is to Blame?* His radical contemporaries, who welcomed its satire of the mores of Nicholas's Russia, failed to notice that that satire was double-edged: from the perspective of the Sandian code of sexual liberation, the novel was distinctly heretical. The wife cannot bring herself to leave her husband for her lover, not, as contemporary commentaries on the novel suggested, because she is insufficiently liberated from conventional morality: Herzen was at pains to stress the moral independence of his heroine, who was modeled on his adored wife, Natalie. She is bound to her husband by a loyalty that owes nothing to externally imposed moral or social conventions and by affection—Herzen reveals that she loves both men. Her husband decides on the noble gesture of offering her her freedom, together with his fraternal friendship—the only decent role open to discarded mates in the Sandian code—but jealousy prevents him from carrying out his intention, and Herzen comments, "We shall not blame him. Such unnatural acts of virtue and premeditated self-immolation are not at all in keeping with human nature: they belong to the realm of imagination rather than reality."[48]

In its simple solutions to complex problems, Herzen suggests, the new radical ethic showed as little regard for the realities of human nature as the old. This double-edged critique became more explicit when, after emigrating to the West, Herzen encountered the new morality at first hand among French radicals whom he accused, along with George Sand, of preaching "notions of abstract duty, obligatory virtues" unrelated to ordinary life. He pointed out that in their attempt to force human nature into a straitjacket of their own devising, these thinkers were following a familiar pattern. Women had once been stoned for infidelity: now jealousy was outlawed as the expression of an impermissible possessiveness: "Against the marriage of legal contract [the novelists] have set up a dogma of psychiatry and physiology: the absolute infallibility of the passions and humans' inability to struggle against them. Those who yesterday were slaves of marriage have now become slaves of love."[49]

The new moralists had asserted the independence of the human personality from God and the devil, only to subject it to the irresistible force of passion. In real human relations, unlike the abstract dialectic of the philosophers, Herzen argues, "a brusque *entweder/oder* (either/or) will lead us nowhere. At the moment of the complete negation of one of the terms, it returns." To reduce the relationships of men and women to casual sexual encounters was as unacceptable as to bind them in indissoluble marriage: "Healthy, normal human life shuns the monastery just as much as the cattleyard." Instincts such as jealousy were an ineradicable part of human nature: instead of outlawing them, one should seek to ensure *"that they flow humanely . . .* that they be equally far removed from monastic poison, bestial ferocity, or the howl of the wounded property-owner." The morality of the future should seek not to stifle and proscribe, but "to introduce more harmony into our conduct," to reconcile personal feelings with universal goals in what Herzen, reminding his readers of the "aesthetic harmony of Plato's Republic," calls "an *elegant* balancing of passion with sacrifice."[50]

That felicitous phrase could equally well characterize the ideal society outlined in the *Aesthetic Education.* Herzen first read the work when, under the influence of Left Hegelian ideas, he was beginning to explore the relationship between moral and political freedom. The profound impression that Schiller's treatise made on him is recorded in a diary entry of July 1843: "A great and prophetic work ... much in advance of its time. Schiller has not been given his due in recent times. These letters were written in 1795 or thereabouts, when Schelling had hardly begun to write. Schiller started out from the standpoint of Kant—but what juicy, vital, beautiful fruits! He went far beyond the views of the critical school. Here, as in some pages of Goethe, are the first poetic and sonorous chords of the new science."

In November of the same year he describes the work as "a colossal step forward in the development of the idea of history."[51] Such a grasp of the originality, scope, and political significance of Schiller's work was rare, as we have seen, until the mid–twentieth century. But for more than a decade Herzen had been approaching the problem of human self-alienation from a very similar perspective. He encountered the *Aesthetic Education* when he had completed *Dilettantism in Science,* the first of two series of essays in which he explores the ways that consciousness has historically misrepresented the external world. These are commonly known as Herzen's Hegelian works, and few critics have remarked on their prominent use of aesthetic criteria. But his diary note on Schiller should alert us to the importance of that feature; Herzen's comment conveys the shock of recognition that he and Schiller had conceived a common project: the aesthetic education of human beings.

Dilettantism in Science attacks the forms of social quietism prevalent in Russian philosophical circles at that time, which Herzen identifies with two one-sided intellectual types. The dilettantes cling to a comforting belief in transcendent entities, whether religious or philosophical, and dabble in philosophy as a form of escapism, demanding only that it confirm their illusions (Herzen had in mind particularly the romantic conservatism of the Russian Slavophiles). Their attitude to the external world is dictated by their egotistical feelings: they equate reality with their subjective desires, which they refuse to submit to the scrutiny of reason.

The opposing intellectual type, buddhists or formalists, dominated by their rational drive, seek to order experience by reference to universal rules and absolute principles. Herzen's criticism was aimed specifically at conservative Hegelians who had defended the existing order in Russia as an inevitable stage in the fulfillment of a schema of universal progress. He accuses them of repressing their compassionate instincts and cultivating an indifference to "all the dark side of contemporary life,"[52] on the ground that the sufferings of transient individuals were a necessary precondition for the realization of history's transcendent goals. Herzen argued that, like the otherworldliness of the dilettantes, the fatalism of the buddhists represented a dualistic approach to reality that isolated elements of the historical process which could be understood only in their dynamic interplay in the flux of events. To grasp the complexity of these relationships, to be able to distinguish in the headlong movement of history between what had outlived its time and what contained the seeds of growth, individuals must achieve a similar tension and balance between their generalizing and particularizing powers, a state that Herzen saw as the prologue to the political transformation of society.

He could only hint at this eventuality in print and concentrated on conveying the nature of that integrated perception of reality which he believed to be the precondition of effective action. As he began work on his second series of essays, *Letters on the Study of Nature*, a history of thought modeled on Hegel's, he turned to the natural sciences for examples of thinking that was tied to close observation of the physical world. In this respect the *Aesthetic Education* harshly criticized the science of Schiller's day:

> One of the chief reasons why our natural sciences make
> such slow progress is obviously the universal, and almost
> uncontrollable, propensity to teleological judgments, in
> which . . . the determining faculty is substituted for the
> receptive. However strong and however varied the impact

made upon our organs by nature, all her manifold variety
is then entirely lost upon us, because we are seeking nothing in her but what we have put into her; because, instead
of letting her come in upon us, we are thrusting ourselves
out upon her with all the impatient anticipations of our
reason. . . . This violent usurping of authority by ratiocina-
tion in a field where its right to give orders is by no
means unconditional, is the reason why so many thinking
minds fail to have any fruitful effect upon the advancement of science; and it would be difficult to say which has
done more harm to the progress of knowledge: a sense-
faculty unamenable to form, or a reasoning faculty which
will not stay for a content.[53]

The meager results of Herzen's search for inspiration in scientific
methodology suggest that half a century after Schiller wrote this
passage, the situation had not greatly changed. Herzen embarked
on an intensive program of reading combined with attendance at
lectures on anatomy and physiology, but the principal result of
these efforts was to lead him to a deeper appreciation of the Renaissance thinker whose inductive method had first impressed him
as a university student: Bacon's insights seemed to him "startlingly
new."[54] But in the *Letters* he stresses that, although adumbrated by
men such as Bacon and by Hegel himself, an approach to reality
that could grasp the unifying principles of phenomena without di-
vorcing them from their material manifestations and thereby fal-
sifying our representations of the visible world was still an ideal for
the future. But an "ecstatic poetic anticipation" of that ideal already
existed—in art, in whose unity of form and content "thought is
immediate and immediacy spiritualized." Herzen argues that such
a synthesis was evident in the culture of ancient Greece, expressing
itself in "a subtle harmony of parts, a virtuosity in life, science, and
institutions."[55] The main source for his discussion of Greek philosophy was Hegel's lectures on this theme, but he prefers the term
realist to Hegel's word *materialist* as a characterization of Greek
thought; and his use of the myth of Greek wholeness as a model

for modern humanity (together with his emphasis on the limitations of that model) recalls Schiller's treatise.

Herzen defines the principal characteristic of the Greeks as a sense of measure: "[They] never confused the sublime with the massive, the elegant with the overwhelming. . . . They understood that the secret of grace lies in a high degree of proportionality between form and content, inner and outer. . . . Greek life . . . flows serenely between two extremes, between existence sunk in sensual immediacy, in which the personality is lost, and the loss of actuality in universal abstractions."[56]

But he reminds us that the harmony of Greek culture was a function of its limited vision of the human personality; the human race's subsequent progression toward rational autonomy had led to the estrangement of spirit from matter, humanity from nature. Herzen suggests that the most important task facing the human intellect in the future will be to combine the actuality and realism of Greek thought with the insights produced by the tormented introspection of the modern age. As an example of the kind of thinking that came close to this ideal, Herzen points to Goethe. While preparing the *Letters* he had read Goethe's scientific treatise *On the Metamorphosis of Plants* and noted in his diary, "What a giant! The poet was not lost in the naturalist. His science expresses . . . the poetry of real life."[57]

Goethe's scientific writings seemed to Herzen to exemplify both the dynamism and the monism of the type of perception that he was struggling to define. Anticipating Hegel's dialectic, Goethe was concerned not with finished objects but with processes: the emergence of new forms through the interplay of opposing forces, all of whose manifestations, from inorganic matter to the highest forms of human creativity, must, he insisted, be understood as part of a single living totality. Distrusting conventional scientific methods of classification, dissection, and analysis, Goethe demanded that his readers think not in concepts (*Begriffe*) but in mental images (*Anschauungen*); he readily accepted a contemporary's definition of his thought as "object-thinking" (*gegenständliches Denken*).[58] In that part of the "Letters" devoted to the modern age Herzen argues that, after Kant's doctrine that things-in-themselves could never be known had threatened to plunge philosophy into despair, it had been rescued by Goethe's "profound realism." Neither a philosopher nor a scholar, he was a "thinking artist" whose vision of reality was "immediate to the highest degree":"[He] instantly plunges *in medias res* (into the center of things) . . . as an experimentalist, an observer . . . but see how the idea of a given object grows and develops under his gaze, how it unfolds inseparably from its contingent existence, and how finally the all-embracing idea is revealed in all its depth. . . . For him nature is life—the same life as exists within him. Hence he understands it: more than that—as it vibrates in him it reveals its secret to us."[59]

In reality Goethe's approach to science was unscientific by any generally recognized standards—the rigorous testing of inspired intuitions by evidence and logic which Herzen admired in Bacon's inductive method was anathema to Goethe. But this discrepancy appears to have escaped Herzen's notice. Goethe interested him primarily as an illustration of a state of psychic harmony that was supremely difficult to define in the terms of abstract argument. The "artistic profundity" of Goethe's thought was epitomized for him by a fragment on Nature, which Herzen quotes, emphasizing its tone of rapturous enthusiasm: "Intoxication with existence . . . emanates from every word."[60]

Repeatedly in *Dilettantism* and the *Letters*, Herzen stresses that a sense of the self-sufficient value of the transient manifestations of life and an aesthetic delight in their interplay are essential concomitants of reason in the understanding of historical reality: "Thought must take on flesh, . . . unfold in all the splendor and beauty of transient existence."[61] The analysis of historical events must be accompanied by a sympathetic insight into the experiences of those caught up in them. It is this humanist empathy with his age that Herzen admires in Schiller, contrasting it with the conservative Hegelians' approach sub specie aeternitatis to the historical process. He laments their lack of warmth and sympathy toward the life around them, their indifference to its poetry, embodied in the extravagant multiplicity of the concrete forms of existence, whose endless variations on a single theme seem chaotic and superfluous to the systematizing intellect. Paraphrasing a quotation from Hegel, Herzen accuses them of hearing all the sounds, but not the harmony. To grasp the headlong movement of reality an understanding of formal relationships is not enough: he describes Hegel's vision of the dialectical development of consciousness (as interpreted by the Left Hegelians) as a lyric poem that must be "lived through" by the entire personality.[62] For an orthodox training in Hegel's dialectic he substitutes an aesthetic education aimed at the cultivation of a play-drive, the ability to approach phenomena as living form (to use Schiller's expression),[63] without enclosing them in a straitjacket of ultimate ends and purposes.

In *Dilettantism* Herzen declares,

> Peoples would be something pitiful if they saw their lives as only a step toward an unknown future; they would be like bearers who have only the weight of the burden and the difficulty of the way: the treasure they bear is for others. Nature does not treat her unconscious children like this—all the more so, in the world of consciousness there can be no stage without its own satisfaction.
>
> Each stage in history . . . has its own fulness—in a word, its personality, seething with life . . . each phase of historical development has had its end in itself, and consequently its own reward and satisfaction.[64]

Compare the passage in Schiller's treatise in which he attacks those forms of specialization that advance the progress of humanity at the cost of the development of individuals:

> In what kind of relation would we stand to either past or future ages, if the development of human nature were to make such sacrifice necessary? We would have been the serfs of mankind; for several millennia we would have done slaves' work for them, and our mutilated nature would bear impressed upon it the shameful marks of this servitude. And all this in order that a future generation

might in blissful indolence attend to the care of its moral
health, and foster the free growth of its humanity!

But can Man really be destined to miss himself for the
sake of any purpose whatsoever?[65]

Like Schiller, Herzen urges that instead of submitting to total-
izing systems we make our drive toward totality of character the
determinant of our moral and social ideals. The individual personality, ignored by philosophy, "has come to demand its rights, to
demand a life palpitating with passion, and self-sufficient through
free and creative action alone.... The need for personality has been
revealed." The ideal for each period, Herzen asserts, "is its own
self, purged of contingency, a transformed contemplation of the
present. Of course, the richer the present is, the more it embraces,
the more universally valid its ideal will be."[66]

"Human beings cannot rest until everything around them has
been brought into unison with them": it is likely that here Herzen
was quoting from a passage in a letter from Schiller to his friend
Körner, outlining the theme of his poem "Die Künstler" (The artists): "The human being, once stirred and animated by a feeling of
beauty, harmony and symmetry, cannot rest until he has brought
everything around him into unison with him, ... until he has given
the most perfect possible shape to everything around him."[67] Herzen puts the same idea in another way: one's actions acquire "aesthetic completeness and vital plenitude" only when one works for
the common goals of humanity as though one were seeking to
satisfy a personal, inner need. Both writers are centrally concerned
with the same paradox: the cultivation of aesthetic delight in the
play of reality, by releasing the personality from subjection to
future-oriented or goal-directed activity, enables it to pursue universal goals more fruitfully and efficiently, guided by that sense of
proportion and measure which Herzen describes as "the main condition for harmonious development."[68]

This view of progress contrasts sharply with the apocalyptic vision then being propagated in the West by the other great radical
of Herzen's generation, Mikhail Bakunin. "The Reaction in Ger-

many," Bakunin's Left Hegelian tract of 1842, forecast that a "new heaven and a new earth" would emerge after the root and branch destruction of the existing order by the "party of negation."[69] In the last essay of *Dilettantism in Science,* published a year after Bakunin's manifesto, Herzen declares the two pillars of his view of the world to be faith in the future and love for the present. Once he gained the freedom to spell that view out in full, it became clear how dissonant a note it struck in the radical chorus of his time.

Herzen's Russian Socialism and the aesthetic ideal of moral freedom that inspired it have been commonly interpreted as one of the last fruits of a vanishing aristocratic culture. In Soviet jargon, Herzen was a "gentry revolutionary" who anticipated the revolutionary democracy of the future but also looked back to the aristocratic rebellion of the Decembrists. Western critics, too, have situated him at the beginning of a radical tradition leading from abstract idealism to Marxist revolutionary theory.[70] These attempts to place Herzen in a retrospectively constituted revolutionary tradition reveal the continued influence (even on non-Marxist scholarship) of the historicist schema first formulated by Marx in his polemics with his socialist rivals, which traced the development of socialism from utopian forms characterized by abstract moral ideals to more objective or scientific forms that gave central importance to socioeconomic relations. Herzen's emphasis on reconciling socialist goals with the values of personal dignity and moral freedom has been ascribed to a lack of realism—part of a gentry mentality that allowed him to keep his head in the clouds of idealism and avoid facing the difficult choices of everyday life.[71]

Undeniably, Herzen's social conditioning as an aristocrat from a preindustrial country—which led him to idealize the Russian peasantry and to approach the European bourgeoisie primarily as an ethical phenomenon, with scant interest in its economic role—imposed significant limitations on his grasp of the causes of conflict and change in advanced societies. But he was much less a victim of his conditioning than he has been made out to be. His extraordinary powers of intellect and observation enabled him to put his

predicament to good use: his reflections on the mentality of alienated intellectuals such as himself produced a critique of the intellectual and emotional roots of ideological thinking that was unsur-
passed in his century. This aspect of his thought has been
undervalued, whereas others have been given disproportionate emphasis by being integrated into a typology of utopian thought. Herzen himself, as we shall see, believed that his main significance as
a thinker lay not in the specific ideal that he advanced, but in his
search to identify the intellectual and emotional sources of authoritarianism in morality and politics. I shall briefly outline the way
in which, after his emigration in 1847, Herzen translated his Schillerian vision of moral freedom into a model for political thinking.

Herzen's view of freedom inspired an analysis of the Revolution of
1848 in France that estranged him from all the radical groupings
of his time. As Schiller had done with regard to the Revolution of
1789, he saw the failure of 1848 to realize its ideals as rooted in
the relations of individuals with themselves, a psychic imbalance
reflected in the polarization of reason and instinct among the
protagonists of progress. On the one hand, the masses (Schiller's
savages) were impelled by "dark instincts" toward a vengeful destruction; on the other, the French liberals and radicals, having
constructed an idealized model of the "sovereign people," had set
it up along with other abstractions (the common good, progress,
humanity, and so on) as an idol demanding human sacrifices.
When Louis Blanc harangued Herzen on a person's duty to renounce his ego for the good of society, the argument was all too
familiar; "The divorce between society and the individual, ... the
fictitious hostility between them" is, Herzen declared, "the last form
of the religion of slavery."[72] Herzen would find the same tendency
toward idolatry of abstractions among the young Russian radicals
of the 1860s, whose doctrines, he argued, had far more to do with
the metaphysics of the French Revolution than with the perceived
needs and aspirations of the Russian peasant.[73]

   "If only people wanted to save themselves instead of saving the
world, to liberate themselves instead of liberating humanity, how

much they would do for the salvation of the world and the liberation of humanity!":[74] this is the leitmotif of Herzen's political writings, which faithfully reflect the aesthetic education that began for
him with his reading of Schiller's critique of Kant.

"Through centuries of unnatural existence . . . we have disturbed
the equilibrium," Herzen wrote. To heal the rifts in our nature
created by dualistic systems that always favor the general and abstract over the individual and particular, we must declare our independence from their authority. "There are no eternal rewards or
punishments"; "the truly free man *creates* his own morality" in
response to circumstances, guided solely by the need not to enter
into contradiction with himself. In a letter to his son Herzen declares, "There are no general rules, but there is improvisation of
behavior, understanding, tact, an aesthetics of action, which a developed person strives to attain, and which constitutes the ground
of his activity in the moral sphere."[75] Remarks such as this led some
of Herzen's contemporaries (and later critics) to define the philosophical outlook of his mature years as a pessimistic moral nihilism.[76] But his meaning was identical with Schiller's: that the equilibrium of the faculties that characterizes aesthetic play, by testifying
to the fundamental unity of human nature, should serve not as a
substitute for moral imperatives, but as a model of how these imperatives are to be reconciled with other drives.

In *Ends and Beginnings,* his polemic with Ivan Turgenev at the
beginning of the 1860s on the nature of progress,[77] Herzen agrees
with the primacy that Turgenev gives to the role of art in human
societies, echoing Schiller's description of the function of the play-
drive in offering an insight into the mystery of human destiny:
"Together with the summer lightning of personal happiness, [art]
is our only indubitable good: in all the rest we work, or draw water
for humanity, our country, for fame, for our children, for gain,
trying all the while to solve an eternal riddle. In art we enjoy ourselves, in art the aim is attained." But Herzen questioned whether
art could continue to serve this function in the West, where the
"aesthetic element" was fast vanishing from social existence, killed
off by a new vulgarity:

> Art is not fastidious: it can depict anything . . . from the
> wild and terrible fantasy of hell and the Last Judgment to
> the Flemish tavern with its back view of a peasant. . . .
> But even art has its limits. There is a stumbling block
> which can absolutely never be overcome either by the
> bow, the brush, or the sculptor's knife—to hide its impo-
> tence before it, art satirizes it. This stumbling block is the
> *bourgeoisie*. The artist who can superbly sketch a man
> quite naked, covered in rags, or so fully clothed that one
> can see nothing except armour or a monk's habit, stops in
> despair before a *bourgeois in a frock coat.*[78]

Herzen argues that great art was the product of periods characterized by restless creativity in the field of ideas, by sublime faiths
and ideals; but the materialist values of the bourgeoisie had pro-
moted a mass culture governed by norms of standardization and
quantification, a culture in which the individual was replaced by
the type, "in which the moral basis of behavior consists in living
like the rest." Such a culture, which confused form with content,
had advanced under the "arithmetical banner" of universal suffrage,
which defined truth "by addition and multiplication, where it could
be rattled out on an abacus and marked out with pins."[79] As has
been frequently pointed out, Herzen's aristocratic conditioning led
him to exaggerate the aesthetic deficiencies of bourgeois culture and
Western liberalism's indifference to the social content of political
forms, but this does not detract from his argument that the phenomenon of formalism in all its manifestations is destructive of
that aesthetic sense of relationships which is the premiss of moral
freedom. Art, "which consists above all in elegance of proportion,
cannot tolerate the measuring rule."[80] Hence the lyrical passages in
which, to borrow Schiller's terminology, he challenges the abstracting, generalizing form-drive of political doctrinaires both of the
Right and Left with a play-drive that approaches historical reality
as an aesthetic whole. He accuses them of being afraid of facts that
do not fit their theories: "What you want is that the world should,
out of gratitude for your devotion, dance to your tune, and as soon

as you realize that it has its own step and rhythm . . . you're cross, you despair. You haven't enough curiosity to watch it doing its own dance." The fact that we cannot impose our ideals on history does not mean we should let ourselves be passively borne along on its currents. Instead, we should study their fluctuations in order to open up new possibilities and new avenues of action: "Having neither a program nor a set theme, nor an inevitable dénouement, the tattered improvisation of history is ready to go along with anyone who can insert into it his verse, and if it is resonant, it will remain *his* verse, until the poem breaks off, as long as the past ferments in its blood and memory."[81]

Herzen frequently uses the word *play* to describe the historical process: those who seek to see a logical progression in it are "misled by categories not fitted to catch the flow of life": "And what, pray, is the end of the song the singer sings? . . . The sounds that burst from her throat, the melody that dies as soon as it has resounded? If you look beyond your pleasure in them for something else, for some other end, you will find that the singer has stopped singing, and then you will have only memories, and regrets, and remorse because, instead of listening, you were waiting for something else."[82]

The present should be thought of as an end in itself, rather than a means to something else: "Everything is included in this—the legacy of past efforts and the seeds of all that is to come, the inspiration of the artist, the energy of the citizen, and the rapture of the youth . . . stealing his way towards some secret arbour where his shy love awaits him—giving herself completely to the present, with no thought of the future or of an aim . . . and the joy of a fish, splashing—there—in the moonlight, . . . and the harmony of the entire solar system."[83]

. All Herzen's writings after 1848 revolve around one central paradox: that serious thinking about history and society must be founded on a play-drive. Although he does not use the term, no other can describe so well the quality of "poetic curiosity"[84] which he contrasts with the goal-directed thinking of his opponents. That poetic intoxication with the diversity of concrete existence that he had once seen reflected in Goethe's science he continually asserts to be the necessary ground for all fruitful generalizations about social ideals. He did not always practice what he preached: although he claimed to base his critique of European culture and his faith in Russia's potential on empirical evidence, they also owed something to the lingering influence of romantic nationalism. But Schiller had not promised that aesthetically modulated persons would be free from aberrations; only that they would never be permanent victims of some imbalance of perception, that they would respond to changing situations flexibly, with the fullness of their rational and intuitive powers—and this Herzen constantly strove to do, modifying his objectives and changing course under the pressure of events, seeking to navigate a precarious path between the two extremes toward which, as he once wrote, human thought is eternally drawn: "drowning in the ideal or being swallowed up in the real."[85] The function of ideals in his thought has often been misunderstood. Like Schiller's liberal state, the federation of communes envisaged in Herzen's Russian Socialism was presented not as a universal goal, but as a model of that kind of social balance, "removed alike from uniformity and from confusion," which would give the greatest possible latitude to the individual's personal development. Herzen observed that political visionaries tended to forget that the task of social transformation had its prosaic as well as its poetic side: "People are unhappy with the economic conditions of labor, . . . with the slavery of the worker, the abuse of wealth, but, . . . along with renewal and rebirth, they want to preserve as much as possible of their familiar life, . . . to harmonize it with the new conditions. On what rational basis can one . . . reconcile such complex, contradictory demands? This is the whole problem; the whole social question comes down to this, when stripped of its aura of thunder and lightning."[86]

Shortly before his death in 1870 he reminded Bakunin, specialist in revolutionary thunder and lightning, that the future upheaval must be not only a "sword of destruction" but also a "protecting force;" it must preserve what was vital and original in contemporary society, not stifling some such elements in favor of others, but contriving "to harmonize them all, for the common good": "Woe to that revolution, poor in spirit and meager in aesthetic significance, which will turn all the gains and experience of the past into a dull workshop, whose whole advantage will consist in subsistence alone."[87] The experience of the past twenty years had shown that the radical idealists of 1848 (themselves included) had seriously underestimated the attachment of the masses to beliefs and allegiances whose logical absurdity was self-evident. There were two ways to deal with this problem: to attempt to speed up the process of change by force, thereby ushering in the new world by the despotic methods of the old, or to begin to introduce the new by gradual means; but he notes that in radical circles far greater courage was needed to utter the word *gradualism* than to call for the most extreme measures.

In the last two decades of his life, Herzen expressed increasing impatience with the doctrinal squabbles among his compatriots over the comparative merits of political forms and systems. As he wrote in the aftermath of 1848, "The harmony between the individual and society is not established once and for all. It *comes into being* in each period, almost in each country, and it changes with circumstances, like everything living. There can be no universal norm, no universal decision on the matter." The path of progress could be neither predicted nor prescribed. Whether it came about from above or below, through the initiative of governments or through popular revolts, was a matter of "the poetic caprice of history."[88]

The self-styled conservative liberal Boris Chicherin, to whom this last remark was addressed, retorted that this was the language of "an artist, observing the chance play of events."[89] What Chicherin saw as Herzen's weakness was in fact his greatest strength, the source of his originality as a political thinker. He was the thinking artist that he had set out to become. His writing on politics and history has a rare vividness and immediacy. His most powerful points are often made in the form of dramatized dialogues, and he frequently depicts the malaises of modern societies through psychological types. The political and personal tragedies of 1848 are crystallized in his portrayal of the Don Quixotes of the revolution, while the issues dividing the Russian intelligentsia are presented through a comparison of the superfluous people (*lishnie liudi*) of Herzen's generation with the jaundiced ones of the next: an example of Goethean object-thinking peculiarly suited to the exploration of one of Herzen's central concerns: the way in which oppression creates a mirror image of itself in the vengeful spite of some of its victims.[90]

Accused of logical inconsistency and a lack of objectivity in his approach to history, Herzen retorted that the paths of logic did not coincide with those of history, which "as well as dialectical development, has its own development through passion and accident; as well as reason, it has its romance."[91] Hence feeling and passion were essential components of sound historical judgments, inconsistency and improvisation the sine qua non of serious political thought.[92] Even more shocking to the conventional political wisdom of his time was his declaration that conflict between the individual and society was not a transitory evil that would be eliminated by progress; in certain forms it was a necessary condition of creative existence: "The individual posits himself as his own end. Society posits itself in the same way. These kinds of antinomies . . . constitute the poles of everything alive: they are insoluble because in effect their resolution would be the indifference of death, the equilibrium of rest, whereas life exists only in *movement:* with the total victory of the individual or of society, history would end with predatory *individuals,* or with a peacefully grazing herd."[93]

He emphasizes the poetic quality of the type of perception that can grasp the dynamic tension between "those great contradictory forces that rend one another apart in strife, while continuing all the while to form the basis of modern societies."[94] In order to determine the limits within which one can quicken the pace of events without damaging the developments one seeks to promote, one needs "as well as logical calculation and readiness for self-sacrifice, a sense of measure and inspired improvisation." He believed that Russian radicals possessed the first two qualities in abundance but were conspicuously lacking in the last: "We advance in a fearless front . . . to the limit and beyond, in step with the dialectic, but out of step with truth . . . forgetting that the real meaning . . . of life is revealed precisely when one stops short before extremes; it lies in the *halte* (pause) of moderation, of truth, of beauty, in the oscillation of the organism in perpetual balance."[95]

Herzen's Schillerian combination of faith in the future with love of the present set him apart from all the political groupings of his time. He noted bitterly that while fact after fact "with needless prodigality" corroborated the few propositions he had devoted his life to preaching, such was the resistance of people's minds to them that he was continually identified with parties and doctrines whose basic principles he opposed.[96]

His ideas still tend to be categorized in ways that obscure the originality and the continuing relevance of his view of freedom. I shall conclude by recalling his confrontations in the last decade of his life with the leaders of the next generation of Russian revolutionaries, whose ascetic ethic demanded that they sacrifice their personal development in the name of duty to the people. Shocked by Herzen's revelations that his own circle in the 1840s had combined serious discussion with the enjoyment of food, wine, and good fellowship, they accused him of being an aristocratic dilettante who was playing at revolution: what for them was a stern duty was for him merely a poetic gesture. Herzen retorted that the young radicals' prescriptions on personal conduct had the ring of barrack-room orders and official ukases and protested against the "monkish asceticism" which, denying virtue to acts issuing from inclination, "values highly only those duties which it is most repugnant to perform."[97]

This distant echo of Schiller's polemic with Kant reminds us of that aesthetic model of individual freedom on which Herzen's political philosophy was based. There could be no better summary of his view of the relation between moral and political liberty than the lesson that Schiller drew from the French Terror: a person who is deaf to the claims of humanity within himself will be deaf to those claims when they come from without.

Herzen and Proudhon:
Two Radical Ironists
CHAPTER THREE

If one looks for the final aim, then the purpose of everything is—
death.

—Aleksandr Herzen

Concerning a system. I do not have one, I do not want one, I formally
reject the assumption. The system of humanity will not be known
until the end of humanity.

—Pierre-Joseph Proudhon

"The intellectual human being has the choice ... of being either an ironist or a radical; a third choice is not decently possible. What he proves to be ... is decided by which argument is for him the final, decisive, and absolute one: life or intellect. ... For the radical, life is no argument. *Fiat justitia* or *veritas,* or *libertas, fiat spiritus*—*pereat mundus et vita!*—Thus speaks all radicalism. 'But is truth an argument—when life is at stake?' This question is the formula of irony."[1] This passage from Thomas Mann's *Reflections of a Non-Political Man,* a work that equates political radicalism with spiritual death, sums up the fratricidal war that irony has waged with utopia ever since both emerged, in their modern form, from the revolution in thought brought about by post-Kantian idealism. Hegel's dialectic gave utopian faith for the first time the appearance of rational certainty by presenting a community embodying freedom as the necessary culmination of objective historical processes. In contradiction with this static ideal, but more consistent with Hegelian historicism, was the vision of romantic irony, which saw conflict and impermanence as the only permanent features of a world without transcendence and encouraged the artist to exploit the creative possibilities of an unprogrammable present and an unrepeatable self. I use the term *irony* here in the sense in which Richard Rorty has defined it, as a vision of the self, freedom, and progress clearly distinct from the rationalist metaphysics underpinning most radical theories of society.[2] The metaphysician (to use Rorty's term) posits an ahistorical, rational core of the self as arbiter of the meaning and purpose of human existence, the source of moral imperatives and of universal criteria for happiness. Initially an affirmation of human autonomy against a divinized vision of the world, the rationalist ethic in turn divinized what it considered to be the individual's intrinsic rational nature, as the source of eternally valid precepts about the one correct way to live. The metaphysician defines freedom as the recognition of necessity, of an antecedent order whose principles are innate in our rational consciousness and to which it is our destiny to conform; progress is perceived as the movement from social conflict toward a state of rational harmony in which all purposes will coincide. In contrast, ironists reject the notion of overarching meanings and final resolutions of the conflicts and absurdities of finite existence and build their freedom on the acceptance of their contingency, exploiting the opportunities of their specific time and place in order to shape a unique self, unprogrammed by transcendent powers. Ironism sees the aim of social existence (as of art) as being not static harmony but fullness of content; not unanimity but a plurality which seeks to accommodate the maximum of individual purposes and creative fantasies.

Ironists have not been prominent in the defense of social justice and equality; the names of Nietzsche and Heidegger are sufficient to evoke the kind of politics that tend to be associated with philosophies of self-creation. But the commonplace equation of irony with moral relativism and social nihilism has been contested by powerful voices, such as that of Isaiah Berlin. Noting how rationalist metaphysics has lent itself to the support of authoritarian visions of society, Berlin has argued that libertarian goals are better served by individuals who combine commitment to them with an awareness of the contingent nature both of their ideals and of the vocabulary in which these are expressed.[3] Rorty echoes this view but contends that while it is possible for the same person to be both an ironist and a liberal (in the very broad sense in which Berlin uses that term), historical experience is not encouraging in this respect. While metaphysics, in the shape both of Christianity and Marxism, has in its time served human liberty, "it is not obvious that ironism ever has."[4]

It has—as we shall see in the political lives and thought of the two radical ironists with whom this chapter is concerned. The relations of Aleksandr Herzen and Pierre-Joseph Proudhon are of far more than mere historical interest. One can trace through them the shaping of a vision of the world which offers a clear alternative both to the rationalistic universalism that has caused so many disasters in the twentieth century and to the nihilistic relativism that threatens to cause still more. But the originality of their ideas has long been concealed by the label *utopian* commonly attached to them both. Of the handful of Russian thinkers (apart from novelists) known outside their own country, Herzen has aroused the widest interest in the West. There have been numerous translations of his memoirs and his philosophical reflections *From the Other Shore,* and since the late 1960s there has been a steady flow of studies of his life and thought which have drawn on the vast corpus of Soviet research on the subject.[5] But while Western scholars have acknowledged the originality of his moral philosophy, sometimes crediting him with being the precursor of existentialism, they have tended, as Berlin once noted, to dismiss his political ideas as "yet another variant of early socialism"[6]—an assessment not far removed from what was the standard Soviet interpretation, based on Lenin's view that Herzen represents a transitional stage between utopian socialism and Russian Marxism. (This view was unlikely to endear Herzen to the postcommunist intelligentsia; his place in Russian thought, like that of many other thinkers mangled by Soviet ideologists, has yet to be properly assessed.) His image in the West owes much to Martin Malia's portrait of him as a utopian fantasist, a gentleman dilettante who, as claimed by another com-

mentator, retained the ideals of "a gentler, more romantic age"—
ideals that had become anachronistic long before his death in 1870.[7]

In discussing the formative influence of early French socialism
on Herzen's thought, Malia presents that movement as a collection
of visionary dreams, offering in place of concrete programs the
magic promise of "an infinity of nameless bliss."[8] This common
view of the European socialism of the 1830s and 1840s is strongly
challenged in K. Steven Vincent's study of Proudhon, which reminds us that the pejorative connotations of the term *utopian* socialism originated in Marx's polemics against his rivals, whom he
accused of failing to understand correctly the real, dialectical movement of socioeconomic relations. The influence of this verdict per-
sists: many historians who regard Marx himself as utopian see his
predecessors as even more so. Accustomed to think of socialism as
preeminently a body of economic doctrines, they have tended to
equate the strong moral dimension of early socialism with a lack
of realism.[9]

The fate of Marx's own historical scenario would seem, as Vincent contends, to underline the need for reopening the question of
the utopianism of the so-called utopian socialists. This chapter has
a narrower aim: to reassess the relationship between the founder
of the Russian socialist movement and the French anarchist to
whom he acknowledged a substantial intellectual debt.

Herzen's association with Proudhon has been too well documented
to need more than a brief summary here.[10] In Moscow in the mid-
1840s his reading of Proudhon, along with other French socialists,
helped to strengthen his suspicion of Western parliamentarianism
and the liberal bourgeoisie and to turn his attention to the question
of social revolution and the anarchist potential of the Russian peasant commune. Soon after his arrival in Paris in 1847, he was introduced to Proudhon by Mikhail Bakunin. He did not pursue the
acquaintance, the reason given in his memoirs being his reluctance
to court celebrities; but he shared Proudhon's dislike of the authoritarian tendencies of the French Left and admiringly followed
his career in the National Assembly in 1848. The Left's ostracism

of Proudhon served to confirm Herzen's view that most European intellectuals were too attached to systems and dogmas to be truly revolutionary in their outlook. He needed a platform for his views, and when in September 1849 Proudhon (then in prison) approached him through an intermediary with a request to provide the guarantee money for a new newspaper, *La voix du peuple*, he agreed, on condition that he would become editor of its foreign section. In a letter accompanying the contract, Herzen hails Proudhon as the only free man in France. Proudhon's reply notes that they share a common ideal, but their subsequent collaboration revealed significant differences between them in both principles and tactics. Proudhon, who hoped for a peaceful social transformation in France, wished to convince the French bourgeoisie of the fundamental identity of their economic interests with those of the masses, while Herzen saw the new paper as an organ of an international revolutionary struggle to replace the discredited foundations of society with a wholly new order. It was suppressed in 1850, and Herzen was expelled from France in the same year. In his memoirs he records his disillusionment on reading Proudhon's work of 1858 *On Justice in the Revolution and the Church,* whose conservative view of the family convinced him that not even this Frenchman had succeeded in freeing himself from the traditions and authorities of the old order. He would also differ sharply from Proudhon in his attitude to such issues as the Polish question. Nevertheless, they maintained a warm if infrequent correspondence, and Herzen was deeply touched by Proudhon's support in the tragedies of his personal life. In his obituary of Proudhon, he refers to him as his teacher. More specifically, in a draft of a letter to him in 1851, he asserts, "I am obliged to you more than you think. You and Hegel between you are responsible for half my philosophical education."[11]

This acknowledgment of indebtedness has puzzled later commentators, who have pointed out that Herzen did not owe any of his basic ideas specifically to Proudhon. As Raoul Labry noted in the first detailed study of the relationship, the central theme of Herzen's writings—the view that the subordination of human be-

ings to transcendent ends is the source of all forms of oppression—
owed more to his reading of Feuerbach than to Proudhon, and the
anarchism that was a logical extension of his intellectual iconoclasm
seems to have been more directly influenced by his observations of
municipal structures in Italy and comparisons with the Russian
commune than by any of Proudhon's works. Labry concluded that
Proudhon was not Herzen's teacher, but rather his guide along a
common path.[12]

Labry saw both thinkers as innovators in their application of
radical philosophy to politics; but subsequent commentators, echoing Marx's dismissive classification of Proudhon's ideas, have concluded that his main influence on Herzen was to encourage him
in a nihilistic rejection of the present and a utopian vision of the
future.[13] The most detailed study of the relationship since Labry's
is an explicitly Marxist analysis: Michel Mervaud argues that while
both were utopians in the sense defined by Marx, Proudhon clung
to the romantic illusion that class struggle and revolution were not
a historical necessity. Herzen, more militant than Proudhon at the
time of their association, was thus more progressive, and his belief
in his ideological affinity with Proudhon must have been due to a
misunderstanding of Proudhon's fundamental orientation.[14]

Few scholars now have such faith in the Marxist version of the
march of history as to lecture past thinkers so confidently about
the true nature of their ideas and goals; but it is significant that no
commentator since Labry has given serious attention to Herzen's
own assessment, expressed at length in letters, essays, and memoirs,
of Proudhon's importance and his own debt to him.[15] Vincent suggests that it is not for us to instruct the founders of socialism on
what they meant by the term. Among those who have sought to
instruct Herzen, some admit to remaining puzzled about what he
saw in Proudhon, who, as one account claims, had far less importance than other socialists of the time with whom he might have
collaborated.[16] But the mystery can be resolved by abandoning ret-
rospective and historicist criteria in favor of a more contextual approach and viewing the relations of the two in the light of their
own perceptions of their aims and ideals.

In his *Confessions of a Revolutionary*, written from prison in 1849, Proudhon attributes the doctrinaire and bullying spirit of French radical politics to the fact that the Left took themselves far too seriously; his generation had its Robespierres and its Bonapartes, but not its Voltaire. He concludes the *Confessions* with a poetic eulogy of irony:

> Liberty, like Reason, . . . manifests itself only through its
> constant disdain of its own creations; it perishes as soon
> as it begins to adore itself. This is why in all ages irony
> has been the mark of philosophical and liberal genius, the
> . . . irresistible instrument of progress.
>
> Irony, true liberty! it is you who frees me from the de-
> sire for power, the tyranny of parties, respect for routine,
> scholastic pedantry, adulation of important persons, politi-
> cal machinations, the fanaticism of reformers, the supersti-
> tious fear of this great universe, and the adoration of my-
> self. . . . You were the familiar demon of the Philosopher,
> when he unmasked at one stroke the dogmatist and the
> sophist, the hypocrite and the atheist, the epicurean and
> the cynic. You consoled the Just Man when, dying on the
> cross, he prayed for his executioners: *Forgive them, Father,*
> *for they know not what they do!*

With just one spark of the reconciling grace of irony in the souls of his compatriots, Proudhon concludes, "the inevitable revolution might be made in serenity and joy."[17]

On reading the *Confessions*, Herzen drank a toast to the author: the concluding passage on irony was "the most sublime poetry," expressing "the most profound understanding of the reality of life." Sadly, he noted, the French radicals would make nothing of it— their brains had not developed sufficiently to grasp this kind of thinking.[18]

Here is the reason for Herzen's sense of a special affinity with Proudhon: he believed him to be the only contemporary socialist to have perceived, as he himself had done, the need to start constructing a new moral and political language.

There is a common view that Herzen's early years in Russia turned him into a utopian; his own belief was that they made him an ironist. Explaining the phenomenon of the Russian intelligentsia to a Western audience in the 1850s, he defined their principal virtues as "an implacable spirit of negation, a bitter irony, a tortured self-questioning." Their existence was founded on paradox: the most talented and idealistic group in their society, they were thereby the most superfluous. The state had forcibly Westernized their ancestors; now their culture cut them off from the people on whose slavery their privilege was built and made them suspect to the state. Victims of tyranny and exploiters in their turn, they had founded their hopes for the future on their loathing of the past and their guilty repudiation of the present. The self-satisfied patriotism of the French and the abstract theoretical negation of the Germans were alien to Russian thought. Its irony, *semper in motu,* could never be restrained by respect for the past. The great national poet, Pushkin, had begun one of his finest works with the somber lines: "All say there is no justice on earth, / But neither is there justice in the world above!" How could such a nation have faith in any easy solution of the fundamental conflicts of existence?[19]

In reality, while their alienation turned some of the Russian intelligentsia into ironists, it led rather more of them to seek an escape from their predicament in a variety of messianic faiths—a fact that Herzen does not stress in the picture that he presents to the West. As we shall see, he himself had strong inclinations in that direction; but, with the detached involvement of the true ironist, he used his own inner struggles as source material for an analysis of the self-delusions through which people seek to blind themselves to the more painful aspects of the human condition. Observing such phenomena as the Slavophile movement, which based a rosy vision of Russia's future on an idealization of its past, he notes how an agonizing awareness of the emptiness of their stunted lives made his generation "ready to grasp at any nonsense, just to fill the dreadful void." His letters and diaries of that time reveal how vulnerable he was to the same temptation. Sentenced in 1834 to an indefinite period of political exile in a remote province, he coped with his barren existence by weaving elaborate fantasies in his correspondence with his distant fiancée, Natalie, casting them both as protagonists in a religious drama of sin, suffering, and redemption, guided by the hidden hand of Divine Providence; but on returning to Moscow at the end of the decade he gradually surrendered the consolations of a belief in predestination in favor of a sober recognition of what he saw as overwhelming evidence of the dominant role of chance in all the processes of life. Unlike some of his Hegelian contemporaries, he refused to accept the suffering and injustices of the present as part of a rational process whereby history was marching to its mysterious goals: "The absence of reason in the determination of individual life is plain." At first he felt nihilistic despair in the face of the "terrible slough of contingencies into which human life is drawn." The delicate health of his wife and the deaths of three children in infancy make him reflect that the fragility of all that we value most in life "is enough to drive one to insanity." He reflects with helpless anger on the way chance can destroy "by a single stupid blow" everything a human being has constructed with infinite labor, with sweat and blood, and suffering. But, observing how his generation was consuming its energies in utopian dreams, he began to sense that coming to terms with the lack of a rational or predictable order in history could lead to freedom and fulfillment, by releasing the mental and affective energies that allow us to make maximum use of the only reality we possess—the present. The fact that we have no control over the future should teach us that "the aim of life is life itself—life in that form, at that stage of development at which a given creature finds itself to be." One must "seize the present, actualize all one's potential for happiness—and by this I mean both the happiness that comes from social action and the happiness that comes through knowledge, as well as that which is brought by friendship, love, and family attachments—and thereafter?—well, what will be will be: the responsibility for that won't be mine."[20]

He found support for this standpoint in Ludwig Feuerbach's transformation of Hegel's philosophy, which presented human history as a movement toward liberty through the reappropriation of the qualities that humans had projected onto idealized transcendent entities. But while the radical Hegelians hoped that the worship of God would give way to the cult of a future perfected humanity, Herzen foresaw clearly that the new religion of humanity represented at least as great a threat to individual freedom as the fetishes it sought to replace. In the two cycles of essays on Hegel's philosophy he wrote in the 1840s he argues that (when properly understood) Hegel's principle of dialectical becoming leads inescapably to the denial of all absolutes, outlaws the worship of all collective abstractions, and demands the replacement of future-oriented visions of history and the human race by one that concentrates on the contingent needs of the present.[21] Herzen attacks the inhumanity of all philosophies that approach finite phenomena as instances of universal principles: individuals, like nations and historical periods, might be links in a chain, but they are also ends in themselves, and only by pursuing their own self-fulfillment can they maximally extend the possibilities of what, retrospectively, we regard as progress.

Herzen sensed that a new kind of language was required to express a view of the world that focused on the self-sufficient value of individual and unrepeatable phenomena and on the open-ended potential of the present. As he observed in 1841, "Philosophy has not yet mastered the concept of individuality—it still treats it with coldness."[22] His eclectic reading during his years in Russia leaned toward thinkers who, like himself, were interested in the intellectual and emotional roots of the human attachment to vast and impersonal entities and who sought to articulate a new way of thinking which would in turn transform social behavior. As I have argued in the two previous chapters, there were two seminal influences on his thought in this respect—Bacon and Schiller. Bacon's critique of idols that cloud human understanding inspired Herzen's own search for a method that would allow him to investigate the contingent world without forcing it into the confines of systems, while Schiller's aesthetic notion of moral freedom as expounded in his polemic with Kant is echoed in Herzen's essays of the 1840s on personal morality, in which he concludes that the best hope for freedom lies not through self-transcendence but through self-creation. We must cease to lay claim to some intrinsic nature or eternal essence as the source of universally correct rules for moral behavior and accept full responsibility for molding our conduct in response to circumstances—a "terrifying" prospect of indeterminacy that explained why people were so eager to cling to the transcendent norms of traditional ethical systems.[23]

An ironist, Herzen was also a liberal in the most general sense of that word, believing that the central concern of social thinking must be the search to protect the individual's dignity and right to self-determination against institutionalized bullying and violence.[24] His early writings reveal an aristocratic sense of personal dignity, combined with a loathing of the humiliations that the Russian system inflicted on the weak. He resolved the dilemma of reconciling an ethic of self-creation with the demands of social solidarity in terms very similar to Schiller's treatise *On the Aesthetic Education of Man*—a work that he perceived to be much in advance of its time. He once described virtuous behavior as an "aesthetics of action," by which, like Schiller, he meant conduct governed not by universal rational precepts but by a response of the integral personality to the specific demands of individual situations.[25]

Herzen believed such a poetic sense of relationships to be both the premiss of moral freedom and a prerequisite for an understanding of the nature of historical movement. In his Hegelian essays he argues that to be able to distinguish between what contains the seeds of the future and what has outlived its time, the observer must possess a sense of form that does not deny the contingent and the concrete its self-sufficient value. It is to aesthetic perception that he turns for analogies with the new kind of language that will be spoken by free persons, believing that the traditional vocabulary of philosophy was inimical to the perception of reality that was born with Hegel's historicism. He repeatedly stresses that it is not just a question of revising our catalogues of ultimate goals and purposes; we must cease to derive the significance of the individual and the contingent from its place in some imagined a priori scheme of things. By cultivating an aesthetic receptivity to the transient and

unrepeatable manifestations of life we can counter our tendency to
rationalize and universalize and learn to exploit the limitless possibilities for self-creation that each historical moment presents.

In the mid-1840s Herzen began to develop this view of the relations between the self and the world through a critique of the
two dominant schools of thought on the future direction of progress in Russia. Each believed that there was only one correct path.
According to the Slavophiles, this led away from the decadent rationalism of the West to a new religious togetherness (sobornost)
based on the virtues of Russian peasant life. For the Westernizers,
it led to the modern Western state—the summit of Hegelian rational progress. Against the exclusivism of both camps, Herzen suggested an approach consistent with his view of the moral self: faced
with the ferment of nationalist and universalist, conservative and
revolutionary aspirations in his awakening country, to start seeking
ways of reconciling aspects of all these tendencies that had the
greatest potential for creative development. Reproached by the
Westernizers for consorting with the opposite camp, he declared
himself an unrepentant advocate of "that lucid and scrupulous humanism which always shuns exclusivist, *haineux* [hate-filled] theories and opinions."[26]

When Herzen left Russia in 1847, he had laid the foundations of
an ironist philosophy; Proudhon's influence would help him complete it.

Herzen's rejection of transcendent authorities was the result of an
aristocratic education that had steeped him in European literature,
philosophy, and history. Proudhon, the largely self-taught son of
peasants, arrived at a similar standpoint through the exercise of a
sharp intellect combined with a down-to-earth suspicion of philosophical systems. On first reading Hegel in the early 1840s, Proudhon was repelled by the extreme abstraction of Hegel's language:
"I call a cat a cat, and don't believe that I gain much by saying that
that animal is a differentiation of the great Whole, and that God
arrives at consciousness of himself in my brain."[27] He was the only
French socialist of his time to embrace Feuerbach's critique of re-

ligious alienation, earning the admiration of Marx, who in 1846 invited him to become a corresponding member of his international socialist organization. In a famous reply Proudhon warned against the doctrinaire intolerance already evident in the new socialist movement: "For God's sake! after having demolished all a priori dogmas, let's not contemplate indoctrinating the people in our turn . . . let's not set ourselves up as apostles of a new religion, even if it's the religion of logic and reason. Let us welcome and encourage all alternative opinions. Let us condemn all exclusivism, all mystification. Let us never regard any problem as resolved. And when we have used up our last argument, let us begin again, if need be, with eloquence and irony. On this condition, I shall be delighted to join your association. If not, no!"[28]

This opposition between religion and irony was developed in *System of Economic Contradictions, or the Philosophy of Poverty,* published later that year. The prologue to this work and the final chapter of the first volume are a discussion of the historical role of religion, in which Proudhon mounts an attack on the historiosophical monism of the German idealists and their ideological descendants. He argues that the atheistic humanists of the Hegelian Left have stopped halfway in their demystification of the universe. Their view that humanity can reappropriate the qualities projected onto the divinity was based on a belief in the intrinsic rationality and harmony of human nature that contradicted historical experience. Proudhon was unimpressed by the humanists' response that the all-powerful creator of the future would be not the individual, but the collective force of the human race. Once again, he observed, we are being invited to seek the real essence of living individuals outside time and space, "to desert the finite for the infinite," thus going back full circle to religious alienation, with humanity subjected to a new master—its own collective ego. Mysticism masked as humanism, superstition parading as science, had created the most dangerous illusion of the age, namely,

> that humanistic philosophy which turns man . . . into a
> holy, sacred being . . . despite the heart-breaking proofs

that he ceaselessly gives of his dubious morality; attributing his vices to the compulsion under which he has lived,
and expecting from him . . . acts of the purest devotion,
because in the myths in which this philosophy has inspired humanity to depict itself, one finds two eras described in opposing terms, . . . an age of compulsion and
punishment, and an age of happiness and freedom! With
such doctrines, man has only to discover (as he inevitably
will), that he is . . . neither saint nor sage, for him at once
to throw himself anew into the arms of religion, so that in
the last analysis, all that the world will have gained by
the denial of God will be the resurrection of God.[29]

In *System of Contradictions* Proudhon expressed regret that his
refusal to assent to the rationalist deification of humanity had estranged him from "the most intelligent faction of socialism"—the
school of Feuerbach. It alienated him equally from such contemporary French radicals as the Jacobin socialist Louis Blanc and the
Christian communist Etienne Cabet, whom he accuses of holding
that the conflicts of modern societies are the result of "a mere
mistake of common sense, which could be corrected by a decree
from the public authority." Such beliefs "were summed up long
ago by Plato and Thomas More in a single word, UTOPIA—that is,
no-place, a chimera." In a work published in 1851 he notes the
general tendency among the Left to see socialism not as a practical
program for remedying specific social ills, but as an all-embracing
system of existence requiring the total destruction of the existing
order: "Let humanity perish rather than the principle! That is the
motto of the utopians, as of the fanatics of all epochs."[30]

Proudhon believed, like Herzen, that the reaffirmation of Divine
Providence in the form of historical determinism was an act of
intellectual cowardice, provoked by insecurity in a world stripped
of metaphysical authorities. Suspicious of the lurking transcenden-
talism in Hegel's dialectic, he tried (with little success: his philosophical talents were inferior to Herzen's) to express a vision of
social existence as a web of contingent relations, to be approached

without recourse to metaphysical notions of causality or substance.[31]

All Proudhon's thinking was based on the proposition, which he
held to be empirically evident, that conflict between the individual
and society was "the very condition" of social existence and of
progress. Failure to perceive "the inherent contradictions in things"
had hitherto been the principal source of error in social theorizing.
Conflict had been suppressed by coercion in the only two models
of society that the human race had known: community (or communism) and property—the first representing coercion by a collective, the second exploitation by a caste. The greatest threat facing
modern societies was that the search to correct the injustice of the
concentration of property in the hands of a few would lead them
to founder again on the rock of community: by confusing the principles of equality and leveling, contemporary communist doctrines
threatened to impose a gray uniformity on human societies. It was
time to develop a third social form; but this required a radical
revision of our perception of the self and its relation to the social
whole.[32]

Proudhon argued that the human race would not achieve political liberty until it ceased hankering after the quality of immutable harmony traditionally attributed to the divine. The socialist
ideal of a wholly rational society in which all individual purposes
coincide was founded on the "hallucination of a collective ego"
that took no account of the real natures of human beings, who
were an untidy "cluster of potentialities" that could not be prepro-
grammed for a single collective destiny. To claim, as did thinkers
like Blanc, that individuals yearned to deny themselves "for the
abstraction called society" was to base social theory on a "dangerous hypocrisy." There were no empirical grounds for believing that
egoism—the source of initiative and creativity—was any less legitimate than the drive to association, or social solidarity. Proudhon
suggests to his fellow socialists, "We would come close to a mutual
understanding if, instead of considering the dissonance and harmony of human faculties as two distinct . . . consecutive periods in
history, you consented like me to see them as merely two aspects

of our nature, always opposed, always in process of reconciliation, but never entirely reconciled." The goal must therefore be not the final elimination of conflicts, but their containment in a dynamic balance, a sort of "general equation of all our contradictions."[33]

Like Herzen, Proudhon called for an aesthetic sense of appropriateness and balance to replace a rigid adherence to norms and rules in personal and social morality. He argued that societies should be based not only on the principle of justice but also on that of equity, or "social proportionality," which he describes as "a mixed product of justice and aesthetic taste"—the form that the human instinct of solidarity takes in intellectually and morally developed individuals. He uses the terms *humanitas, politesse,* and *urbanité* to describe this "noble" sense which makes a person rebel against the social enforcement of equality, "desiring to give service when prompted by reason, not by command, to sacrifice himself as an act of egoism, not of servile obligation."[34] While equity should not be allowed to compromise justice, it can enrich it with aesthetic feeling, love, esteem, and the noble human capacity to idealize. In other words, in Proudhon's model of society, it is the aesthetic sense of equity (or moral grace, to use Schiller's term)[35] that would maintain the delicate balance in which genius and talent would neither exploit nor be effaced by egalitarian mediocrity.

The parallels with Herzen (and Schiller) are close: rejecting the notion of virtue as submission to universal norms, Proudhon proposes a model of moral behavior as a reciprocal regulation of the psyche's drives in response to changing priorities. He defines a free individual as one whose rights and duties exist in a state of balance with those of his fellow citizens.[36] He was acutely aware that his revolt against absolutes threatened to lead to moral relativism: a problem that he lacked the philosophical competence to resolve. As Pierre Haubtmann has noted, the works in which he attempts to steer a course between these extremes are full of contradictions.[37] But on one point all his writings are unambiguous: he believed that the glue of society should be not a set of universal prescriptive norms, but the imaginative empathy that allows one "to sense one's dignity in the person of one's neighbor as much as in oneself, to affirm oneself simultaneously as individual and species."[38] He defines the guiding principle of such a society variously as positive anarchism, mutualism, and reciprocity.

Proudhon perceived an embryonic version of his ideal in the workers' associations for mutual aid that had begun to attract the attention of French radicals in the 1830s. He envisaged the progressive organization of labor into mutualist structures for production and consumption that would avoid the extremes of both anarchic individualism and authoritarian restraint, encouraging a variety of aptitudes in their members, and developing through their practice new kinds of persons, who would no longer need to justify their goals and actions by reference to powers outside themselves. He hoped that these structures would increase in social and economic power until they replaced the state, which would then become (in the Saint-Simonian conception) an organization for the administration of things.

There is much that is naive and ill-thought-through in Proudhon's social ideal. His hope that the mutualist structures of his time would grow to replace the state was based on simplistic economic notions and a greater faith in human nature than his theories allowed. His concept of liberty had its limitations: as Herzen noted with disapproval, he maintained a traditional French peasant's attitude to the role of women and the family. But it should be remembered that the dismissive image of Proudhon as a utopian was created by thinkers whose own pseudo-science Proudhon exposed with clarity and wit. The proposition (as advanced by Marx and Engels) that a revolutionary "act of universal emancipation" was a "historical necessity" and the "mission of the modern proletariat"[39] now seems rather more fantastic than Proudhon's hopes for the peaceful transformation of modern societies through shifting and pragmatic accommodations between sectional interests.

Whatever the value of Proudhon's positive ideals, his principal significance is as a demythologizer. He was the first socialist to debunk the notion of a society without conflict, as a mere variation on the ancient myth of an earthly paradise—and he emphasized that his own ideal could never be a universal panacea. Like all other forms of human association, it would restrict individual liberty and initiative, which in some cases might be better served by different arrangements. No theory could be more than a pragmatic response to contingent needs. The unpredictability of those needs meant that historical progress should be conceived not as movement toward a final goal, but, on the contrary, as "the negation of all immutable forms and formulas, of all doctrines of eternity, permanence, of infallibility, of all permanent order, not excluding that of the universe." Proudhon himself believed that his most important achievement had been to "light up the dual face of things."[40] As his letter to Marx suggests, his aim was to create a political discourse founded on the language of irony, which, by constantly subverting its own creations, could never harden into dogma.

His principal weapons in the war against the "religion of logic and reason" were contradiction and paradox, designed to subvert those sanctities that, as he remarked in his disquisition on irony, his contemporaries took far too seriously. In the shifting web of contingent existence, distinctions dissolve and opposites attract. In his *System of Contradictions* he pointed to profound similarities between atheist and theist visions of the world and, on the question of political economy and social organization, between the doctrinairism of the traditionalist Right and the utopian Left. The truth, he declared, "lies in a formula that shall reconcile these two terms: *Conservation* and *Motion*." On the one hand, he famously pronounced property to be theft. Less famously, however, he remarked that property is also liberty and that purist attempts at its eradication led inevitably to its apotheosis in the state as the owner of its citizens.[41] He described his philosophy as "nothing other than permanent reconciliation," a concept that he did not see as incompatible with permanent revolution (to which, at a radical banquet, he proposed a toast).[42] In his *Confessions* he noted with relish that he had been attacked from all sides: by the communists for upholding the rights of individuals, by the propertied classes for questioning the moral basis of their ownership, and by politicians of all persuasions for equating democracy with the dissolution of government.

Nowhere is his ironic ambivalence more marked than on the question of religion. He rejected both religious belief and atheistic materialism, on the ground that both posit a universal and necessary order which leaves no place for human autonomy. Whether that order issued from an omniscient creator or blind necessity was of little significance. He declared himself an antitheist dedicated to war against all absolutes, all occult powers, all fictions designed to crush the freedom of individual human beings. But he notes that while he is an atheist in practical matters, he leaves open the question of whether in some infinite sphere of existence (the possibility of which, he observes, is not excluded by science), a reconciliation of being and knowing might finally come about.[43]

Opinion is divided on the question of whether, in the final analysis, Proudhon was an atheist or a believer.[44] The answer is that he was an ironist. His antitheism is the clumsy construction of a self-taught philosopher, but it bears a striking resemblance to the rebellion of Ivan Karamazov—the creation of one of the greatest of modern paradoxists. It is based on the acceptance of what Rorty describes as the unresolvable tension in the human psyche between "an effort to achieve self-creation by the recognition of contingency and an effort to achieve universality by the transcendence of contingency."[45] Proudhon believed that the latter urge, if allowed to determine social practice, led to tyranny; but to ignore its existence was an equally dangerous self-delusion. He concedes that in progressive circles at that time even to raise the hypothesis of a Supreme Being is seen as evidence of a feeble intellect. But he insists that a sense of infinity is an integral part of human consciousness and, as such, a legitimate subject of discussion and hypothesis. Much of Proudhon's own treatment of this theme (in *System of Contradictions* and in his notebooks) is a poetically immediate expression of the predicament of a creature whose reach exceeds his grasp, whose finite reason confronts infinity in science, whose sense of unbounded potential is belied by his meager achievement, who experiences an "incomprehensible emptiness" when he rejects God and seeks him in humanity, but equally rebels against the notion of transcendence as an insult to his reason and a denial of his autonomy; and who in despair is driven to imagine a malevolent deity who, having made us "contradictory . . . in our thoughts, contradictory in our words, contradictory in our actions," laughs to hear us gravely discuss the meaning of justice and injustice.[46]

Contrary to the view of some critics, there is no coded certainty in these texts. The intensity of psychic conflict in modern human beings, their obsessive yearning to be otherwise constituted than they are, had led Proudhon's socialist contemporaries to conclude that the moment of transfiguration was close. Proudhon's originality consisted in his insistence that there were neither logical nor empirical grounds for this belief. The discord between the human race's sense of infinity and the conditions of its finite existence was, he believed, the "fundamental antinomy, of which I find modern critics have not taken account."[47] The progress that humanity had made so far had been brought about through its inherent mutability and propensity for struggle—qualities that could not generate the changeless harmony for which it yearned; but this fact could be reconciled with social hope if we learned to speak the poetic language of irony.

As Herzen observed in his memoir on Proudhon, this was not a language acceptable to the radical intelligentsia, who were accustomed to clear classifications, binding prescriptions, and stories with a moral at the end. He stressed repeatedly that Proudhon's strength lay in the force of his negation, which respected no sanctities.[48] These passages have been interpreted as reflecting the influence of Proudhon's utopianism on Herzen; on the contrary, it seems clear that Proudhon's brand of iconoclasm had the effect of making Herzen more consistently antiutopian than he might otherwise have been.

When Herzen arrived in Paris from Russia in March 1847 amid the political ferment that would erupt in revolution in the following year, his ironist vision of moral freedom became the criterion by which he judged the activities and ideals of the French Left. He concluded that in their readiness to sacrifice individuals to abstractions they differed little from the Right: "the tyrannical *salus populi* and the bloody, inquisitorial *pereat mundus, fiat justitia* are in-scribed in the consciousness of royalists and democrats alike. . . . The French have in no way freed themselves from religion. . . . Read George Sand and Pierre Leroux, Louis Blanc and Michelet—their work is full of Christianity and romanticism, adapted to suit the customs of the time; it's full of dualism . . . , official, rhetorical mo-rality with no relation to practical life."[49]

During the same period Proudhon was expressing very similar views about the French Left, whose moral confusion he saw ex-emplified in the phenomenon of Jacobinism: an ambiguous mix-ture of "liberty and authority, monarchy and democracy, superficial philosophy and sentimental religiosity—capable, according to choice, of inspiring an insurrection or a coup d'état, of protecting the citizen or proscribing him."[50]

Reflecting in 1847 on the strangeness of the fact that many con-temporary socialists sought to free people from poverty and injus-tice only in order to stifle them in a communistic system, Herzen commented, "To grasp all the breadth and reality, . . . all the sanc-tity of the rights of the personality and not destroy society, not shatter it into atoms—this is the most difficult of social tasks . . . in the past it has never been resolved." This passage seems to echo Proudhon's definition, in a work of 1839, of the central problem of social theory: "*To find a state of social equality which is neither community nor despotism, nor disintegration, nor anarchy, but liberty in order and independence in unity.*"[51] Herzen's answer to this prob-lem, which he began to sketch out on his arrival in Europe, was a model of social relations based on the self-governing structure of the Russian peasant commune. The role of the commune in his thought has been much misunderstood. It was not, as Turgenev claimed, a new idol to replace those that he had cast down, but rather, like Proudhon's associations, a rough sketch for a type of social structure that would be flexible enough to maximally accom-modate the changing needs and aspirations of disparate human beings. He pointed out that the unpredictability of those needs meant that no social form could be regarded as inherently "very good or absolutely bad"—all were relative in that they had to adapt to a living, developing content. Herzen emphasized the difference between his approach and traditional political thinking, which was based on what he called formalism: faith in the existence of an optimal form of political association that would put an end to social conflict. Such attempts at harmonization, he remarked, always led to the dominance of one or other of the warring principles. Nineteenth-century liberalism had used the "arithmetical pantheism" of universal suffrage to sanctify the predatory instincts of the strong; communism would justify the tyranny of the herd. In his vision of history, as in Proudhon's, conflict and contradiction were to be welcomed, not suppressed. As he puts it in 1866, "Self-will and law, the individual and society and their endless battle . . . in this lies the whole drama of history. The individual, who may *rationally* liberate himself only within society, revolts against it. Society, which cannot exist without individuals, subdues the rebellious individual. . . . These kinds of antinomies . . . constitute the poles of everything that lives; they are insoluble because in effect their resolution would represent the indifference of death, the equilibrium of rest, whereas life exists only in *movement*."[52]

There seems no doubt that Herzen's reading of Proudhon helped him develop his model of social existence: but if the two thinkers agreed on the end, in the late 1840s they differed significantly on the question of means.

In characteristic style, Proudhon had followed his 1839 definition of the aim of social theory with the following declaration: "Having solved the first question, we come to the second: *to indicate the best form of transition*. There we have the whole problem of humane philosophy." Herzen, with no direct experience of processes of social change, was inclined at first to regard revolution as the solution to the most pressing problems of the century. We have seen that his insight into humanity's predisposition to compensating fantasies did not prevent him from succumbing to them himself when exposed to factors that he knew from observation to be their cause: intellectual isolation, a lack of contact with concrete social realities, and a frustrated need to participate in a meaningful historical process. In his first exile in the 1830s he had consoled himself with faith in the saving hand of Providence. At the beginning of his permanent exile in Europe, he was a passive observer of great historical events in which his own country had no part, and whose economic and political causes he as yet only dimly understood, and he had few contacts apart from his fellow Russian exile Mikhail Bakunin, who was then in the process of formulating a revolutionary nationalism based on a romantic cult of young, primitive peoples. Herzen's own embryonic nationalism became infected with Bakunin's millennial impatience; in commentaries to his friends in Russia on events in France in 1848–49 he argues that the revolution can be saved only by the violent destruction of the state and compares the current situation in western Europe to the last days of Rome before the barbarian invasion from the East. In the short term, tsar Nicholas's Cossacks might deal the deathblow; in the long, the energy as yet slumbering in the Slav soul might hold out new hope for mankind.

It was in this spirit that in response to Proudhon's request for assistance with his paper he wrote a letter that he called his confession. In the surviving draft of that document, he greets Proudhon as the first thinker to have declared that "there is no salvation within the boundaries of this putrefying world." He therefore flatters himself that "for this reason . . . you will sympathize with my barbarian way of seeing things"—namely, his pleasure at the imminent demise of the old order. It was the French radicals' reluctance to break completely with the past that had led to the failure of the revolution, but this, Herzen declares, was no bad thing. Liberty born at the hands of such midwives would not be worth having—"let's rather have barbarism to toughen our slack morals, our effeminate souls."[53]

Herzen's draft letter reveals that at that time he saw no significant difference between Proudhon's views and Bakunin's bloodthirsty belief in the creative nature of the urge for destruction. But Proudhon's reply was a model of the conciliatory approach that was central to his political philosophy. While agreeing that a future revolution would demand "fearful leaps," he argues that it is not for them, as journalists, to welcome or justify such violence; they would only make themselves hated and lose their influence. He informs Herzen that he too has written a confession but fears Herzen will find it disappointing: destined for the French, it is devoid of "that *verve barbaresque* to which your German philosophers . . . have accustomed you."[54]

The ironist in Herzen must have felt the force of this remark, which points with devastating precision to the unacknowledged paradox underlying the romantic cult of primitive spontaneity. Not long afterward, Herzen read and was deeply impressed by Proudhon's *Confessions,* which explored in depth the self-deceptions of radical utopianism. In the following year he published his own considered reflections on 1848. In its critique of the faith that history can be fashioned to conform to an ideal, *From the Other Shore* was something of a *volte-face,* but it did not represent the end of the conflict between irony and utopianism in Herzen's attitude to events in his own country. In the early 1850s he argued that the autocracy could not survive because the bureaucratic state created to support it was an artificial structure founded on Western models and alien to the nature and aspirations of the Russian people. This dichotomy of state and people, recalling the polarities of romantic thought, was challenged by Proudhon in a letter of 1855. He agrees to be one of the titular editors of a periodical that Herzen had just established in London but notes that while Herzen has focused his attention on the despotism of governments, his own target is rather different:

> Is it not true that despotism is so difficult to destroy only
> because it is supported by the deepest instincts of its op-
> ponents—or rather, I should say, its rivals—so that a
> writer who is sincerely liberal . . . often doesn't know
> against which side to direct his blows: against the coali-
> tion of oppressors or the suspect motives of the oppressed?
>
> Do you believe, for example, that the Russian autocracy
> is the mere product of brute force and dynastic intrigues?
> Does it not have its hidden foundations, its secret roots in
> the heart of the Russian people?[55]

Proudhon reminds Herzen that "nothing resembles a tyrant so much as a popular tribune." (Always open to the possibility that progress could come from unlikely sources, on hearing reports of the new tsar's intention to give the Poles their freedom he speculates as to whether the Russian autocrat might not revive the moral sense "that has been destroyed in the west by bourgeois egoism and Jacobin stupidity.")[56]

Herzen responded to Proudhon's criticism by denying that his view of the Slav world was "idealist or *exaltado*,"[57] but his knowledge of it was then based on distant and selective memories. This situation changed three years later, when he began in London to publish (first monthly, then fortnightly) his review the *Bell*, which became the only forum for the free expression of Russian opinion on the eve of the emancipation of the serfs. The *Bell*'s offices were flooded with material smuggled out of Russia: leaked details of official projects for the coming reforms and reports of conditions in the cities and the countryside that ranged from dry statistical surveys to denunciations of corrupt or tyrannical officials. There was also no shortage of Russians bearing the latest news and gossip from the homeland; with the promise of reform in the air, it became the fashion for Russians traveling abroad, from government officials to radical dissidents, to call on their most celebrated political exile.

Amid this deluge of complex and contradictory facts and opinions, Herzen's journalistic line was very similar to Proudhon's in the late 1840s, opposing extreme and doctrinaire solutions with a pragmatic and conciliatory approach to the problem of progress. Like Proudhon, he was attacked from all sides: by the Russian Left when he urged them to explore every possibility of peaceful change before resorting to violence and tried to dissuade the Poles from a premature rising; by the liberals for supporting the rising when it broke out and for questioning their view that Western-style constitutionalism was the only suitable form of government for their country.

The political outlook of his mature years is summed up in his essays of 1869 *To an Old Comrade*, addressed to Mikhail Bakunin, who had been tirelessly working for a Europe-wide revolution since his escape from Siberian exile in 1861. He tells Bakunin (as he himself had been told by Proudhon twenty years before) that although they have a common goal, they differ on the question of means. He had long ceased to share Bakunin's faith in the cleansing power of violence, observation and experience having convinced him of the futility of using brute force against institutions whose power was based in part on the acquiescence of those whom they exploited. Bakunin yearned to reduce the field of history to ashes, but "that field, with its wheat and its cockle, constitutes the immediate ground of the people's entire moral life, of all its customs, all its consolations."[58] Herzen urged him not to underestimate the Russian peasantry's innate conservatism—its attachment to the tsar and to the church that upheld his power. The aim should be not to destroy the old in the name of the new, but to seek through education and persuasion to reconcile the new with what was worth preserving of the old. But the transformation of human consciousness took time; the path to freedom was not a straight line, but a series of zigzags, the result of endless compromises.

To an Old Comrade echoes many of the themes of *System of Contradictions*. This was no coincidence. In an assessment of Proudhon written in the mid-1850s, Herzen ranks the *Contradictions* with Hegel's *Phenomenology of the Spirit* as the two most significant works of the first half of the century—a highly original view: unnoticed in France on its publication, Proudhon's work is remembered only for Marx's contemptuous attack on it in *The Poverty of Philosophy*. But Herzen, on the ground that only Proudhon had dared to complete the demystification of the world begun by Hegel, perceived it as the most revolutionary work of its age. In precluding the possibility of escape from the contingent self into idealized collectives, Proudhon had "transformed the language of revolution, freed it not only from heavenly phantoms, but also from those of the earth ... [from] the sentimental apotheosis of humanity, the fatalism of progress."

Those who have not "*lived through* [the *Phenomenology* and the *Contradictions*] ... who have not passed through that furnace ... are not truly modern":[59] this image conveys with great economy the intensity of Herzen's personal struggle against the phantoms of utopia, and the passage as a whole leaves little doubt as to Proudhon's role in that process. In Herzen's view, Proudhon's particular genius lay in the skepticism that had made him a pariah on the French Left. In his memoirs he recalls how offensive they had found Proudhon's lack of reverence for their idols: "Men of faith, they hate analysis and doubt"; party men, they could not tolerate independent minds.[60]

In 1849 Herzen had been struck by the profundity of Proudhon's observation that irony was the safeguard of liberty. In the following year he published his own profession of faith on this theme. A rethinking of the nature of the self in a world stripped of transcendence and thereby of rational harmony and inevitability, *From the Other Shore* effects what Thomas Mann held to be impossible—the marriage of irony with radicalism.[61]

Herzen argues in this work that we cannot achieve political liberty without first making our moral vocabulary consistent. In spite of Hegel's revolution in thought, our language remains the language of Christian dualism: "Our imagination has no other images, no other metaphors." Dualism pervades all our judgments, siding "with one shadow against another, granting spirit the monopoly over matter, species the monopoly over the particular, sacrificing man to the state, the state to humanity." The rhetoric of "*réchauffé* Christianity, diluted with the muddy water of rationalism" produces contradictions at every step: "the Gospel and political economy, Loyola and Voltaire, idealism in theory and materialism in practice, an abstract rhetorical morality and behavior directly opposed to it." Its most absurd construction is the *Religion des Diesseits*, "the religion of science, of universal, hereditary, transcendental reason." Why should belief in God and the kingdom of heaven be ridiculous, and belief in humanity and earthly utopias not?

> The world will not know liberty until everything religious
> and political is transformed into something simple, human,
> susceptible to criticism and denial. . . . It is not enough to

despise the crown, one must give up respecting the Phryg-
ian Cap. It is not enough not to consider *lèse-majesté* a
crime, one must look on *salus populi* as being one.

It is time for men to put the republic on trial, along
with its legislation, its system of representation, all our
notions about the citizen and his relations to other citizens and to the State.[62]

The essays that comprise the work are mainly in the form of
dialogues between successive radical rationalists and an ironist, who
argues that the events of 1848 have amply demonstrated that "life
has its own embryogenesis which does not coincide with the dialectic of pure reason."[63] He invites his interlocutors to see how
things look if one bases one's freedom on an acceptance of contingency.

Herzen's alter ego points out that historical development is much
closer to the "physiology" of Nature, with its experiments, abor-
tions, and improvisations, than we like to think.[64] One of his interlocutors finds the view that history lacks a clear direction morally
repulsive: it deprives human strivings of their dignity, turning them
into "mere idle play."[65] Herzen seizes on the last word: the eternal
play of life, which makes nonsense of our deterministic schemas,
is the source of our freedom. By denying us the consolation of self-
transcendence, history maximizes the possibilities of self-creation.
The absence of an objective, universally binding system of moral
values means that individuals are free to create their own morality,
with one proviso—that they should not enter into contradiction
with themselves. Of course, the possibilities of self-creation are not
identical for all: throughout human history only a minority had
sought knowledge, loved beauty and truth, and craved moral independence. Such people were stifled by the old world, but they
could also not identify with the harbingers of the new—the doctrinaire theorists who were inciting the dispossessed to seek revenge
through a leveling communism.

From the Other Shore has been seen as a work of remarkable
philosophical originality, a precursor of existentialist theory; but

studies of Herzen's political thought have kept a wary distance from it. A common view is that it reflects a temporary mood of despair after the disasters of 1848.[66] But Herzen, once again at odds with his interpreters, later described it as his most important work. It was not a withdrawal from idealism into skepticism, but a rethinking of the relations between the two. Herzen's attitude to the masses in this work has been compared to the aristocratic contempt of Nietzsche, but it is the down-to-earth Proudhon whom he presents as the embodiment of freedom: ostracized by the Left for his "merciless irony,"[67] Proudhon could have mended his bridges with them, but only at the cost of confusing his message and losing his strength. His isolation was his most powerful political act. If one could not identify with the new world, one could still point to the defects of the old. If one's ideas answered a contemporary need, they would survive in some form into the future; if not, that did not mean we had not the right to pursue our personal vision of self-creation.

Throughout his career as a radical journalist, Herzen would devote himself to preaching this new moral language, out of which new institutions could grow. When Bakunin protested that it was time for deeds, not words, Herzen retorted in *To an Old Comrade*, "As though *words* are not *deeds?*" People could not be liberated politically if they were not already morally free. Prejudice and ignorance could not be eradicated by terror: "One must open people's eyes, not tear them out." Such a process did not produce the quick results desired by radical theorists; often, it would produce no results at all. Herzen was a much more thoroughgoing ironist than Nietzsche. Indignation with a world that will not dance to one's tune, he tells his interlocutors in *From the Other Shore*, is "a mean and prosy attitude": one should have the curiosity to watch it doing its own dance.[68]

Herzen, like Schiller, understood the seriousness of poetic play. To the *memento mori* of metaphysics, he opposes the *memento vivere* of nature and art; he finds it comforting that we cannot control the future—proof that "every historical phase . . . has its own good that is peculiar to it alone," allowing the creation of a unique self.[69]

His fascination with the inexhaustible variety of human aspirations and inventiveness saved him from the lofty subjectivism of a Nietzsche or the destructive nihilism that often passes for irony. He would have agreed with Friedrich Schlegel that "nothing is more trivial than the empty form of irony without enthusiasm, and without tension between the real and the ideal."[70]

Herzen perceived this tension very differently from most of his radical contemporaries: not as a struggle between present darkness and future light, but as a process akin to aesthetic creation, based on an artist's sense of the plasticity and three-dimensionality of things. He invites us to take up the challenge offered to our creative powers by the openness and unpredictability of history by inserting our own verse into its "tattered improvisation."[71] This aesthetic sense of history's flow enabled Herzen, seventy years before the beginning of the Russian Revolution, to predict the manner of its end: "Socialism will develop in all its phases, until it reaches its own extremes and absurdities. Then once again a cry of denial will break from the titanic breast of the rebellious minority and once again a mortal struggle will begin, in which socialism will play the role of contemporary conservatism and will be overturned in the subsequent revolution, as yet unknown to us."[72]

On the eve of the Russian Revolution, Thomas Mann remarked that the twentieth century, like the eighteenth, seeks to forget what one knows about the human being, "in order to adapt him to its utopia."[73] Now that that kind of thinking has gone through all its repertoire of extremes and absurdities, we are better able to appreciate the originality of Herzen and Proudhon in showing it to be possible to combine political idealism with what experience has told us about human behavior. They developed a political language that reversed the accepted wisdom, setting up as a model an intellectual type for whom a radical uncertainty was the sign of moral independence and maturity. A "need and capacity for endless revision and self-correction, for questioning and suspending judgment, for living 'hypothetically and subjunctively,' as Kierkegaard says, and keeping alive a sense of an infinity of possibilities":[74] this definition of irony encapsulates the type of thinking that they represented. Again, contrary to traditional political wisdom, they held that such an approach to reality would lead not to social chaos, but to the kind of dynamic balance of forces that is conducive to the maximum of individual liberty. Theirs was an ironist utopia of an "endless, proliferating realization of Freedom,"[75] delighting in experiment and respecting no absolutes. Such a society would be aesthetically incapable of tolerating dictatorship. As Mann notes, "Irony is always irony toward both sides; it directs itself against life as well as against intellect, and this takes the grand gesture away from it, this makes it melancholy and modest."[76]

Why did thinkers of such originality have so little impact on the radical movement? Herzen suggested an answer by emphasizing the strength of psychological resistance to his thinking: "What is most offensive of all is that people seem to understand you, agree with you, and yet your thoughts remain alien in their heads, without ever acquiring relevance to reality."[77] Rorty has argued that what people most resent about ironists is their "inability to empower": they can never promise to regenerate human societies by uncovering the goals of history or the true nature of the self.[78] It is significant that Bakunin, whose certainties on these points Herzen subjected to such devastating criticism, nevertheless enjoyed so great a following on the Left that at one time he seemed capable of wresting the leadership of the International from Marx.

In their attempts to describe things in new ways, Herzen and Proudhon fell foul of the conservatism and inertia of ideological thought: their ideas are known principally through the distorting and often hostile interpretations of the traditions they sought to subvert. Proudhon's reputation was destroyed by Marx's ridicule, while Herzen suffered a more grotesque fate. His canonization by Lenin as a precursor of Russian communism means that he is rarely read by Russians now engaged in seeking new paths. Herzen's "other shore," where freedom is built on the acceptance of contingency, is never likely to be heavily populated: Its climate is too uncertain and its landscape too exposed for most of us to bear. But the insights into the nature of moral freedom that he shared with

Proudhon would give greater depth to current discussions about new directions in radical thought. Against the background of those discussions, it has been claimed that the utopian vision was the best thing that nineteenth-century Russian intellectual history bequeathed to the twentieth century.[79] I propose, instead, another of Herzen's predictions: that the spirit of irony "is our hope and our salvation, the progressive element in the Russian nature."[80]

A European Nanny:
Herzen and Mill on Liberty
C H A P T E R F O U R

The beliefs which we have most warrant for, have no safeguard to rest on, but a standing invitation to the whole world to prove them unfounded. If the challenge is not accepted, or is accepted and the attempt fails, we are far from certainty still: . . . if the lists are kept open, we may hope that if there be a better truth, it will be found when the human mind is capable of receiving it; and in the meantime we may rely on having attained such approach to truth, as is possible in our own day. This is the amount of certainty attainable by a fallible being, and this is the sole way of attaining it.
—J. S. Mill

People like things to be decorative. Even in truth they see only the side that looks the best; they don't care if round the back the grass is growing wild. But *real* truths have three dimensions, and all three are essential to their existence.
—A. I. Herzen

I n mid-nineteenth-century Russia there took place a series of polemics that have been interpreted as an archetypal conflict between two political temperaments: the gradualist and the extremist. A despot had just died; his successor had declared his intention to free the masses from serfdom and to reform the legal system and local government. The most prominent members of educated society—liberal professors, jurists, and writers—hoped that the promised reforms would be the first step in the slow transformation of Russia into an industrialized democracy on a Western pattern. This prospect was vigorously opposed by Aleksandr Herzen, the publications of whose Free Russian Press, smuggled from London into Russia, played a dominant role in the political discussions of the time. He pointed out that parliamentary democracy had done nothing to prevent the economic exploitation of the masses in the West. Russia could avoid the terrible human cost of large-scale industrialization on the Western model by developing its peasant communes into cooperative units of consumers and producers. Instead of a slow evolution toward Western bourgeois democracy Herzen proposed a direct transition to an advanced form of socialism, preferably by an initiative from above, but if necessary by revolution from below.

If, as liberal historians have argued, Herzen's confrontation with the Russian liberals was a clash between utopian extremism and sober pragmatism, it is Herzen who has the better claim to being the pragmatist. His chief opponents, the historian Konstantin Kavelin and the jurist Boris Chicherin, were Hegelians who interpreted the historical process as the dialectical development of universal reason toward its supreme incarnation in the modern state. This in its perfected form (Hegel's *Rechtsstaat*) they held to be the goal of human history. The commune, they argued, was a survival of the earliest phase in this process and was destined to be discarded as Russia, according to the ineluctable laws of progress, followed in the wake of its more advanced neighbors, There was no going back to the commune: history could not retrace its steps.[1]

Herzen retorted that such doctrinairism had blinded the liberals to the empirical advantages of the commune as a solution to Russia's urgent social and economic problems. As a functioning institution with a self-governing structure, it had the potential, with the help of Western technology and social theory, to combine economic development and social justice in a way that the West had signally failed to do. There was no empirical evidence that the path taken by the most developed states in western Europe was obligatory for all other countries. Moreover, the doctrine that historical development was a linear advance toward a single goal could not be reconciled with the liberals' expressed belief in the human right to self-direction. On this point he could cite a powerful authority in his support. Toward the end of his life, Herzen observed that, as Russians tended to have far more respect for Europeans than for other Russians, whenever he wished to be taken seriously he took the precaution of placing his ideas under the protection of a "European nanny."[2] When attempting to wean the Russian liberals from their fixation on the obligatory virtues of Western bourgeois democracy, he quoted John Stuart Mill.

Herzen's use of *On Liberty* as a weapon against the Russian liberals was not just an astute polemical move. There are deep affinities between his view of freedom and Mill's. Both men found themselves isolated from the political groupings of their time, and their philosophies have since proved difficult to categorize. The Russian liberals of the nineteenth century saw Herzen as a dangerous radical; many radicals believed him to be a liberal. He has subsequently been classified both as a utopian optimist and as a precursor of modern pessimism.[3] Mill's contemporaries debated over whether he was a liberal or a Tory, and subsequent efforts to define his outlook have led to the theory of "two Mills."

Herzen and Mill took an ironic view of such attempts to label them. They saw themselves as innovators, seeking to persuade their contemporaries to adopt new ways of talking about the self and the world, and they were resigned to being misunderstood by those who remained obstinately attached to old habits of thought. They belonged to a very small number of thinkers (among them, Proudhon) who rejected all forms of rational determinism, from Hegel's system to the materialistic scientism of the midcentury, while distancing themselves equally from the limitless subjectivism of romantic revolt. In this respect their approach bears a striking resemblance to that of one of the most original—and still one of the most undervalued—of post-Enlightenment texts on liberty: Schiller's treatise *On the Aesthetic Education of Man*. My discussion of this three-sided relationship has two aims: to draw attention to significant confluences in the history of ideas and to establish the relevance of Herzen's and Mill's views on liberty and morality to the beginning of the twenty-first century, when appeals to timeless and impersonal standards have become generally suspect.

Herzen's celebrated onslaughts on the tyranny of abstractions over living human beings owed much to the revolutionary negation of the German Left Hegelians, but he went further than most thinkers of his time in extending his critique to the concept of progress itself. In his profession of faith *From the Other Shore,* reflecting on the shattered hopes of 1848, he observes that radicals no less than conservatives had perpetuated the belief (inherited from religious eschatology) that individual lives derive their meaning and purpose from transcendent authorities and powers. Those who sought to free people from the tyranny of monarch and church were happy to enslave them to such empty abstractions as progress, humanity, universal reason, and the common good. It was time to confront the fear of freedom that pervaded all traditional notions of personal morality, society, and the state: the desire to evade responsibility for one's fate by surrendering one's autonomy to some collective noun.

As we have seen, in the early 1840s Herzen had been much struck by the resemblance between his views on the relation of inner liberty to political freedom and those set out by Schiller in his treatise of 1795 on aesthetic education. Schiller's model of the aesthetically modulated personality (capable of maintaining a shifting balance between affective and rational drives in appropriate responses to specific situations) was intended to counter the regimenting tendencies of modern societies, which were supported, Schiller points out, by the Kantian model of virtue as successful self-coercion in the name of universal norms and imperatives furnished by reason. Herzen pronounced the work prophetic, regretting that Schiller, known only as the romantic poet of the "beautiful soul," had not been given his due. More than a century later the British philosopher Stuart Hampshire would make the same point.[4]

Mill came to his unorthodox views about the ends and means of progress by the same route as Herzen: through painful reflection on the emotional cost of his preoccupation with philosophical abstractions. Stifled by the hothouse atmosphere of the Russian intellectual circles of the 1840s, the young Herzen had diagnosed his generation's excessive addiction to speculative thought as "a kind of madness" that destroyed their chances of finding self-fulfillment in everyday reality.[5] Mill has left his famous account of his breakdown in 1828, when at the age of twenty he found himself "stranded at the commencement of my voyage, with a well equipped ship and a rudder, but no sail; without any real desire for the ends which I had been so carefully fitted out to work for; no delight in virtue or the general good, but also just as little in anything else. The fountains of vanity and ambition seemed to have dried up within me, as completely as those of benevolence." He concluded that his extraordinary education in the spirit of Benthamite utilitarianism had turned him into "a mere reasoning machine."[6]

The conviction to which Mill's devastating experience led him is expressed succinctly in a passage from Schiller's *Aesthetic Education:* "It is not, then, enough to say that all enlightenment of the understanding is worthy of respect only inasmuch as it reacts upon character. To a certain extent it also proceeds from character, since the way to the head must be opened through the heart. The development of man's capacity for feeling is, therefore, the more urgent need of our age, not merely because it can be a means of making better insights effective for living, but precisely because it provides the impulse for bettering our insights."[7]

Such, precisely, was the project on which Mill embarked, seeking to reawaken his impulse to the good by immersing himself in poetry, music, and art. Cultivation of the feelings—not as a substitute but as a corrective for the habits of rational analysis—became a central point of his ethical and philosophical creed.[8] In the process of resolving his personal crisis, Mill's aesthetic education broadened and deepened his vision of human nature. He remained an empiricist, but the Benthamite definition of happiness as consequent on a rational calculation of pleasure and pain had become too narrow a creed for him. As he wrote to Thomas Carlyle in 1834, he continued to pursue the utilitarian goal of the greatest happiness of the greatest number, but he now believed that "this end can in no other way be forwarded but . . . by each taking for his exclusive aim the development of what is best in *himself*."[9] This in turn Mill believed could be achieved only by what he describes as "the maintenance of a due balance among the faculties."[10] His view of liberty, like Herzen's, rests on an aesthetic model of the individual's relations with himself.

The resemblance of Mill's model of virtue to that of Schiller's treatise is the more remarkable in view of the fact that, unlike Herzen, Mill seems not to have known the work.[11] As J. M. Robson has pointed out, for Mill the end of morality was a state of being, not conformity to an abstract formula.[12] Insisting on the "psychological fact" of our self-awareness as social beings, he rejects the dualistic concept of the psyche implied in a rigid distinction between egoistic and altruistic acts; instead he presents the curbing of inclinations in the name of the general good as part of a reciprocal ordering of drives in the interests of the optimal harmonization of all aspects of the self. He acknowledges the primacy of reason in determining moral goals and directing and controlling selfish and irrational impulses but maintains that this is best achieved by forming character through an aesthetic education which makes feeling reason's ally, furnishing images of beautiful conduct which we long to emulate and developing our imaginative empathy with particular individuals and cases.[13] This, he insists, is a securer foundation for morality than the habit of obedience to general principles, the great majority of good actions being intended "not for the benefit of the world, but for that of individuals, of which the good of the world is made up." Rejecting, like Schiller, the view that all acts of self-renunciation are necessarily virtuous, he maintains that social utility is best served by those in whom the cultivation of feeling has created a disposition to do good that is independent of any system of prescriptions and sanctions. The formation of character in this way will, moreover, constitute a safeguard against the excessive influence of such systems which in the name of service to humanity threaten to "interfere unduly with human freedom and individuality."[14]

Schiller had warned that moral freedom would not be attained through political reforms that substituted one set of universal norms for another: "The old principles will remain; but they will wear the dress of the century, and Philosophy now lend her name to a repression formerly authorized by the Church."[15] Alexis de Tocqueville was among the first to point out that the new dress of popular sovereignty was cut to a familiar pattern; but while his influence on Mill was considerable, Mill's aesthetic self-education was a no less important factor in shaping his perception of the threat to freedom posed by the advent of mass democracies.

Like Schiller's work, *On Liberty* is structured around the opposition between a dualistic and an aesthetic vision of the individual's relations with himself. In Mill's nightmarish picture of Victorian society the stern rigor of moral attitudes founded on Kantian dualism and Christian asceticism has combined with the zeal of reforming rationalists to secure the ascendancy of "collective mediocrity." Tocqueville had noted the part played by puritanism in enforcing moral conformity in America; in England Mill calls attention to the influence of the "pinched and hidebound" type of character favored by the more mean-minded varieties of Protestantism, whose power was reflected in such monstrosities as Sabbatarian legislation. Social reformers, too, seemed bent on making people all alike, regulating their thoughts and actions by a common set of rules and maxims. The growth of mass communications and the standardization of the conditions of material existence were moving society in the same direction. Spontaneity and eccentricity were frowned on as obstructions to the right way of doing things; this "liberticide" was favored even by heretics and dissidents who occupied themselves "rather in inquiring what things society ought to like or dislike, than in questioning whether its likings or dislikings should be a law to individuals."[16]

Mill notes that the moral coercion of public opinion is applied more fiercely against deviations from the norm in private than in public conduct: the improvement of morals being conceived as the standardization of conduct through the discouragement of excesses, the suppression of the strong desires that constitute individuality.

He was justly accused of caricaturing Victorian society for his polemical purposes. Contemporary critics reminded him that eccentricity still flourished in England: a society that listened attentively
to such personalities as Thomas Carlyle could scarcely be said to
be fleeing from independence of thought.[17] But Mill insisted that
he was seeking to define an incipient tendency: it was as yet insufficiently perceived that the term *self-government* denoted "not the
government of each by himself, but of each by all the rest." The
collective tyranny of popular sovereignty offered fewer means of
escape than other kinds of oppression, "penetrating more deeply
into the details of life, enslaving the soul itself"; the personality
divided against itself submits unprotestingly to the yoke of uniformity:

> In our times, from the highest class of society down to the
> lowest, all live under the eye of a hostile and dreaded cen-
> sorship. Not only in what concerns others, but in what
> concerns only themselves, the individual and the family do
> not ask themselves—what do I prefer? or, what would suit
> my character and disposition? or what would allow the
> best and highest in me to have fair play, and enable it to
> grow and thrive? They ask themselves, what is suitable to
> my position? What is usually done by persons of my sta-
> tion and pecuniary circumstances? or (worse still) what is
> usually done by persons of a station and circumstances su-
> perior to mine? I do not mean that they choose what is
> customary, in preference to what suits their own inclina-
> tion. It does not occur to them to have any inclination,
> except for what is customary . . . until by dint of not fol-
> lowing their own nature, they have no nature to follow:
> their human capacities are withered and starved. . . . Now
> is this, or is it not, the desirable condition of human na-
> ture?[18]

"But can Man really be destined to miss himself for the sake of
any purpose whatsoever?"—thus Schiller had protested against the
hypothesis that the increasing regimentation of modern societies

was a prerequisite of progress.[19] Mill, like Tocqueville, insisted that the extension of the powers of society over the individual, both through legislation and opinion, was not an essential feature of mass democracies but a creeping perversion, against which it was imperative to raise "a strong barrier of moral conviction."[20] There is, he insists, no necessary contradiction between the self-realization of individuals and social utility, provided that social utility be not too narrowly interpreted.[21] The following passage could be Schiller contesting Kant's ideal of virtue as self-renunciation:

> There is a different type of human excellence from the Cal-
> vinistic; a conception of humanity as having its nature be-
> stowed on it for other purposes than merely to be abne-
> gated. . . . There is a Greek ideal of self-development,
> which the Platonic and Christian ideal of self-government
> blends with, but does not supersede. . . .
>
> It is not by wearing down into uniformity all that is in-
> dividual in themselves, but by cultivating it and calling it
> forth, within the limits imposed by the rights and inter-
> ests of others, that human beings become a noble and
> beautiful object of contemplation; and as the works par-
> take the character of those who do them, by the same pro-
> cess human life also becomes rich, diversified, and animat-
> ing, furnishing more abundant aliment to high thoughts
> and elevating feelings, and strengthening the tie which
> binds every individual to the race, by making the race infi-
> nitely better worth belonging to. In proportion to the de-
> velopment of his individuality, each person becomes more
> valuable to himself, and is therefore capable of being more
> valuable to others. There is a greater fulness of life about
> his own existence, and when there is more life in the
> units there is more in the mass which is composed of
> them.[22]

Hence the famous principle of *On Liberty:* "The sole end for which mankind are warranted, individually or collectively, in interfering with the liberty of action of any of their number, is self-protection.

... The only part of the conduct of any one, for which he is amenable to society, is that which concerns others. In the part which merely concerns himself, his independence is, of right, absolute."[23]

Although *On Liberty* is regarded as a key text of classical liberalism, its central principle has been much criticized for making a distinction between self-regarding and other-regarding acts that is unworkable in a modern society and implies a false antithesis of the individual and the state.[24] This would seem a perverse reading of a text whose aim is to remind us that (as Mill put it in another context) mankind "after all are made up of single human beings";[25] and whose concluding paragraph contains the following prescient insight into the fate of societies that ignore this truth: "A State which dwarfs its men, in order that they may be more docile instruments in its hands even for beneficial purposes will find that with small men no great thing can really be accomplished; and that the perfection of machinery to which it has sacrificed everything, will in the end avail it nothing, for want of the vital power which, in order that the machine might work more smoothly, it has preferred to banish."[26]

It was as a moral barrier against such dehumanization that Mill's principle was conceived: the hostility it has encountered from some political philosophers seems based on so radical a misreading of his intentions that one is tempted to explain it by resistance to the introduction of an alien style of reasoning into a field of enquiry long dominated by the discourse of Enlightenment rationalism. (The same reason has been advanced for the fact that Schiller's treatise was interpreted for so long as preaching an ivory tower aestheticism.)[27] Mill himself was well aware of the heretical status of his principle. It might, he wrote, seem a truism that "the only freedom which deserves the name, is that of pursuing our own good in our own way"; but no doctrine was more directly opposed to the general tendency of existing opinion and practice. Such a view had been held only by a minority of thinkers in any age, and in his own, "few persons, out of Germany" would not be amazed to find so high a value attached to individuality. In asserting his "very simple principle" Mill stood like Herzen on a lonely shore.[28]

Like Herzen's dissection of the illusions of 1848, *On Liberty* hits out in all directions, presenting a view of human autonomy clearly distinct from all the mainstream varieties of idealist metaphysics, rationalist determinism, and romantic doctrines of protean self-creation. It is significant that of those thinkers who anticipated his ideas, Mill describes it as appropriate to mention only one: Schiller's admired friend and correspondent, the Prussian scholar and statesman Wilhelm von Humboldt. *On Liberty* is headed by an epigraph from Humboldt's book *The Sphere and Duties of Government:* "The grand, leading principle, towards which every argument unfolded in these pages directly converges, is the absolute and essential importance of human development in its richest diversity."[29]

One commentator has defined Humboldt's distinctive characteristic as a sense of the complexity of our attitudes toward and need of other people which gives his thought a particular kind of tension as he interweaves a number of intellectual strands, achieving a certain coherence between them in his search to reconcile the ideal of the self-determining moral agent with the values of diversity and spontaneity.[30] Accepting Kant's categorical imperative but not his dualistic model of moral consciousness, he drew on German idealism and aesthetic theory for a liberal view of the relations between the individual and the state which would reconcile the goal of maximum receptivity to experience with the limiting conditions imposed by the rights of others. His minimalist state would protect rights against encroachment but not lay down institutional forms for an equilibrium that he saw as necessarily unstable; rather, he favored a voluntary associationism of a sort more readily identified with anarchist than liberal theory. It has been observed that there are liberalisms of harmony and liberalisms of dissonance: the former see rational consensus as the ultimate goal of social organization, while the latter emphasize the need for unceasing compromise and negotiation to accommodate the diverse and conflicting ways in which individuals seek to fulfill themselves.[31] Humboldt's was a liberalism of dissonance. His ideal of human interaction, expressed in aesthetic metaphors, is situated within the kind of moral framework, "removed alike from uniformity and confusion," that is outlined in the *Aesthetic Education of Man*[32]—a work that Humboldt helped to shape during his daily discussions with Schiller.

It has been said of Humboldt that he enlarges one's sense of what a liberal theory may be.[33] The same is true of Mill. His mental breakdown having taught him that human needs were too complex to be explicable in terms of any unitary system of rational purposes, he began to seek illumination from mutually exclusive doctrines—a procedure that, as Isaiah Berlin has commented, was "greatly daring" in one brought up in a puritanical Benthamite radicalism.[34] The ideological wrangle of the nineteenth century with the Enlightenment came to seem to him a battle between half-truths; following Goethe's motto of many-sidedness, he turned to idealist philosophies of history, rejecting their metaphysical a prioris but using their dialectical vision of an evolving truth to deepen his sense of the creative potentials of an unprogrammed world. (A few years later in Moscow, the young Herzen, exasperated by what he saw as the incompleteness of idealist and materialist explanations of reality, would follow a similar path.)[35] Respecting no ideological boundaries, Mill found inspiration in sources as diverse as the Saint-Simonians' revolutionary views on the relations of the sexes and the conservatism of Carlyle, from which he benefited "not as philosophy to instruct, but as poetry to animate."[36] Asked to explain his system, he retorted, as Proudhon had done, that he neither had nor aspired to have one.[37] Instead, he had a method, whose basic premiss can be summed up in Schiller's dictum: "Reason does indeed demand unity, but Nature demands multiplicity; and both these kinds of law make their claim upon man."[38]

Much of what Mill's critics took to be his inconsistency derived from his efforts to maintain in his thinking a dynamic equilibrium between these competing orders of law. In this he believed, like Herzen, who recommended a training in the methods of the experimental sciences to any budding political philosopher, that science was on his side: the inductive methods of the natural sciences supported moral instinct and aesthetic insight by demonstrating the incompleteness and provisionality of all generalizations about contingent phenomena. Hence, while sharing Auguste Comte's opti-

mism about the possibility of a future science of society, Mill
viewed the range and competence of such a science very differently
from Comte, whose ideal of a society ruled by a body of scientist-
philosophers seemed to him both despotic and unscientific: "It is
one of M. Comte's mistakes that he never allows of open questions";[39] his love of system and certainty was in contradiction with
his positivism. Observation showed human nature to be not an
unchanging totality of characteristics, but a thing of "extraordinary
pliability" whose achievements were built on historically accumulated experience.[40] By plotting regularities in that experience, science could make increasingly accurate predictions but should not
presume to extrapolate the future forms of society from the present.
A true science of society would be experimental, not prescriptive.

It is as sources of experiments, always open to revision and rejection, that Mill approaches all social theories, including his own.
In *From the Other Shore* Herzen predicts that one day socialism
"will play the role of contemporary conservatism and will be over-
whelmed in the subsequent revolution": such was the "eternal play
of life." Mill regarded the validity of representative democracy as
"a question of time, place and circumstance." He sees nothing sacred in the principles of the liberal political economy of his time.[41]
In revised editions of his *Principles of Political Economy,* written
with Harriet Taylor, he speculates on the advantages of communal
systems of ownership and production. Their attempts to reconcile
the principles of individual liberty and social justice led the two to
class themselves "decidedly under the general designation of Socialists,"[42] while distancing themselves equally decidedly from every
form of collectivism. With this exception, Mill welcomed all "experiments of living"—such as those of Robert Owen's followers—
which, by offering alternative models of organization, could shake
society out of that complacency which he saw as the greatest danger
facing modern democracies.[43]

Given Mill's perspectivist approach to institutions, it is not surprising that his work contains no formulas for the structure and
conduct of representative government, other than the general prin-

ciple of the necessity of counterbalances to the ascendancy of any
single power or elite (as a check to the evil described in *On Liberty*
he favors a form of proportional representation.) On the definition
of the areas of competence of government he offers only one "simple and vague" rule—that the interference of government should
never be admitted except "when the case of expediency is strong."[44]

Such remarks have been cited as proof of the abstractness of
Mill's political philosophy. On the contrary, they can be said to
spring from his respect for the particularity of context in the future
as well as the present and past. To reproach him for not giving
more concrete examples of the permissible extent of government
interference is to misread the guiding intention of his work, which
is to convey not a theory of the relations between state and individual, but the rudiments of an aesthetic education that would
equip his readers to discern for themselves what, in any given context, those relations should be. He looked forward, he tells us, to a
future in which "convictions as to what is right and wrong, useful
and pernicious, deeply engraven on the feelings by early education
and general unanimity of sentiment, [would be] so firmly grounded
in reason and the true exigencies of life that they shall not, like all
former and present creeds . . . require to be periodically thrown off
and replaced by others."[45] His *Autobiography*, the *Inaugural Address
to St. Andrews*, and *Utilitarianism* are manuals in the cultivation of
a plasticity of vision based on a moral sensitivity to the contours
of particular cases. Mill is no more sanguine than Herzen about
the ease and speed with which "education, habit and the cultivation
of the sentiments" can ensure that such a vision is no longer confined to a small minority. Contrary to the belief of idealists, Herzen
insisted, humanity did not love freedom: "Man loves to obey, always seeks to lean upon something."[46] Thinkers who sought to
remove those traditional props had to contend with the awesome
power of heredity and habit. Mill warns against the folly of premature attempts to introduce enlightened reforms in the face of
the resistance of beliefs which, however intellectually discredited,
continue to form the moral framework of most lives: "All political
revolutions, not effected by foreign conquest, originate in moral

revolutions. The subversion of established institutions is merely one consequence of the previous subversion of established opinions."[47] Mill's personal experience had shown him that moral revolutions came about through the interaction of individual character and circumstance, that the self was not an unchanging rational core which orders the rest according to universal norms, but rather, to use a phrase of Proudhon, "a cluster of potentialities," from which each human being creates a unique personality.[48] Thus, while attaching great importance to the role of education in developing the imaginative empathy that he saw as the basis of social cohesion, Mill strongly opposed any centralized system of instruction that would force people into a single mold: "It is essential that different persons be allowed to live different lives. . . . whatever crushes individuality is despotism, . . . whether it professes to be enforcing the will of God or the injunctions of men."[49]

In Herzen's polemics with the ideologists of Russian liberalism we see the same insistence on the three-dimensional untidiness of all real truths about history, society, and human nature, and the same warning against the efforts of systematizers to seat reason on religion's empty throne. He told them that the empirical evidence did not support their view of history as a linear progression toward a final goal. It was an improvisation formed from the combination of general laws with the unpredictable effects of chance and environment: "Neither nature nor history *are going anywhere,* and therefore they are ready to go *everywhere* they are directed, if . . . nothing obstructs them." Hence his method was not to prescribe a path of development, but to study the reality around him in order to distinguish and encourage those elements that seemed to have the most creative potential. The final outcome was not in his power to predict: that was up to the "poetic caprice of history"—a phrase calculated to enrage the proponents of rational progress.[50]

In "the complete anthropological view," Schiller had declared, "content counts no less than form and living feeling too has a voice."[51] It was just such a vision that Mill and Herzen sought to articulate, and in so doing they both embarked on what (with reference to Humboldt) J. W. Burrow has described as the perilous journey from one set of metaphors to another.[52] Mill's *Autobiography* is commonly approached as a source of anecdotes about his extraordinary upbringing. But this account of a mind "which was always pressing forward, equally ready to learn and to unlearn either from its own thoughts or from those of others"[53] was intended, like Proudhon's *Confessions of a Revolutionary* and Herzen's monumental memoirs *My Past and Thoughts*, to serve as an exemplary text. Thought takes on flesh as Mill portrays his intellectual development not as the gradual uncovering of timeless truth, but, using a more prosaic metaphor drawn from the unfinishedness of contingent existence: a fabric of thought, incessantly rewoven as it gave way in ever fresh places under the pressure of new events, personalities, and ideas.[54]

Mill's countrymen, like Herzen's, tended to operate with a different set of metaphors. During his brief parliamentary career he disappointed the many Tories who had expected to find an ally in the author of *On Liberty:* "As I was able to see the Conservative side of the question, they presumed that, like them, I could not see any other side."[55] Something of the reasoning of the Tory Party can be found in the debates among later commentators as to whether Mill was ultimately a libertarian or a utilitarian. At the cost of a considerable distortion of his arguments, he has been portrayed as an individualist who stressed liberty to the detriment of values like community and justice; and conversely, as tolerating diversity only within the limits of a rationally agreed social consensus. A less reductive approach—the theory of the two Mills—presents him as alternating between mutually incompatible philosophical doctrines.[56] It is odd that the point is still having to be made that Mill himself did not see the matter like that.[57] His *Autobiography* leaves no doubt that the doctrinal inconsistency which so perturbs some critics was for him a sine qua non of that truly anthropological perspective that takes account of the two kinds of law to which consciousness is subject. This is not to say that Mill was always consistent by his own criteria. As Berlin has noted, rigorous argument was not among his accomplishments,[58] and some of his many ambiguities stem, like Herzen's, from the fact that his irony is not always proof against utopian hope.[59] His belief in the steady improvement of humanity through science, education, and a free rein to creativity was based, he claimed, on empirical observation; but it took little account of the kind of creativity that prefers chaos to order and mocks reason and self-interest by asserting its preference that $2 + 2$ should equal 5.

Yet Mill was no less a subversive than Dostoevsky's underground ironist, who declares that the human race is not programmed to construct "one marvelous building, eternal and indestructible."[60] His early training in Enlightenment optimism left a permanent mark on him, but the unity for which he hopes is far closer to Proudhon's "general equation of all our contradictions" than to the static harmony of a Benthamite or Comtian consensus.[61] The passage in On Liberty calling for the maximum divergence of opinion to be encouraged "until man is more capable of recognising all sides of the truth" has been cited as evidence that Mill saw freedom of discussion as only a means to the establishment of a body of universally agreed truth.[62] But in its context the meaning of the phrase is clear: that in free discussion an empirical, perspectivist approach to questions of social organization will gradually come to prevail over varieties of belief in a single right way. For Mill as for Herzen, the role of contingent circumstances as a necessary dimension of all meaningful truths about human beings and society meant that society's many sides could never coexist in static harmony or perfect symmetry. Stressing the supreme importance of "giving full freedom to human nature to expand itself in innumerable and conflicting directions," noting the provisional status of all political theories as the basis of "experiments of living," insisting that a "plurality of paths" is essential for historical progress, Mill does not predict that the conflicts will be resolved, the experiments end, or the paths ultimately converge.[63] His ideal of harmony is dynamic, unstable, open-ended, maintaining a shifting Schillerian accommodation between general moral principles and the "exigencies of life." It is his respect for these demands in their untidy unpredictability and infinite variety that leads him to con-

demn what he saw as Comte's narrow conception of social improvement: "The united forces of society never were, nor can be,
directed to one single end, nor is there, so far as I can perceive,
any reason for desiring that they should. Men do not come into
the world to fulfil one single end, and there is no single end which
if fulfilled even in the most complete manner would make them
happy."[64]

As Mill notes in *On Liberty*, propositions of this kind might seem
self-evident; but they ran counter to deep-seated habits of thought.
Herzen declared in the aftermath of 1848 that the time had come
to put on trial "all our notions about the citizen and his relations
to other citizens and to the State." Mill, too, demanded of his
audience that they change not merely their opinions but "the fundamental constitution of their mode of thought."[65] Even for the
sake of the improvement of humanity, this was a lot to ask.

In 1859, at the height of his polemics with the Russian liberals,
Herzen published in his periodical the *Polar Star* a memoir on
Proudhon, another of his European nannies whose iconoclasm, directed against the reigning orthodoxies of Right and Left alike, had
been a formative influence on his thought. He contrasts Proudhon's
mode of thinking—constantly developing, changing, and reflecting
events—with the sluggishness of thought characteristic of all doctrinairism: the stubborn narrow-mindedness of those who are at
ease only with fellow-believers and indifferent or hostile to new
ideas and influences. Herzen cites "an excellent expression regarding these truths settled once and for ever: 'The deep slumber of a
decided opinion.'"[66] The quotation is from *On Liberty*, which, by
a happy coincidence, had just been published and which Herzen,
under the title "Mill on Liberty," proceeded to review in the same
journal.

Mill's writings seem to have come to Herzen's attention only
after he had spent some years in England; his first published reference to them (recommending them to the readers of the *Bell*)
occurs in 1857.[67] But the appearance of *On Liberty* was an event of
great importance for him. Since his arrival in the West he had been

unsparing in his criticism of the defects of bourgeois democracy and culture. He contended that the experience of 1848 had shown representative systems to be "a cunningly conceived device to transmute social needs . . . into words and endless arguments."[68] He accused Western liberals of a superstitious reverence for political forms, characteristic of a culture dominated by the shopkeeper's yard-rule, where form took precedence over content as a measure of virtue and value. Herzen's liberal friends had dismissed these views as Slavophile ranting. Hence the note of triumph with which his review of *On Liberty* begins: "Thanks be to those who after us confirm with their authority what we have said, and with their talent clearly and forcefully pass on what we have feebly expressed." Nicely balancing modesty with a claim to precedence, he greets Mill as one of the few serious minds in Europe who have come to share his sense of a deep crisis in European thought. When he had voiced this opinion in *From the Other Shore,* he had been scolded for presuming to criticize his elders and betters; now a similar pessimism was being expressed not by some "angry socialist exile" like Proudhon or himself, but by a man of "enormous, well-merited authority," a celebrated political economist "long versed in affairs of state and theories deeply thought through, accustomed to regard the world calmly, like an Englishman and a thinker."[69] For Herzen, ritually denounced by both the Russian government and much of Russian progressive society, it must have been comforting to discover this distinguished fellow-heretic who, unlike him, could not be patronized by liberal intellectuals.

In his autobiography Mill expressed regret that the desire to placate common opinion had on occasion made him suppress "the more decidedly heretical part of my opinions, which I now look upon as almost the only ones, the assertion of which tends in any way to regenerate society."[70] Herzen's first reference to Mill in print, two years before *On Liberty*'s appearance, shows a keen sense of this predicament. Surveying current Western publications in the *Bell,* he welcomes Mill's writings along with the new scientific positivism, as spearheading an attack on all forms of idealism by approaching history and nature without theological or metaphysical preconceptions. He notes the enormous distance between the ideas of this avant-garde and popular prejudices: hence the regrettable tendency of scientific popularizers to water down their message "so as not to scare the crowd and to have a full auditorium."[71]

He would make no such criticism of *On Liberty*. Presenting the work to his Russian readers, he points to the similarity between Mill's plain speaking on the aesthetic poverty and moral despotism of bourgeois culture and his own critique, much derided by his liberal friends when he had expressed it a decade before. Now his critics would be forced to reflect on the fact that in a country renowned for its political freedoms, an eminent thinker should find it necessary to publish a book "in defense of *liberty of thought, speech, and the individual.*" As Herzen had asked Proudhon after Louis Napoleon's coup of 1851, "Can there be any idea in the world more impoverished than that of order?"[72] Mill's answer to this question was so much in sympathy with his own thinking that the term *collective mediocrity* would henceforth be a refrain of his commentaries on Western democracies. His review gives much emphasis to Mill's warning that progress is not a universal characteristic of human history. Were the despotism of custom to become institutionalized in European societies, they could reach a state of inertia so complete that Europe would become another China, with one difference—the bitterest drop in Mill's cup of wormwood: the European bourgeoisie would continue in its restless pursuit of change and fashion. In proscribing singularity the spirit of conformism did not proscribe change, "provided all change together."

Herzen seizes on Mill's image of a new China to develop the analogy between historical and evolutionary processes that had long been a central feature of his writing on history. He notes that Mill is describing something akin to the formation of "herd types," the ultimate result of a long succession of consummations and attainments:

> The antediluvian beasts represent a kind of heroic age in
> this Book of Being: they are the Titans and the knights;
> they grow smaller, adapt to a new environment and, as

soon as they attain to a type that is sufficiently skillful
and stable, they begin to repeat themselves in conformity
with their type, to such a degree that the dog of Ulysses
in the *Odyssey* is as like all our dogs as two drops of water. And that is not all: has anyone said that political and
social animals, not only living in a herd but with a degree
of organization, like ants and bees, established their anthills or nests straight off? I do not think so at all. Millions
of generations lay down and died before they built and
stabilized their *Chinese* anthills.[73]

In human societies, Herzen suggests, an analogous process occurs when the active, historically significant segment of a population reaches a form of social organization that suits it and gives up
the struggle for something better in favor of preserving what has
been achieved so far. To maintain this state of equilibrium requires
neither wars, revolutions, nor eccentric individuals. On the contrary, a passive absorption in the herd is one of the prime conditions for self-preservation. There are signs that Europe is approaching such a state: "Individuals do not come out of the ranks because
there is not sufficient cause for them to do so. For whom, for what,
or against whom should they come forward?" This, Herzen observes, is not a question that Mill addresses: frightened by the moral
worthlessness of his environment, he seems to want people with
the mentality of shopkeepers "to turn, from some poetic necessity,
by some spiritual gymnastics, into—heroes!" Instead of remon-
strating with the sick man, we should admit the pathological fact:
the absence of the passionate convictions that were the creative
inspiration of Europe from the Middle Ages to the eighteenth century. Catholicism, Protestantism, science, and revolution had all
played their part in this respect, but one searched in vain in the
contemporary world for ideals of the kind that had led people in
the past to walk with a firm step to the scaffold or the stake:

Look around you: what is capable of inspiring individuals,
uplifting peoples, moving the masses? The religion of the
pope with his Immaculate Conception of the Mother of

God, or the religion with no pope and its dogma of absten-
tion from beer on the Sabbath Day? The arithmetical pantheism of universal suffrage or the idolatrous worship of
monarchy? Superstitious belief in a republic or in parliamentary reforms? . . . No, no: all this is fading, ageing,
and being stowed away, as once the gods of Olympus were
stowed away when they descended from heaven, ousted by
new rivals risen from Golgotha.

Unfortunately our blackened idols have no new rivals,
or at all events Mill does not point them out.[74]

Herzen notes that Mill is strangely silent on one question: "For
what reason are we to wake the sleeper? In the name of what shall
the flabby personality, mired in mediocrity, be inspired, be made
discontented with its present life of railways, telegraphs, newspapers, and cheap goods?" If no such principle can be found, Mill's
nightmare will be realized in different ways in all those countries
where the benefits of education and technology have prepared the
ground for an improved variety of oriental stagnation. England will
retain her trade and may even extend her freedoms, the growth of
obligatory custom providing a more effective rein on the will than
legal sanctions; France will perfect its martial centralization until it
becomes a new Persia: "The transition . . . will take place impercep-
tibly; not a single right . . . will be lost, not one freedom will be
diminished; all that will be diminished is *the ability to make use of
these rights and this freedom*."[75]

In Herzen's interpretation of Mill's scenario, the human urge for
liberty was in danger of withering away like an organ rendered
superfluous in the evolutionary process. The only hope of a different path of development lay with those for whom that organ still
performed a vital function, as the instrument of a struggle with a
hostile environment: the working masses. The aim of social revolution might recover from its recent defeat to become that idée fixe
which could steer Europe to new destinies. But he suggests that the
chances of this are small: to pursue his metaphor, it was not an
adaptation profitable to Europe's governing classes.

"Mill on Liberty" makes no reference to Herzen's hopes about the potential of the Russian commune: he used the weapon that had come so conveniently to hand to concentrate his fire on what he defined as the major impediment to all constructive discussion about Russia's post-Emancipation options—the "fanatical" faith of the liberals that their favored political option was the desired and destined goal of all humanity.[76] But in the mid-1860s—after Mill published the revised edition of his *Political Economy* with its reflections on the potential advantages of systems of communal land tenure—Herzen would point out to his Russian readers that he had long attempted without success to persuade "*our* liberals and economists" to give the commune the attention that had now been bestowed on it by Mill.[77]

The themes of Herzen's review of Mill's book were subsequently developed in the long essay "Robert Owen" and in *Ends and Beginnings*. Published in 1861 and 1862–63, respectively, they were his last extended philippics against the Westernizers' doctrine of progress (the first was addressed to Kavelin, the second to Turgenev). Together with the supremacy of the European middle classes, he predicts, "there will develop the degradation of the whole of moral life, and Stuart Mill . . . did not exaggerate at all when he talked of the narrowing of people's minds and energies, of the effacement of individuality, of the constantly increasing pettiness of life, of general human interests being constantly excluded from it, by its being reduced to the interests of the trading-house and bourgeois prosperity."[78]

In Herzen's attitude to bourgeois culture there is a strong element of what one critic has described as "an aristocrat's reaction to a world of shopkeepers."[79] But these essays also contain far-sighted observations on what we now call mass culture. The bourgeoisie interested him not as an economic category but as an ethical type—the antithesis of his aesthetic ideal of man. If he was guilty of exaggeration in describing this type, it was the same kind of exaggeration as Mill's contention that modern democratic societies were moving toward "liberticide." Both men sought to dramatize the moral consequences of those ways of conceptualizing the world that pervade all our notions about human relations with the self and with society. They saw modern human beings as schooled by religious dualism and rationalist universalism to accept conformity as a virtue and leveling, standardization, and rationalization as imperative social goals. Both stressed that the development of democratic institutions and mass communications imbued with these values had resulted in a narrowing of horizons that could be fatal to what Herzen called the aesthetic element in individual and social existence: the development of many-sided individuality through the love of originality and diversity, creative experimentation, and the pursuit of virtue as moral beauty. Much has been made of the fact that Herzen was an aristocrat from a preindustrial society; but his critique of bourgeois values was not inspired by nostalgia for an idealized past. He notes that the vast multitude who aspire to bourgeois status have good grounds for doing so. With the growth of the middle class, personalities become more effaced, but such effaced persons are better fed and clothed: in that respect, the bourgeois state is "an *immense step* forward."[80] Herzen was concerned not to denigrate the rational progress so prized by the liberals but to observe, as Mill and Tocqueville had done, that this had been accompanied by regression on other fronts. He remarks on the identical curious phenomenon in the advanced democracies of Europe and North America: "The freer a country is from government interference, the more fully recognized its right to free speech, to freedom of conscience, the more intolerant grows the mob: public opinion becomes a torture chamber; your neighbor, your butcher, your tailor, family, club, parish, keep you under surveillance and perform the functions of a policeman."[81]

There were many reasons for this moral despotism, among them fear of the anarchic instincts of the masses; the educated classes were prepared against their convictions to walk on a leash themselves, provided the masses not be released from it. But the principal cause was the fear of freedom: "The fear that children feel when they begin to walk without leading-strings . . . the habit of clinging to those handrails steeped in sweat and blood, to those boats that have become arks of salvation, in which peoples have survived more than one dark day." People "will believe anything, submit to anything, and are ready to sacrifice much; but they recoil in horror when, through the open chink between two religions, which lets in the light of day, there blows on them the fresh wind of reason and criticism."[82]

There were no quick or simple cures for the waning of the soul; the main hope lay in the indeterminability of history which the Russian liberals were so eager to deny. Accidents of time, place, and individual character would, for good or ill, prevent Russia from faithfully following Europe's path and committing all the old errors in a new way. The same contingent factors made it impossible to predict whether the moral stagnation of the most advanced Western democracies represented a settled condition or the prelude to new beginnings: "There are in life and nature no monopolies, no measures for preventing and suppressing new biological species, new historical destinies and political systems—they are limited only by practical possibility. The future is a variation on the theme of the past."[83]

"Mill on Liberty" was composed against the background of an upheaval of seismic proportions in the history of ideas: the publication in November 1859 of Darwin's treatise on the origin of species. In the transformed intellectual landscape that it left behind, Herzen's and Mill's vision of history's unpredictability no longer stood out as a poetic fantasy: it had received the sanction of science.

On the Origin of Species and
From the Other Shore
CHAPTER FIVE

In history, writes Aleksandr Herzen, "all is improvisation . . .
all is *ex tempore*": there is no libretto.[1] Among political thinkers of the nineteenth century Herzen stands out above all for
his insistence on the dominant role of chance in human life.
His "philosophy of chance"[2] has often been compared to Nietzsche's. It has arguably a far closer affinity with the thought of
Charles Darwin. In 1849 Herzen, then an obscure Russian socialist
who had recently emigrated to western Europe, completed the collection of essays that were published under the title *From the Other
Shore*. These reflections on the nature of history, inspired by his
observations of the events of 1848 in France, are an astonishing
anticipation of Darwin's writings on the role of chance in evolution.

As Stephen Jay Gould has observed, we are scarcely beginning
to come to terms with the enormous implications of Darwin's discoveries for our understanding of *Homo sapiens*. We have been
culturally conditioned to believe in our centrality to the cosmic
process and to see history as a purposive march of progress: if we
are only "a kind of cosmic accident, just one bauble on the Christ-
mas tree of evolution,"[3] all our assumptions about the meaning of
life and the basis of morality need to be reviewed. We are now
familiar with critiques of the traditional grand narratives of progress, which sought to impose a fictional order and direction on
the flux of events; but there is little consensus on how an understanding of our own contingency should affect our attitudes to
society and morality, and some critics fear that the campaign to
free discourse from metaphysical illusions may end in the destruction of all meaningful notions of truth and objectivity. This is why

it is timely to recall Herzen's views on the nature of freedom and choice in an unprogrammed world, in the context of the fear and anger aroused by the publication of the *Origin of Species*. He is remarkable both for anticipating one of the greatest intellectual revolutions of modern times and for orienting himself without confusion or dismay in the unmapped territory it opened up. In essays of great vividness and power he would assert that not only are freedom and responsibility possible in such a world, but that they are not possible in any other. His responses to despairing pessimists—remarkably similar to Darwin's—have lost none of their force today.

The immediate audience for Herzen's reflections on the failed revolution in France were his liberal friends in Russia, who viewed history as an ascent toward the ideal rational state—Hegel's *Rechtsstaat*. They would have seen his comparisons between historical and evolutionary processes as no more than colorful metaphors: in 1849 it was still considered axiomatic that historical development and natural evolution were two separate types of process, with their own laws and goals. That belief was exploded scientifically ten years later, with the publication of *On the Origin of Species*. The first edition sold out in one day, and the Darwinian revolution began.

As the philosopher John Dewey observed, the theological clamor that attended the publication of the *Origin* concealed the true nature of the crisis in systems of knowledge and representation that it brought about. The issue was not primarily between science and religion, but within science itself.[4] It is now generally accepted that the most far-reaching implications of Darwin's theory of natural selection lay in its challenge to teleological thought in all branches of intellectual endeavor. The notion of species change and the descent of man from apes had been discussed before Darwin. What was new was the hypothesis that evolution was not a goal-directed process, but rather the by-product of adaptive responses to changes in local environments. Half a century later Dewey, whose pragmatism claimed direct descent from Darwinian methodology, stressed the magnitude of the intellectual revolution that Darwin had set in motion: "The conceptions that had reigned in the philosophy of nature and knowledge for two thousand years ... rested on the assumption of the superiority of the fixed and final; they rested upon treating change and origin as signs of defect and unreality."[5] Philosophy, science, and religion were rooted in the idea (inherent in the Greek formulation of the term *species*) that knowledge of individual phenomena meant referring their peculiarities to a general regulative principle: the phenomenal world could be rendered intelligible and given sanction and worth only by reference to concepts of ultimate purpose and design. These conceptions, part of the familiar furniture of the mind, were made redundant by a new logic: with some exaggeration, Dewey maintained that philosophy after Darwin "forswears enquiry after absolute origins and absolute finalities in order to explore specific values and the specific conditions that generate them."[6] Of course, elements of such a logic had existed as a skeptical strand in European science at least since Francis Bacon's time. In the immediate pre-Darwinian era, as Gertrude Himmelfarb has observed, every possible doubt about the meaning and purpose of life had been expressed: "What the *Origin* did was to focus and stimulate the religious and nihilist passions of men. Dramatically and urgently, it confronted them with a situation that could no longer be evaded, a situation brought about not by any one scientific discovery, nor even by science as a whole, but by an antecedent condition of religious and philosophical turmoil."[7]

Such a turmoil had existed in the Russian intellectual circles of the early 1840s. It was there that Herzen had first encountered the ideas of Feuerbach and the Left Hegelians, which strengthened his revolt against the tyranny of abstract concepts over individuals. When the Darwinian revolution broke out, he was at its center in London. All around him, in lecture halls, academies, learned journals, and the popular press, raged a debate over questions to which he had already given more than a decade of reflection. The strength and originality of his historical vision can be appreciated best in the context of the issue of chance versus design which lay at the heart of the controversy over the *Origin of Species*.

The question dividing Darwinian and anti-Darwinian parties in England and the Continent was less the origin of species than the origin of man. Darwin himself wished to avoid discussion of this subject "as so surrounded with prejudices"[8] (*On the Descent of Man* was not published until 1871, by which time his ideas had been accepted in the scientific community.) But the continuity between animals and humans was clearly implied in the argument of the *Origin,* and scientists expressed a surprising degree of unanimity with the clerical establishment in their opposition to the new theories. As Darwin's most ardent supporter, T. H. Huxley, later declared, "There is not the slightest doubt that, if a general council of the Church scientific had been held at that time, we should have been condemned by an overwhelming majority."[9] Even those who accepted that Darwin had killed off the old conception of the immutability of species often refused, like the Catholic *Dublin Review,* to condone the expansion of his theory to "such unreasonable lengths" as to include man.[10] Behind the resistance to Darwinism there was what Himmelfarb describes as a "primitive and pervasive revulsion" against the idea that human beings were no more than the last stage in a natural order encompassing primal matter and savage beasts; hence George Bernard Shaw's ironic opinion that though Darwinism could not be disproved, no decent-minded person would accept it.[11]

Acutely aware that he was treading on hallowed ground, Darwin had concluded the *Origin* with a reassuring reference to "the laws impressed on matter by the Creator": "as natural selection works solely by and for the good of each being, all corporeal and mental endowments will tend to progress towards perfection."[12] But when others equated natural selection with the intervention of a purposive power, he was moved to state that if he believed in the existence of such a power, he would reject his theory as rubbish. If all variations were designed to lead to a "right" end, "natural selection would be superfluous."[13]

As the furor over the *Origin* died down, Darwin began to express himself with increasing forthrightness on the question of design. In a work of 1867 he affirms that "no shadow of reason can be assigned for the belief that variations ... which have been the groundwork through natural selection of the formation of the most perfectly adapted animals in the world, man included, were intentionally and specially guided."[14] In the *Origin* he contends that adaptations which, when viewed in hindsight, appeared to be goal-directed are the outcome of "many complex contingencies"[15] such as changing physical conditions and the nature of other, competing inhabitants. Believing in "no fixed law of development," Darwin marvels at the ignorance and presumption that lead us to invent overarching designs to explain the extinction of a single organic being: in the dynamic equilibrium of living things the forces are "so nicely balanced" that, while "the face of nature remains uniform for long periods of time ... assuredly the merest trifle would often give the victory to one organic being over another."[16] Any such fluctuation would set in motion adaptive changes whose extent had no necessary limits and whose direction could not be plotted in advance. Hence the irrelevance to Darwin's scheme of the two dominant interpretive categories of teleological thought: perfection and progress. Natural selection precluded universal standards of perfection, requiring rather that each organic being be "as perfect as, or slightly more perfect than, the other inhabitants of the same country with which it comes into competition."[17] The notion of perfection was further qualified by the existence of independently evolving and functionally similar solutions to complex problems like that of flight. Darwin did not reject the notion of biological progress, which he tended to identify with increasing complexity, but gave it a relativist interpretation. If, as he believed, evolutionary change tended toward a maximum economy in the use of resources, a retrogressive development—such as the loss of eyes in cave-dwelling animals—could increase the chances of survival of a particular organism. Nature in the Darwinian scheme was not a fine-tuned instrument created by the Divine Artificer for the ideal performance of its allotted tasks, but rather a collection of contingent structures adapting themselves with the help of whatever improvisations lay to hand in a never-ending process of crisis management. The cherished myth of Creation's plan was thus replaced by an undignified scramble, in which Darwin had the audacity to include the human race. In the democratic world of nature, where the sole criterion of fitness is the ability to reproduce, it is (as he reflects in his Notebooks) "absurd to talk of one animal being higher than another. *We* consider those, where the cerebral structure/intellectual faculties most developed, as highest. A bee doubtless would where the instincts were [most developed]."[18] Nor are human attributes so distinctive as to justify placing man in a category apart: "The mental faculties of man and the lower animals do not differ in kind, although immensely in degree."[19] One of Darwin's most revolutionary hypotheses—for which, he notes, he was much abused)[20]—was to attribute the origin of the moral sense, as well as the historical variations in value systems, to demands contingent on socialization: "The imperious word *ought* seems merely to imply the consciousness of the existence of a persistent instinct, either innate or partly acquired, serving [humans] as a guide."[21] The process of humanization was not nature straining upward to create her most perfect work, but the cumulative result of ad hoc modifications dictated by immediate needs: "What a chance it has been . . . that has made a man!"[22]

Darwin seems sometimes to have been tempted to draw back from the abyss which this discovery opened up. It has been pointed out that in arguing against belief in designed adaptations, he "retained the rhetoric of deliberate, piecemeal design": as used in the *Origin*, his central metaphor, natural selection, often carries voluntaristic and anthropomorphic connotations.[23] In later editions of the *Origin* he emphasizes that by the term *nature* he meant "only the aggregate action and product of many natural laws"; but he admits that when writing the work he had not been entirely able to free himself from the prevalent teleological habits of thought.[24] Although such ambivalence helped reassure those who sought to superimpose human values on natural processes, Darwin never supported the social Darwinists, who attempted to justify their models of social progress by appealing to the principle of the struggle for existence. When the efforts of German "scientific socialists" in this regard were brought to his attention, he dismissed them as foolish.[25] The Darwinian revolution was neither so tidy nor so abrupt a break with former mentalities or methodologies as it has sometimes been made out to be, but its logic led irresistibly in one direction. As Robert Young admirably puts it, Darwin and the evolutionists on whose ideas he built "together, by a confused mixture of metaphysical, methodological and scientific arguments which depended heavily on analogical and metaphorical expressions... brought the earth, life and man into the domain of natural laws."[26]

> In nature conservatism is just as powerful as the revolutionary element. Nature allows the old and the useless to live on, but she did not spare the mammoths and the mastodons when she was arranging the world. The revolution that destroyed them was not directed *against* them; if they could have escaped it they would have survived and then quietly and peacefully degenerated in an unpropitious envliuriment. The mammoths whose skins and bones are found frozen in Siberia probably escaped the geological revolution; they are the Comneni, the Paleologoi of the feudal world. Nature has nothing against that, any more than history. We superimpose upon her a sentimental personality and our passions; we become oblivious to our metaphors and take the turns of phrase we use for reality. Unaware of the absurdity of it, we introduce our own petty household rules into the economy of the universe for which the life of generations, peoples, of entire planets, has no importance in relation to the general development.[27]

This passage is from the cycle of essays that Herzen published when the *Origin* was still a bundle of notes. The parallels between nature and history that he drew in *From the Other Shore* strikingly anticipate ideas that Darwin would express with much greater circumspection in his scientific writings.

Herzen presents his argument principally in the form of dialogues with companions driven to disillusionment and despair by the failure of the revolutionary ideals of 1848. He accuses one of

his interlocutors of speaking as though there were a stone wall
between nature and history:

> If we had not learnt from the age of five that nature and
> history are two different things, it would not have been
> difficult for us to understand that the development of na-
> ture passes imperceptibly into the development of man-
> kind, that these are two chapters of one novel, two phases
> of one process, very far apart at the extremities, very close
> together in the centre. It would not have surprised us,
> then, that part of everything that takes place in history is
> influenced by physiology, by dark forces. It is true that
> the laws of historical development are not opposed to the
> laws of logic, but their paths do not coincide with those of
> thought, just as nothing in nature coincides with the ab-
> stract norms constructed by pure reason. Knowing all this,
> we would have striven to study, to discover these physio-
> logical forces. But do we do so? Has anyone ever given se-
> rious thought to the physiology of social life, of history as
> an objective science? No one: neither conservatives, nor
> radicals, nor philosophers, nor historians.[28]

The sacred phrases that we use to describe human virtues dis-
guise a simple physiological truth: "Man is an animal with a remarkably well organised brain. Therein lies his power." Lacking the
tiger's litheness and the lion's strength and the acuteness of their
senses, "he discovered within himself infinite cunning and a multitude of tame qualities which, together with a natural inclination
to live in herds, placed him on the first rung of social life." Among
these qualities is a strong inclination to obedience, a trait observable
also in the animals the human race has domesticated:

> The wolf eats the lamb because it is hungry and because
> the lamb is weaker, but the wolf doesn't demand slavery
> from the lamb, the lamb doesn't submit; it protests with
> cries, with flight; man introduces into the animal world of
> savage independence and self-assertion an element of loyal

and humble service, the element of Caliban. That alone
made possible the development of Prospero. And here
again is the same merciless economy of nature, her calculation of means, whereby an excess in one direction is paid
for by unfulfilment in another, so that having stretched
the neck and front legs of the giraffe to fantastic lengths,
she stunts its hind legs.[29]

We must cease to believe that humanity lives under some special
dispensation. History's path, like nature's, is subject to deviation
and disease; it could continue for millions of years—or a comet or
geological cataclysm could end it tomorrow:

In nature, as in the souls of men, there slumber countless
forces and possibilities; under suitable conditions they develop—and develop furiously; they may fill the whole
world, or they may fall by the wayside, take a new direction, stop, collapse. The death of one man is no less absurd than the end of the whole human race. Who guaran-
teed the immortality of a planet? It will be as little able to
survive a revolution in the solar system as the genius of
Socrates could the hemlock—possibly it will not be offered
hemlock . . . possibly. . . . On the whole, nature is perfectly
indifferent to the result. . . . Having buried the whole human race, [she] will lovingly begin all over again, with
monstrous ferns and reptiles half a league long, probably
with certain improvements suggested by new surroundings,
new conditions.[30]

This vision is greeted with horror by Herzen's young companion:
if such is the nature of history, "we have nothing to die for and
nothing to live for."[31] Their interchange anticipates the famous
exchange of letters between Darwin and the Christian evolutionist
Asa Gray, who feared that Darwin's theory could be held to imply
that the world was shaped entirely by blind chance. Darwin's reply
acknowledges the existence of laws which may or may not have
been expressly designed and which direct the broad channels of

life, "with the details, whether good or bad, left to the working out of what we may call chance."[32] In his response to his friend's protest Herzen makes the same distinction: "Nature has hinted only vaguely, in the most general terms, at her intentions, and has left all the details to the will of man, circumstances, climate, and a thousand conflicts."[33] History is not a random process, but neither is it determined, and among the forces that fashion it are the reason and moral ideals of human beings: "The future . . . is created by the combination of a thousand causes, some necessary, some accidental, plus human will, which adds unexpected dramatic *dénouements* and *coups de théâtre*." Each historical epoch is forged by "the reciprocal action of natural forces and the forces of will, the consequences of which one cannot know in advance." It is this unpredictability that gives history its interest: "All is *ex tempore;* there are no frontiers, no itineraries. There exist conditions, sacred discontent; the flame of life and the eternal challenge to the fighters to try their strength." History improvises, "she rarely repeats herself . . . she uses every chance, every coincidence, she knocks simultaneously at a thousand gates. . . . Who knows which may open?"[34]

But this exhilarating vision is bought at a price: we must surrender the view that a unique destiny has been reserved for the human race. The controversy over evolution would bear out Herzen's observations on the tenacity of this belief, epitomized by Rousseau's "famous absurdity: 'Man is born to be free—and is everywhere in chains!'" What, Herzen asks, "would you say to a man who, nodding his head sadly, remarked that 'Fish are born to fly—but everywhere they swim'?" Every generation has its exceptional individuals, representing the limits of its development. Idealists reveal their contempt for facts in portraying such exceptions as the norm. "You," he tells his questioner, "when speaking of history and nations, speak of flying fish, whereas I speak of fish in general."

The "flying fish" who love beauty and cherish freedom have no grounds for presuming that their values will become generally accepted; the legitimacy of an aspiration in no way guarantees its realization: "Life realizes only that aspect of an idea which falls on favorable soil, and the soil in this case doesn't remain a mere passive medium, but gives its sap, contributes its own elements. The new element born of the conflict between Utopias and conservatism enters life, not as the one or as the other side expected it—it enters transformed, different, composed of memories and hopes, of existing things and things to be, of traditions and pledges, of belief and science."[35] Civilization, Herzen observes,

> dreams the apotheosis of its own being, but life is under
> no obligation to realize such fantasies and ideas. . . . Ro-
> man civilization was higher, far more humane than the
> barbarian world, but in the very confusion of barbarism
> were the seeds of things not to be found in the civiliza-
> tion of Rome, and so barbarism triumphed despite the *Cor-*
> *pus Juris Civilis* and the wisdom of Roman philosophers.
> Nature rejoices in what has been attained, and reaches out
> beyond it; she has no desire to wrong what exists; let it
> live as long as it can, while the new is still growing. That
> is why it is so difficult to fit the work of nature into a
> straight line; nature hates regimentation, she casts herself
> in all directions and never marches forward in step.[36]

Nevertheless, Herzen discerns a movement upward in the historical process; but his conception of progress is not to the taste of his idealist friend. As each human generation builds on experience that is stored in the memory of the species, new demands and methods arise: "Some capacities improve at the expense of others; finally, the cerebral tissue improves. . . . Why do you smile? . . . Yes, yes, indeed, the substance of the brain improves." Comparing the skull of an ancient bull with that of a modern domesticated one, Goethe established that although the newer skull had grown more fragile, the area occupied by the brain had increased. "Why do you consider man less capable of development than a bull?" But Herzen insists that no teleological interpretation should be put on this fact: "This generic growth is not an aim, as you suppose, but the hereditary characteristic of a succession of generations." The organism of the animal gradually evolves an instinct, but the human being has gone further, slowly and painfully developing reason, a variation new in nature: "One has to achieve it and come to terms with it as best one may, because there is no *libretto*." Herzen's companion sarcastically suggests that perhaps the brain has taken a wrong turn—hence the calamities of their age. "Instead of jeering," he replies, "you have said something much more sensible than you think. Any one-sided development always leads to the stunting of the other neglected parts. . . . Through centuries of unnatural existence we have turned ourselves into idealists—we have created a form of artificial life, we have disturbed the equilibrium." Behind the antagonisms of 1848 there had been a disparity in stages of development: some had emancipated themselves sooner than others from the conditioning of the past. Monarchists and socialists "cannot talk to one another nor understand one another; they do not use the same logic; their brains are different."[37]

"As a social being," Herzen writes, "man strives to love":[38] like Darwin, Herzen sees the moral sense as the product of socialization. Idealists, who do not connect this capacity with the development of the brain, have unrealistic expectations regarding the speed of humanity's moral progress. Centuries have been spent in struggle, blood has flowed in streams, "and the result was five or six brains who understood the rudiments of the social process. . . . The wonder is that men under these oppressive conditions ever arrived at their present moral state, at self-sacrifice, at patience, at a peaceful way of life." But our present achievements did not entitle us either to indict the past or to prescribe for the future: "The harmony between society and the individual is not established once and for all. It *comes into being* in each period, almost in each country, and it changes with circumstances, like everything living. There can be no universal norm, no universal decision in the matter." Herzen represents virtue as an adaptive response, prompted by the need to realize an inner potential: "It depends on us whether we are contemporary, in harmony with our development, in a word, whether we *mould* our conduct in response to circumstances."[39]

For Herzen as for Darwin, the role of contingency in the processes of life invalidated traditional teleological approaches to the natural and human sciences. Human beings are predestined to nothing: "Very often we take as an aim what are the consecutive phases of some single development to which we have become accustomed." The fact that such developments are so frequently and unpredictably broken off is comforting proof that "every historical phase has its complete reality, its own individuality." Life "does not try to reach an aim, but realizes all that is possible, continues all that has been realized. It is always ready to go one step further in order to live more completely, to live more, if possible. There is no other aim."[40]

From the fact that one cannot predict the future "one thing alone is clear: that one should make use of life, of the present; not in vain does nature in all her utterances for ever beckon life onwards and whisper in every ear her *vivere memento*." Nature not only never makes one generation the means for the attainment of some future end, "she does not concern herself with the future at all. . . . Nature has the heart of a bacchante, of a *bayadère*."[41]

The Russian liberals who saw inexcusable frivolity in the use of such images possessed a different kind of brain, one that could not easily adapt to the revolution in thought that was beginning to redraw the map of the self and its relations with the world. *From the Other Shore* was a prescient attempt to sketch out the contours of that map. In one of his most brilliant essays, "Robert Owen," begun in the year of the Darwinian revolution, Herzen proceeds to fill in the topographical detail of an unfamiliar and frightening landscape.

Published in the summer of 1861 in Herzen's journal the *Polar Star,* "Robert Owen" was dedicated to Herzen's friend and ideological opponent, the Russian liberal historian Konstantin Kavelin. The utopian optimism of the English socialist is the starting point for a discussion that was calculated to dispel any misunderstandings among Russian liberals as to where Herzen stood with regard to all doctrines of progress: he methodically demolishes the traditional grounds for historical hope before proposing his own.

A successful mill owner turned socialist, Owen set up a factory and school on exemplary communitarian principles in the Scottish hamlet of New Lanark; he followed this philanthropic exercise with a full-scale attack on the existing economic and social order, organized religion, property, and the institution of the family. His ideal was a system of cooperative socialism based on networks of small, predominantly agricultural units. In these, liberty for all would be harmonized (in some undisclosed fashion) with full equality. His nebulous schemes are firm on one point: once society is reorganized in accordance with rationalist and egalitarian principles, it will become apparent that humans are by nature not only rational but benign. His failed utopian experiment in New Harmony in the United States did not affect his serene optimism, reinforced in his old age by spiritualism: in one of his last works he predicts the coming of a peaceful revolution engineered by the "departed spirits of good and superior men and women."[42]

Herzen recalls that when he met him in 1852, Owen was nearing the end of his life with his enthusiasm undimmed: a seemingly pathetic figure, vilified by the English clergy and regarded by liberal opinion with condescending pity as a harmless madman. Herzen found the latter sentiment the more repulsive. He cites an obituary of Owen which, written in this spirit, concludes with faint praise. Why, Herzen asks, should he find such an attempt at evenhandedness more offensive than the rantings of the English clerics? "It is because there you have passion, outraged faith, but here is narrow *dispassionateness*—the dispassionateness not simply of a man but of a judge in the court of first instance."[43]

In the English middle class's attitude to Owen Herzen saw epitomized the calm superciliousness of those who believe their outlook to be eminently rational and their prejudices self-evident truths. This kind of doctrinairism, he observes, constricts the intellect and the soul more even than "crude Christianity and gilded Byzantinism": a religion "without a revelation, without a church and with pretensions to logic is almost ineradicable from superficial minds that have neither enough heart to believe nor enough brain to reason."[44] Owen's sin was to have transgressed the civic commandments of such a credo by teaching that in matters of ethics and education, punishment and coercion are not the best methods of developing human potential. Despite its success, his experiment in New Lanark had succumbed to the intolerance of those who pronounced it a threat to order, authority, and morality.

If Owen *was* mad, Herzen asserts, it was because, with the indestructible faith of the thinkers of the eighteenth century (known so curiously as the century of unbelief), he held the human race to be on the eve of its adulthood. He made the mistake of most prophets and reformers in assuming that simple truths are easily understood. But all the evidence pointed to the contrary: "Simple! Easy! But is the simple always easy? It is positively simpler to breathe air than to breathe water, but for this one must have lungs, and where are they to be evolved in a fish, which needs a complicated respiratory equipment in order to obtain a little oxygen from water? Their environment does not permit, does not challenge them to develop lungs; it is too dense and is differently constituted from air. The moral density, the moral composition in which Owen's hearers grew up called forth their *spiritual* gills; breathing a purer and thinner medium necessarily caused them pain and revulsion."[45]

Do not think, Herzen warns the reader, that this is merely a figure of speech: "Here is a true analogy of identical phenomena at different ages and in different strata."[46] It should be remembered how novel—and, for many, how shocking—such comparisons were in 1861. Ten years later, Darwin's explicit analogies between human and animal behavior in the *Descent of Man* would expose him to the charge of moral nihilism: the London *Times* pointed out that a similar "loose philosophy" was then fanning the flames of the Paris Commune.[47] In the intellectual climate of the time, the implications of the argument that Herzen proceeds to develop would have seemed considerably more subversive than the socialism he preached in his propaganda directed to Russia. He notes that Owen was mistaken in seeing the modern state, with its panoply of threats and penalties, as an asylum for those who had lost their senses: it was a haven for those who had not yet come to them. It was one thing to hypothesize that mollusks contained the potential to evolve into creatures with arms, legs, or wings, and another to do as Owen did: to preach to oysters to lay down their shells and follow him. "Intelligence is the final endeavor, the summit to which development rarely attains; hence it is powerful, but it will not stand up against fists. . . . in comparison with the venerable patriarchs of the Alps, witnesses and participants in geological revolutions, it has hardly been born." The aspiration to break through from instinct to reason was observable in all human societies that had reached a certain state of satiety and security. But in this process, as in all forms of evolution, there is no course laid down in advance: a path must be forged. History hurls itself hither and thither as societies seek to escape from the rule of unreason, and the more mature civilizations produce their prophets and accusers, protesting against social bondage and the bondage of conscience. But these figures represent an upper limit, "an exceptional and rare phenomenon, like genius, beauty, or an extraordinary voice. Experience does not show that their utopias were realizable."[48]

"In all spheres of life we come up against insoluble antinomies, against those asymptotes that are always striving toward their hyperbolas and never coinciding with them. These are the extreme limits between which life fluctuates, . . . touching now one shore, now the other." History testifies, for instance, that societies that have reached a high level of rationality in their arrangements tend to remain in a state of moral subjection. There was the terrible example of the United States. Never before in history had circumstances been so propitious for the development of a free and rational state. Bound by no historical precedents, founded on the teachings of the French philosophes and English common law, but without the militarism of the French and the class system of the English, the new country represented "everything that old Europe dreamed of: a republic, a democracy, a federation, autonomy for every plot of land, all scarcely bound together by a common governmental girdle with a weak knot in the middle." And the result? "Society, the majority, seized the powers of a dictator and of the police." In the North, puritans and quakers sought to make their narrow vision mandatory for all, while in the South slavery had acquired the force of a religious dogma: "The people who eighty

years ago proclaimed the 'rights of man' is disintegrating because
of the 'right to flog.'" Whatever rubbish peoples demand, Herzen
concludes, "*in our century* they will not demand the rights of an
adult."[49]

Herzen could point to developments in liberal democracies (as
interpreted by Mill and Tocqueville) to support the conclusion he
had drawn from the debacle of 1848: history, like nature, has its
own embryogenesis "which does not coincide with the dialectic of
pure reason."[50] He expects the same resistance to this proposition
as he had encountered then: toward the end of "Owen," discussing
the implications for human freedom of this view of history, he
resorts to the polemical strategy of *From the Other Shore*, anticipating his readers' objections and voicing them in an imaginary
dialogue. His opponent protests against such pessimism. Surely it
is merely a question of time before the type of understanding that
has hitherto been confined to a small minority in each generation
becomes universal: it is simply inconceivable that humanity will
never come to understand what is in its best interests. Herzen repeats that the evidence is not encouraging on this point. Owen held
that it was sufficient to demonstrate the absurdity of a custom or
belief for it to be discarded. But history has developed by means
of absurdities; people have set their hearts on chimaeras, have built
cities and created beauty as a result. For absurdities they have suffered with exemplary self-abnegation, gone to their deaths, and
killed others: "Life goes by as a series of optical illusions, artificial
needs, and imaginary satisfactions."[51] One dream gives way to another; the sleep sometimes becomes lighter but never quite passes.
In all the thousand and one nights of history, as soon as a little
education is amassed, a few wake but are unable to rouse others.
Their appearance is definitive proof of humans' capacity to evolve
a rational understanding. But this does not answer the question:
can such an exceptional development become universal? Past experience does not favor a positive verdict. The future may go differently, with forces unknown to us changing the destiny of humanity or a considerable part of it for better or worse. The
discovery of America amounted to a geological upheaval; railways

and the electric telegraph had transformed human relationships in unanticipated ways: "But even at the best estimate we still cannot foresee that it will be soon that human beings will feel the need for *common sense*. The development of the brain demands time. There is no haste in nature: she could lie for thousands and thousands of years in a trance of stone, and for other thousands could twitter with the birds, roam the forests as beasts, or swim in the sea as a fish. The delirium of history will last her for a long time, a magnificent continuation of the plasticity of nature, which in other spheres is exhausted."[52]

Science had knocked down the wall between nature and history just over a year before "Owen" was completed. In the spring of 1860 Herzen had sent a copy of Darwin's treatise to his son Sasha, then studying the natural sciences in Germany; he later expressed approval of a lecture in which his son denied that Darwin had introduced Providence into nature.[53] To the Russian readers of the *Bell* Herzen cited the *Origin* as an eminent exception to the spirit of pietism prevailing in English intellectual circles. Huxley was seeking to propagate the new theories as widely as possible through popular lectures to working men; Herzen recommends that one such series be translated into Russian, in view of its "sound and simple language."[54] His attitude to Darwin's opponents is reflected in "Owen" in his comments on "rationalist iconoclasts" who, while vigorously denouncing idols, are astonished to find that, as fast as they throw some down from their pedestals, others appear before them:

> But for the most part they are not even astonished, either because they just do not notice this, or because they take them for true gods.
>
> Natural scientists, who boast about their materialism, keep harping on preordained plans of nature, about its purposes, its adroit selection of means: one can't understand a word—as though *natura sic voluit* [thus nature decreed] is clearer than *fiat lux* [let there be light]? This is fatalism to the third degree, fatalism cubed: at the first,

the blood of Januarius boils; at the second, the fields are
irrigated by rain in answer to prayer; at the third, the secret designs of a chemical process are revealed, praise is
given to the thrifty qualities of the life force, which stores
up the yolk for the embryo, and so on.

Protestants who scoffed at the miraculous boiling of a saint's
blood in a phial, while prepared to pray for divine intervention
against drought, were guilty only of naive stupidity. There was superstition of an altogether different order in "the pious rhetoric
that we are constantly finding in physiological and geological lectures and treatises, in which the natural scientist talks tenderly of
the goodness of a Providence that has equipped birds with wings,
without which the poor things would fall down and be smashed to
pieces, and so on."[55]

Having a lively interest in the natural sciences, Herzen probably
attended several lectures of this kind during his years in London.
These perhaps included presentations by the eminent exponent of
evolutionary geology Charles Lyell, who welcomed Darwin's theories as scientific confirmation of the notion of a preconceived plan:
"The amount of power, wisdom, design or forethought" required
for evolution was at least as great, he argued, as that required for
a multitude of separate acts of creation.[56] A Darwinian *avant la
lettre*, Herzen was equipped to grasp sooner than most that the new
theories had edged providential design altogether out of the cosmic
scheme. The new science of evolution lent formidable authority to
his long-held view that the human faculty of reason was a chance,
marginal, and terrifyingly fragile development in the history of life:
"Quantitatively, intelligence will always have to give way; its *weight*
is feeble in the extreme. Like the Northern Lights it shines over
great distances, but it hardly exists."[57]

Echoing the dissenting voices in *From the Other Shore*, Herzen's
questioner protests: if humanity's most advanced ideals stand so
little chance of realization, what then is the point of history? Herzen's response, querying the mercenary demands of those who look
to history for a confirmation of their hopes, is familiar from his

earlier essays; but here he develops his argument in some of his
finest writing on the nature of human intervention in history. He
conveys in striking images the inner tensions and the creative freedom of an attitude that approaches the predicament of human
contingency in a spirit of aesthetic play.

To the questioner demanding what moral can be drawn from
his view of history, he replies, "*Liberation from lies—that is the
moral*":

> For everything we have endured, for our broken bones, for
> our trampled hearts, for our errors and delusions—at least
> to decipher a few letters of the mysterious charter, to un-
> derstand the general sense of what is happening around
> us. . . . That is a tremendous lot! The childish rubbish
> which we lose no longer interests us: it is dear to us only
> from habit. What is there to regret in that? The Baba Yaga
> or the vital force? The fairy tale of the Golden Age behind
> us or of eternal progress ahead? The miracle-working phial
> of St. Januarius or a meteorological prayer for rain? The
> secret design of conspiratorial chemists or *natura sic
> voluit?*
>
> For the first minute it is frightening, but only for one
> minute. Everything round us is oscillating, speeding along:
> stand still, or go wherever you like; there is no barrier, no
> road, no authority. . . . Probably the confusion of the sea,
> too, was frightening at first but, as soon as man under-
> stood its aimless bustle, he took his road with him and
> crossed the oceans in a shell.
>
> Neither nature nor history *are going anywhere,* and
> therefore they are ready to go *everywhere* they are di-
> rected, *if this is possible,* that is, if nothing obstructs
> them. They are composed *à fur et à mesure* of an immense
> number of particles acting upon and encountering each
> other, repelling and attracting each other; but man is by
> no means lost because of this, like a grain of sand in a
> mountain; is not more subject to the elements nor more

tightly bound by necessity: he grows up, by virtue of
having understood his situation, into a helmsman who
proudly cleaves the waves with his boat, making the bot-
tomless abyss serve him as a path of communication. . . .
    An infinity of possibilities, episodes, discoveries, in his-
tory and nature, lies slumbering at every step.[58]

Herzen does not exaggerate the fear and disorientation of those
who sensed that science and philosophy were in the process of
destroying the foundations of order and meaning in human societies. The London *Times* expressed a widespread apprehension
when it predicted that, should Darwin's mischievous ideas ever become widely accepted, "morality would lose all elements of stable
authority."[59] (In 1866 Herzen would note in the *Bell* that, scenting
Darwin's influence behind an attempt to assassinate the tsar, the
Russian government had banned his works, along with those of the
materialist philosophers and natural scientists Jacobus Moleschott
and Karl Vogt.)[60]

In the controversy over the *Origin,* many expressed the sense of
being cast adrift in a limitless, purposeless, and unfeeling universe.[61]
"Fear grips one—all is empty, vast, free . . . how can one go without
knowing where: how can one give up what one has, without any
positive prospects?" People have come to fear their own logic and
try to save the remnants of the past. Having repudiated Christianity,
they cling to a secular concept of Providence: thus Herzen had
accounted for the survival of faith in predestined progress after the
catastrophes of 1848.[62] Darwin's ambivalence on the question of
purpose and design has been attributed to the fact that the idea of
progress was too central to his age to be easily and tidily dispensed
with.[63] His correspondence suggests that the conflict of logic with
traditional and cherished beliefs was particularly intense in his
thought around the time of the publication of the *Origin:* "The
mind refuses to look at this universe, being what it is, without
having been designed; yet, where one would most expect design,
viz. in the structure of a sentient being, the more I think on the
subject, the less I can see proof of design." Darwin confesses that

he is "in an utterly hopeless muddle" on the question: "I cannot think that the world, as we see it, is the result of chance; and yet I cannot look at each separate thing as the result of Design." But chance progressively edges out design in his metaphors until, in an autobiographical fragment of 1876, he summarizes his personal views: "There seems to be no more design in the variability of organic beings, and in the action of natural selection, than in the course which the wind blows."[64]

Herzen, who attached great importance to the metaphors we employ to describe the world, would have approved of this one. The conclusion to "Owen" uses a succession of vivid images to familiarize the reader with the novel proposition that to deny a final purpose in nature and history is not, as Darwin seems to have feared,[65] to reduce human beings to the status of mere playthings of blind forces: there is hope after teleology.

The fact that nature is not for us does not mean that she is against us: "Nature never fights against man; this is a vulgar, religious calumny. She is not intelligent enough to fight: she is indifferent. . . . Nature cannot thwart man unless man thwarts her laws; as she goes on with her work, she will unconsciously do his work too." Through science and reason we can influence and change the flow of circumstance as a navigator exploits the elements; but we tend to forget that in history we are simultaneously pilot, boat, and wave, inextricably meshed in processes that we seek to control. It is this that offends the abstracting and systematizing intellect: "In history it is easier [for the individual] to be carried passively along by the current of events or to burst into it with a knife and the cry, 'General prosperity or death!' than to observe the ebb and flow of the waves that carry him, to study the rhythm of their fluctuations, and thereby to open up unending channels for himself." We yearn for maps to direct our journey, not understanding that only if history is not determined can human beings be regarded as objects of serious interest. If the cards are stacked and our future mortgaged before our birth, if history is simply the mise-en-scène of some plot conceived before it began, then we should at least be given dummy swords and shields: "Are we to shed real blood and real tears for the performance of a charade by Providence?"[66]

Herzen's argument was directed above all against those Russian liberals who professed a Hegelian belief that the modern constitutional state was the summit of historical progress. He points out that at least the religious concept of predestination had its aesthetic side: the drama of the rebellious Lucifer, the banished Adam, and the redeeming Christ. But the secular metaphysics of the state has replaced the poetic images of religion with the logical absurdity of a historical *arrière-pensée:* "Why, if it exists already, does it come into being again? But if it does not exist, and is only *becoming* . . . then what new immaculate process of conception has given birth in the temporal to a preexisting idea which, issuing from the womb of history, announces that it has existed before history and will exist after its end?" In its transition from the church to the academy fatalism "has lost all its sense, even the sense of verisimilitude that we demand in a fairy tale."[67]

In *From the Other Shore,* Herzen had declared that the transience and unrepeatability of individuals and their ideals were comforting proof that "every historical phase has its complete reality, its own individuality, that each is an end achieved, not a means."[68] To this proposition, central to his differences with the doctrinaire Russian liberals, he devotes the concluding pages of "Owen." Idealists, he writes, look for the significance of humanity outside the flickering of individual lives; they will not admit that our entire significance consists in the fact that while we live these brief lives

> *we are for all that ourselves,* and not dolls destined to suffer progress or embody some homeless idea. We must be proud of not being needles and threads in the hands of fate as it sews the multicolored cloth of history. . . . We know that this cloth is not sewn without us, but this is not our goal, not our purpose, not the lesson set us to learn, but the consequence of the complex mutual guarantee that links all existing things by their ends and beginnings, causes and effects.

And that is not all; we can *change the pattern of the*
carpet. There is no master craftsman, no design, only a
foundation, and we are alone, quite alone.[69]

But, his questioner objects, if people do not believe that they are
serving some higher end, surely they will sit back and do nothing?
Herzen retorts that if the cheerlessness and crushing fatalism of
deterministic systems did not have that effect on most of the human race, "then there is no reason to fear that this may be done
by a view which rids them of these slabs of stone. The mere sense
of life and its inconsistency was enough to rescue the peoples of
Europe from religious pranks like asceticism and quietism, which
had constantly existed only in word and not in deed: surely reason
and consciousness will not turn out to be feebler?"[70]

Instinct and conscious understanding together tell us that while
we are not independent from our natural and historical environment, neither are we subjugated to it: "Human beings are a long
step ahead of the apes; their aspirations do not vanish without a
trace: they are clothed in words, embodied in images; they are preserved in tradition and handed on from age to age . . . behind us,
as behind the wave on the shore, is felt the pressure of a whole
ocean—of the history of all the world; the thought of all the centuries is in our brain at this moment . . . and with that thought we
can be a power."

Each person can be "an *irreplaceable reality.*"[71] These italicized
words from the concluding paragraph of his essay encapsulate Herzen's aesthetic vision of human freedom and dignity.

The price we pay for the freedom to insert our own verse into
history's improvisation is the absence of a predictable pattern of
linear development: but if history's path is not determined, neither
is it random. The accumulated knowledge of generations and the
methods of experimental science can together supply us with a
"theory of probabilities" on which to base predictions. Herzen's
own hypotheses about Russia's future are no more than such a
theory: "We are terribly concerned to stress the difference between
the possible and the inevitable." Bourgeois democracies might yet

take flight in new directions, the most poetic nations might turn into shopkeepers; who knows how many possibilities will perish, strivings be aborted, and developments deflected? But there is one incontrovertible fact about the historical process: each individual, in his or her particular time and place, has a unique contribution to make to it. "Now do you understand on whom the future . . . depends? . . . *On* YOU *and* ME *for instance! This being the case, how can one sit back and fold one's arms?*"[72]

Herzen attached great importance to "Robert Owen": in the last year of his life he would look back on it as one of his finest essays.[73] This view was not shared by those for whom it was written. Kavelin did not, it seems, respond to Herzen's repeated requests for his reaction; nor did Turgenev, to whom Herzen sent the essay, describing it as "a bold, and, as far as I can tell, successful piece."[74]

Undoubtedly, the boldness of the work accounts for its cool reception. Herzen's liberal friends would probably have perceived it as a brilliant feat of evasion, substituting poetic imagery and rhetorical exaggeration for logical rigor. Nietzsche had yet to give philosophical respectability to a language and style that sought to convey the fluidity of experienced reality. Herzen's writings on the nature of history can be seen as early experiments in that genre, attempting through the use of aesthetic metaphor to retrieve the lived experience and "living truth" of moral freedom that rationalistic systems had obscured. That this was his intention is confirmed by a document which represents his philosophical manifesto: the "Letter on Free Will" of 1866, addressed to his son Sasha and published only after his death.

Herzen took a close interest in the studies of his son, who began in the late 1850s to prepare himself for a career in the physical sciences under the guidance of Karl Vogt, a leading exponent of the crude materialism that was the dominant ideology of mid-nineteenth-century natural science. In letters to his son, Herzen rejects the claim of the new self-styled realists that, in representing phenomena as forces, they had stripped away the mystery with which philosophical idealism had shrouded their essential nature.

He recommends a more modest, Baconian approach that did not
lay claim to knowledge of essences and did not define as goals what
experimental science would recognize only as consequences.[75]

Herzen's correspondence with his son and with his friend and
coeditor Nikolai Ogaryov in the decade after "Owen" reflects his
continuing preoccupation with the problem of retrieving the paradoxical reality of freedom from the reductiveness of philosophical
formulations and the distortions of teleological thought. In the
1830s he had described materialism as characterized by "precise
knowledge of the parts and total ignorance of the whole."[76] This
opinion was confirmed in the spring of 1867, when he and Ogaryov
attended a series of colloquia on the subject of the will organized
by Moritz Schiff, under whom the young Herzen was working at
the University of Florence. Eager to write on the question but lacking the time, Herzen delegated the task to Ogaryov but was unhappy with the result: neither Ogaryov nor Schiff had grasped "the
complexity of the task, particularly in its historical incarnation." He
was especially irritated by the abstraction of Ogaryov's language:
noting his fondness for the word *volition,* he urges him to "call it
practical reason, active reason, and explain its laws and relations in
such a way that when, at this moment, I say that this is a bad
action, I can know that I am not talking nonsense."[77]

Herzen's ideological opponents misconstrued his demand that
philosophy approach the problem of freedom in the embodied particularity of historical events and personalities. The Slavophiles
called him a materialist; but this, he asserted, was a "scholastic
label" which "does not, of course, go to the heart of the matter."
What interested him was not the antithesis of freedom and inevitability, but that margin, "where each term of the antinomy passes
over into the other: that is, where a conscious individual avails
himself of his right to step forward with his left or right foot, although the action is performed according to the laws of physiological necessity."[78]

In the "Letter on Free Will" Herzen observes that philosophy
had alternately deified the will as Absolute Mind and denied its

existence by reducing it to a conditioned reflex of matter; but it had scarcely begun to approach liberty as human beings experience it: "as a phenomenological necessity of the human intellect, as a psychological reality." A response to a pamphlet by his son on the physiology of the will, the "Letter" pays due tribute to the role of the biological sciences in dispelling the last illusions of primitive religious dualism. But Herzen argues that they went beyond their competence when they proceeded to declare the ego a hallucination and the notion of liberty a misconception. As a necessary premiss of social existence, our sense of moral freedom is, at the very least, an anthropological reality. Human reason, passion, and memory are subject to the same laws of organic life as breathing and digestion, but they have an added dimension: shaped by historical and social existence into the faculty of choice, they have created a "moral milieu" with laws of its own, which are no less real for being unverifiable by scientific experiment. By methods of extreme generalization and simplification, consciousness may be reduced to a set of physiological first principles; but by so doing we lose the social dimension, in which individuals define themselves by the freedom to choose between particular options in particular sets of circumstances: "the phenomenalized, differentiated, specific, detailed world,—the one in which we live, and which is our sole reality."[79]

The fundamental problem of knowledge was not, as philosophers had held, to break out of the vicious circle of freedom and necessity, but to comprehend it. As Herzen observes to Ogaryov, the dualistic systems that have taught us to perceive the world as divided into subject and object, mind and matter, body and spirit have ensured that we possess "neither the language, nor the categories, nor the words" to discuss the nature of choice in the nexus of contingency and invariant laws.[80] But that purpose could be served by aesthetic metaphor: Herzen expresses the relationship between physical determinism and moral freedom through the distinction between a sound in isolation—a physical phenomenon subject to the laws of acoustics—and a sound in a musical phrase, where "it acquires for us another value (or existence, if you like)." This aesthetic existence does not exempt it from the physical laws to which it is subject—the string may break, and the sound will disappear:

> but as long as the string remains unbroken, the sound be-
> longs not just to the realm of vibrations, but also to the
> realm of harmony, where it exists as an aesthetic reality,
> functioning in a symphony which allows it to resound,
> dominates and absorbs it, and then leaves it behind in its
> wake.
>
> Human individuality in society is a conscious sound
> which reverberates not only for others but also for itself.
> The product of physiological and historical necessity, the
> individual strives to affirm himself in the course of an ex-
> istence between two voids: the void before birth and the
> void after death. Even as he develops according to the
> laws of the most fatal necessity, he constantly posits him-
> self as free. This is a necessary condition for his activity,
> this is a psychological fact, a social fact. . . .
>
> But what, you will ask, is the objective reality? You
> know that the thing in itself . . . is a *magnum ignotum,*
> like the Absolute, and final causes: what is the ultimate
> objective nature of time, the ultimate reality of space? I
> do not know; but I do know that both time and space are
> essential to me as coordinates, that without them I shall
> sink into the darkness of a chaos without measure or
> end.[81]

Here is the abyss that can be glimpsed behind the notion of history's play with which Herzen teased the Russian liberals. The fleeting and precarious present is our sole domain and our only source of meaning. Herzen's philosophy of existence is built on what, half a century later, John Dewey would describe as the new logic epitomized by Darwin's scientific method. This logic "outlaws, flanks, dismisses—what you will—one type of problem and sub-stitutes for it another type."[82] As at many other turning points in the history of ideas, the old problems were not solved; the new movements merely abandoned them, setting aside enquiries about remote causes and eventual goals as ultimately futile and no longer of urgent concern.

The shift in philosophical priorities to which Dewey refers is strikingly reflected in Darwin's responses to those who pressed him after the appearance of his book for an opinion on the origin and purpose of being. In the last two decades of his life he remained in "the same sort of muddle . . . as all the world seems to be in with respect to free will"; but defining his position on such matters became increasingly unimportant to him.[83] He conscientiously re-hearses the arguments for and against the existence of an intelligent First Cause but admits that his own opinions on the subject are vague and denies that his theories have any relevance to it: "Science has nothing to do with Christ, except in so far as the habit of scientific research makes a man cautious about admitting evidence." Its methods were not conducive to belief in revelation and miracles, but on questions such as that of life after death, "every man must judge for himself, between conflicting vague probabilities." Issues of this sort were "beyond the human intellect, like 'predestination and free will' or 'the origin of evil' "; Darwin asserts that he cannot pretend to throw the least light on such abstruse problems: "I for one must be content to remain an Agnostic."[84]

In what appears to have been Darwin's final word on the matter, he wrote, "The safest conclusion seems to me that the whole subject is beyond the scope of man's intellect, but man can do his duty."[85] Such, too, was Herzen's position in the "Letter on Free Will." Unlike the materialists, he acknowledged the world to be ultimately unknowable by science; but unlike idealists (and anticipating Ludwig Wittgenstein), he concluded that on that of which we cannot speak we had best be silent: what we know of our moral nature derives solely from our experience of action and choice within the nexus of contingent circumstances that is "our sole reality."

The reception of Darwin's theories reveals the strength of resistance to such agnosticism even among those who, like Herzen's son, prided themselves on their freedom from religious superstition. The debate between T. H. Huxley and Herbert Spencer over the moral significance of natural selection was symptomatic of the prevalence of dualistic habits of thought in such circles. Huxley maintained that the evil savagery of natural processes furnishes us with a negative moral example, while Spencer interpreted the struggle for existence as a model for social progress. This view was echoed by the gamut of social Darwinists, whose interpretations of the evolutionary process, whether conservative or radical, individualist or collectivist, democratic or elitist, were all grounded in the assumption that human beings were central to the cosmic process, and that even when, as Huxley maintained, they were at war with it, their reason and moral goals remained the sole criterion of its meaning and purpose: when correctly interpreted, nature would yield guidance for the ever-higher ascent of the human race. While doctrines of inalienable progress, including Marxism, proudly nailed the theory of natural selection to their ideological masts, its author remained consistently aloof from all ethical interpretations of its content. Against those who persisted in representing the evolutionary process as a movement to perfection, he argued that "natural selection is not perfect in its action, but tends only to render each species as successful as possible in the battle for life with other species, in wonderfully changing and complex circumstances."[86]

Herzen's view of moral freedom sprang from a similar delight in what he called the "eternal play of life."[87] Why did the Russian liberals find this notion so offensive and threatening? In his exhilarating interpretation of Darwin's theory as a celebration of "wonderful life," Stephen Jay Gould provides a clue. He argues that our thinking about the history of life is dominated by the idea of a dichotomy—a single line embracing all possible opinions, with the two ends representing polar opposites—in this case determinism and randomness. We may understand that the determinism of a ladder of predictable progress in nature and history cannot apply strictly, "but we think that our only alternative lies with the despair of pure randomness. So we are driven back towards the old view, and finish, with discomfort, at some ill-defined confusion in between." Gould maintains that Darwin's concept of contingency offers a third alternative, inviting us "to step off the line, to a site outside the dichotomy." The principle of natural selection does not make evolution a process without sense or pattern; although the precise route taken by any development cannot be predicted, it can be shown after the event that the final result was dependent, or contingent, upon every stage that had gone before. Contingency is "a thing in itself, not the titration of determinism by randomness." Unlike the two elements of that dichotomy, it offers the possibility of maneuver and control within channels dictated by general laws. By observing that a particular outcome did not have to be, we grasp the causal power of particular events. Every detail of life and history "holds the power of transformation. Contingency is the affirmation of control by immediate events over destiny, the kingdom lost for want of a horseshoe nail. . . . Contingency is a license to participate in history."[88]

Such, we have seen, is the view of contingency that Herzen presents in "Robert Owen," emphasizing the creative responsibility of participation in the "wonderfully changing and complex circumstances" of an unprogrammed historical process. He believed that the chief impediment to such an understanding of our freedom lay in the systematizing rationalism, with its drive to finality and its faith in an unchanging body of truth, that had become equated with an enlightened and progressive mentality. Herzen showed how it had turned Russian liberal theory into a smug orthodoxy; John Stuart Mill pointed to its deadening effect on English morality and social attitudes; the debate over the *Origin* shows how strong was its grip on science. It has been recognized that when Darwinism finally gained respectability a decade after the publication of Darwin's book, it was not because its antiteleological thrust had been accepted, but because ways had been found to reconcile it with more traditional attitudes in religion, morality, and science.[89] Gould has remarked that Darwin's demonstration of the irreducible complexity and unpredictability of the processes of evolutionary change has not dislodged the stereotype of the scientific method which governs popular understanding of the nature of knowledge and truth: according to this, explanations that rest on contingency are less interesting, less valid, and less elegant than those based on universal and invariant laws.[90] Outside intellectual avant-gardes, foundationalist doctrines still command an impressive adherence: it is noteworthy that in his landmark essay of 1962 on the nature of scientific revolutions, Thomas Kuhn found it necessary to stress the fact that science is not an enterprise that "draws constantly nearer to some goal set by nature in advance."[91]

Those who first began consistently to apply this view to the physical and human sciences had to suffer their share of disdainful condescension. In a remark that Darwin described as very contemptuous, a revered elder statesman of British science, Sir John Herschel, referred to the theory of natural selection as "the law of higgledy piggledy."[92] One of Herzen's Hegelian opponents, the legal philosopher Boris Chicherin, admonished him for inappropriate frivolity in referring to the "poetic caprice of history." Later commentators have interpreted Herzen's emphasis on the role of chance as the expression of a deep pessimism.[93] His response to critics of both sorts was always eminently Darwinian: as he remarks in *From the Other Shore*, "I am neither an optimist nor a pessimist; I watch, I examine, without any preconceived notion, without any prepared ideals, and I am in no hurry to reach a verdict."[94]

"Dealing in Pluses":
The Thought of Anton Chekhov
CHAPTER SIX

Chekhov is one of the most deeply subversive writers of his own or any other age, a figure whose originality is as yet poorly understood: this view, increasingly voiced in studies of Chekhov's art, may still astonish many of his most devoted admirers.[1] Unlike the novels of Dostoevsky, which revealed the demonic potential of the human psyche, Chekhov's plays and stories portrayed ordinary men and women leading uneventful, often humdrum lives. While Tolstoy preached anarchism and thundered against the Russian church and state, Chekhov worked peacefully as a country doctor and small-scale farmer, until his health broke down and he was forced to spend his winters in Yalta.

It was a life that to many of his contemporaries seemed perversely uninvolved in the great issues of the time; yet it was precisely their lack of tendentiousness that made his writings so subversive. His ironic approach to the reigning canons of correctness now seems startlingly prescient. He undermined many of the assumptions of modern societies about the nature of progress, freedom, and personal morality, and (unlike Tolstoy) did not replace the myths he demolished with new ones of his own.

The society of his time looked to its writers for ideological commitment and moral leadership in the battle against autocratic rule. Radical critics, whose authority over literature rivaled that of the official censorship, glorified such second-rate writers as N. N. Zlatovratsky and Gleb Uspensky, who presented the conflict between reaction and enlightenment through crude stereotypes: priests, merchants, and army officers were invariably cast as villains, peasants and young radical idealists as pure-hearted heroes. When Chekhov's ideas began to be the subject of debate in progressive circles, he outlined his credo in a famous letter to the fiction editor of a journal that had begun to publish his work:

> I am neither liberal, nor conservative, nor gradualist, nor monk, nor indifferentist. I would like to be a free artist and nothing else. . . . Pharisaism, dullwittedness and tyranny reign not only in merchants' homes and police stations. I see them in science, in literature, among the younger generation. That is why I cultivate no particular predilection for policemen, butchers, scientists, writers or the younger generation. I look upon tags and labels as prejudices. My holy of holies is the human body, health, intelligence, talent, inspiration, love and . . . freedom from violence and lies, no matter what form the latter two take.[2]

Chekhov's loathing of violence and cant sprang from an early and brutal exposure to both. As he once remarked apropos of Tolstoy's idealization of the Russian peasantry, "I have peasant blood flowing in my veins, and I'm not the one to be impressed with peasant virtues."[3] He was born in 1860, the year before the abolition of serfdom in Russia. His grandparents on both sides had been serfs; his father, Pavel, gained a precarious foothold in the merchant class when he acquired a grocer's shop in the south Russian town of Taganrog. A domestic tyrant much given to moralizing, he faithfully reflected the pious and patriarchal traditions of his peasant background: the third of six children, Anton later recalled that for him and his two elder brothers "childhood was sheer suffering";[4] they were thrashed every day by their father and by the choirmaster in the church where they were made to sing for long hours kneeling on freezing stones.

As a schoolboy of sixteen Anton was left to fend for himself in Taganrog when his father went bankrupt and was forced to move most of the family to Moscow in search of work. The destitute, bewildered Chekhov siblings were typical of vast numbers of talented young people set adrift by the crumbling of Russia's patriarchal structures and values. Some, like Anton's two feckless elder brothers, acquired a higher education but remained unprincipled drifters; many others would find a new church and dogma in the radical movement. Anton took a singular path. In three years alone in Taganrog, continuing his schooling while tutoring other pupils, he accomplished what Tolstoy spent his life trying vainly to do: he reinvented himself as a person of moral integrity, free from the disfigurements inflicted by the despotism that pervaded Russian life. He became the effective head of his family, whose survival depended on the money he sent them from his earnings. Meanwhile he civilized himself through voracious reading in the Taganrog public library.

What that solitary process entailed can be deduced from advice he gave some years later to his delinquent elder brother Nikolai: to overcome "the side [of you] raised on birch thrashings beside the wine cellar and handouts," he must cultivate respect for the personalities of others and refrain from all forms of force and deceit. "You must work at it constantly, day and night. You must never stop reading, studying in depth, exercising your will. Every hour is precious." Anton's own achievements in this respect were such that at the age of thirty he was able to protest to the editor of a journal that had called him an unprincipled writer, "I have never toadied, nor lied, nor insulted"; whatever the artistic defects of his work, "I have never written a single line that I am ashamed of today."[5]

Chekhov's literary career began as a means of supporting his family when, equipped with a stipend from his hometown, he was admitted to study medicine at Moscow University. He began submitting humorous sketches to weekly magazines, and their success was such that after graduating in 1884 he was able to divide his time between "medicine ... my lawful wedded wife, and literature my mistress."[6] His short stories were remarkable for the originality of their form and the range of their subject matter, equally masterly in their depiction of the Russian landscape and of the inner worlds of women, priests, peasants, merchants, gentry, and animals. Before he was thirty he was acclaimed as a great writer; in 1887 his play

Ivanov launched him as a dramatist. Solvent at last, he was able to buy his family their first settled home, a small estate within reach of Moscow, where he was lionized in artistic circles. He relished the social round and the company of beautiful women; several of the women with whom he had affairs before his marriage at the age of forty remained his devoted friends. Men also found his personality irresistible. The painter Konstantin Korovin describes him as "*extremely* handsome," with kind eyes and a "special shy smile. His whole appearance . . . inspired in people a special sort of confidence."[7]

The source of this trust was his down-to-earth humanity, which gave him a sharp nose for political cant and hollow generalities: "I acquired my belief in progress when still a child; I couldn't help believing in it, because the difference between the period when they flogged me and the period when they stopped flogging me was enormous."[8]

He admired the moral idealism of many Russian radicals but found their polemical methods too reminiscent of his childhood milieu: "I am physically repelled by abuse no matter at whom it is aimed."[9] He accused intellectuals obsessed with their utopias of ignoring the concrete achievements of the *zemstva,* institutions of local government set up by the Great Reforms of the 1860s, in civilizing Russian society. Citing the advances in surgery in Russia over the previous two decades, he once noted that if he were offered a choice between "the 'ideals' of the celebrated 1860s" (expressed in radical utopias such as that in Nikolai Chernyshevsky's novel *What Is to be Done?*) and the poorest *zemstvo* hospital, "I'd take the latter without the least hesitation."[10]

His own record of humanitarian work was impressive. His book about the prison colony of the Siberian island of Sakhalin, based on a medical-statistical survey of conditions there, brought the horrors of the Russian penal system to public attention. His efforts to alleviate famine in his region in 1891–92 were followed by a spell of exhausting activity traveling, often on foot, through the frozen countryside as an unpaid medical inspector charged with containing a cholera epidemic. He treated thousands of peasants in a clinic on his estate, planned and helped build schools, endowed libraries, and scraped together money and support for a multitude of other causes, including an attempt to rescue a bankrupt journal of surgery and the purchase of horses to be distributed to peasants for transporting grain. This firsthand involvement with day-to-day practicalities made him scornful of all recipes for universal salvation: on a visit to Nice he observed that one of its pleasures was the absence of "Marxists with their self-important faces." He had no faith, he wrote, in the intelligentsia en masse; he placed his hopes on individuals, be they intellectuals or peasants, scattered all over Russia, through whose inconspicuous efforts knowledge and social awareness were slowly and inexorably advancing: "They're the ones who really matter."[11]

Chekhov's early struggles and his medical practice helped to inspire a dominant theme of his art: the conflict of human aspirations with unpropitious circumstances. He had observed and suffered the oppressive power of heredity and environment—he once described his father as "a man of average caliber unable to rise above his situation"[12]—but his own life presented a notable counterexample. His experience in Taganrog taught him that the most important moral battles are won or lost not at points of great dramatic tension but through a succession of individually unremarkable choices. Hence the distinctiveness of the Chekhovian hero—and Chekhov's advice to his editor and friend Aleksei Suvorin, who was writing a play with a traditional melodramatic dénouement: "You can't end with the nihilists. It's too stormy and strident. What your play needs is a quiet, lyrical, touching ending. If your heroine . . . comes to realize that the people around her are idle, useless and wicked people . . . and that she's let life pass her by—isn't that more frightening than nihilists?"[13]

The strangeness of the ordinary, the drama of the undramatic were the subjects of the plays with which Chekhov revolutionized the Russian theater in the last decade of his life. His first major play, *Ivanov*, which retained elements of traditional melodrama, had been positively received; *The Seagull*, in which he first fully worked out his technique, dispensing with conventional plot, was a cata-strophic failure on its opening night in October 1896, but its second production in Moscow in 1898 was acclaimed, as were the subse-quent premieres of *Uncle Vania, Three Sisters*, and, in January 1904, *The Cherry Orchard.* The fact that "nothing happens" in Chekhov's plays was henceforth established as their distinctive mark, but crit-ical discussion of them has tended to resort to cloudy platitudes, such as Chekhov's ability to create atmosphere or mood: they are commonly interpreted as melancholy evocations of a twilight Russia in which the ineffectual representatives of a dying class contemplate their wasted lives.

These clichés were demolished in Richard Gilman's fine study of Chekhov's drama, which owes much to the influence of Francis Ferguson's essay on *The Cherry Orchard* as a "theater-poem of the suffering of change."[14] Borrowing an observation by Henry James on *Hedda Gabler,* Gilman approaches Chekhov's plays as "that sup-posedly undramatic thing: the portrait not of an action but of a condition": the anguish in them derives from our universal pre-dicament as mortal beings subject to the depredations of time and chance. Chekhov's ability to dramatize the undramatic is most striking in *Three Sisters,* in which the passage of time—mentioned on a dozen occasions in the first few minutes of the play—steadily erodes the sisters' hopes of future fulfillment through a return to the city that they identify with an idealized past. "Where has it all gone? Where? Where? . . . We'll never get to Moscow, never. . . . I can see that now": Irina's weeping capitulation toward the end of act 3 encapsulates what Gilman calls the play's "enactment of dep-rivation . . . as our condition."[15] But all the major plays have to do with the losses brought about through time's erosions; in three of them a home is threatened or (as in *The Cherry Orchard*) lost, along with a cherished way of life; hopes of love and creativity are un-realized, or realized differently from what had been expected.

The plays' common subject is the destruction of illusions. Love, work, and the future are each presented as idealized abstractions through which characters try unsuccessfully to redeem, ennoble, or escape their current situation. Six of the characters in *The Seagull* experience romantic longing for an "other" as an agent of salvation. Tuzenbach and Vershinin in *Three Sisters* and Trofimov in *The Cherry Orchard* look forward to a future golden age in which the world will be transfigured by labor. For Irina in *Three Sisters* work ("How wonderful it must be to get up at dawn and pave streets, or be a shepherd, or a schoolteacher.") is part of a sentimental package with love and the future: "I kept waiting for us to move to Moscow, I knew I'd meet my true love there."[16]

As Gilman puts it, many of Chekhov's characters wish to become someone else or to be elsewhere; the plays force them back to where and who they are now. But there is no sense of fatality: *Three Sisters* and *The Cherry Orchard* are each subtitled "A Comedy"; the conventional linear progression to a dénouement is replaced by what Gilman calls a "dramatic field": a range of reactions to a perceived loss.[17] We see the characters only when, confined in their backwaters, they have nothing to distract them from responding to their immediate situation, in dialogue that corresponds to the familiar rhythms of our lives—fragmentary, improvised, oscillating between memory and anticipation, punctuated by gaps and by the irruption of the comic into the serious. In *The Cherry Orchard* the entrepreneur Lopakhin, often wrongly interpreted as the instrument of inexorable social forces, speaks of "this messy, unhappy life":[18] it is life's accidental and unpredictable quality—of which we are constantly reminded by the intrusion of such irrelevancies as the famous breaking of a string—that thwarts the characters' hopes and plans. Some, like Konstantin in *The Seagull*, are destroyed by their disillusionment; others, like Nina in *The Seagull*, the sisters, and Vania's niece Sonia, mature spiritually by coming to terms with the constraints and the narrow potential of their situation. Their stamina, a particular virtue in Chekhov's theater, is leavened by wit, affection, and in some cases hope. By closing off some options, time opens others: acceptance of the loss of the orchard means new possibilities for Ranevskaia and her daughter Ania.

Gilman's exposition of the relation between Chekhov's ideas and his dramatic techniques should be required reading for the producers and critics who persist in interpreting the plays as studies in failure and despair. The *New York Observer*, for example, described the London Almeida Theater's production of *Ivanov* in 1997 as displaying "themes that Chekhov spent the rest of his life writing about—intellectual ennui, brooding Russian melancholia, death of the class system and unforgivable cruelty".[19]

We know that Chekhov was unhappy about Stanislavsky's production of *The Cherry Orchard*. He is reported to have said to another director, "With the exception of two or three parts nothing in it is mine. I am describing life, gray, ordinary life, and not this tedious whining. They make me either a crybaby or simply a bore."[20] Stanislavsky subsequently complained that in rehearsals for the premiere "the blossoms had only just begun to appear when the author arrived and messed up everything for us."[21] The continuing strength of the resistance to Chekhov's perception of ordinary life suggests how subversive he still is. He is telling us something new about the familiar, offering a perspective on everyday experience which contradicts conventional assumptions and offends cherished beliefs about ourselves and the world.

To grasp more fully the perception of the world that is implicit in Chekhov's plays and stories we need to turn to his life and letters. His biographers, however, have tended to focus on the saint to the exclusion of the thinker. The recent opening up of archives in Russia has released much previously unknown detail on his life. But the first biography to benefit from this (Donald Rayfield's) adds very little to the portrait of the wholly admirable man we have already been given by Ernest Simmons, Ronald Hingley, Henri Troyat, Daniel Gillès, and many others: the self-sacrificing son and brother, public-spirited doctor and citizen, and affectionate friend and husband, who also happened to be a writer of genius, but whose inner world remains elusive. Rayfield seems to suggest that no biographer can hope to enter it: whereas we can reconstruct a philosophy from Tolstoy's and Dostoevsky's life and fiction, "it is very hard to say what [Chekhov] 'meant' when he so rarely judges or expounds."[22]

One is reminded of Chekhov's response when accused of writing a story that lacked ideology: "But doesn't the story protest against lying from start to finish? Isn't that an ideology?"[23] To understand the significance of his quarrel with those who complained, like Tolstoy, that "he has not yet revealed a definite point of view,"[24] one needs to know something of the intellectual life of his age. The most illuminating attempt to place Chekhov in that context remains Simon Karlinsky's introduction to his selection of Chekhov's letters.[25] But the best single source on his thought are the letters themselves, which reveal a formidable thinker whose views on a range of issues from female sexuality to conservation of the environment were remarkably ahead of their time.

One of the keys to Chekhov's thought is the autobiographical résumé he wrote for an alumni publication, in which he asserts that his medical training in the empirical methods of the natural sciences had been the formative influence on his literary work. Astonishingly few commentators have found this revelation worth discussing; however, the importance that Chekhov gave to his scientific background emerges clearly enough from his letters.

He insisted that within the boundaries of artistic convention the writer should be faithful to the empirical reality of the world and of human behavior and present his characters' views "with perfect objectivity." He told Suvorin that he had never denied that problematic questions have a place in art, but it was important not to confuse two concepts: "*answering the questions* and *formulating them correctly*. Only the latter is required of the author."[26] He revered Tolstoy but was repelled by his didactic story "The Kreutzer Sonata," whose treatment of human sexuality exposed the great writer as "an ignorant man who has never at any point in his long life taken the trouble to read two or three books written by specialists."[27] He was profoundly out of sympathy with the search to achieve what Russian intellectuals liked to call an integral view of the world *(tselnoe mirovozzrenie),* which interpreted all human experience in the light of ultimate political or religious purposes. He wrote in his diary, "Between 'There is a God' and 'There is no God,' lies a vast stretch which a real sage traverses with difficulty. The Russian knows one or the other of these two extremes,—the

interval does not interest him."[28] He observed that writers with a
smattering of scientific method were prone to the delusion that
mankind was on the verge of resolving the ultimate mysteries of
existence: "[They] want to embrace the scientifically unembrace-
able." When one of his stories was criticized for having taken no
clear standpoint on the question of pessimism, he retorted, "It is
not the writer's job to solve such problems as God, pessimism, etc.;
his job is merely to record who, under what conditions, said or
thought what about God or pessimism." Chekhov often describes
without comment a character's sense of a mysterious eternal force
reflected in nature—a sense that he shared, expressing it with characteristic unsentimentality in a letter to Suvorin: "I feel wonderful
in the woods. It's terribly stupid of landowners to live among parks
and fruit orchards rather than in the woods. There's a feeling of
divine presence in the woods, to say nothing of the practical advantages: no one can steal your timber and you're right there when
it comes to looking after the trees."[29]

Chekhov's view of the limits of knowledge did not lead him to
a moral relativism. His goal was twofold: "to depict life truthfully
and to show in passing how much this life deviates from a norm."
But no one, he said, can define that norm: "We all know what a
dishonest deed is, but what is honor?—we do not know."[30] He will
be guided, he writes, by those concepts of the good that have with-
stood the test of time: liberation of the individual from oppression,
prejudice, ignorance, and domination by his passions.

This empirical approach made him suspicious of all schematic
views of history and literature. One such theory of the rise of the
Russian novel specifically excluded the influence of Nikolai Gogol.
Chekhov objected, "I don't understand that. If you take the standpoint of natural development, it's impossible to put not only Gogol,
but even the bark of a dog outside the current, for all things in
nature influence one another, and even the fact that I have just
sneezed is not without its influence on surrounding nature."[31]

We are now familiar with the "butterfly effect," in which the
flutter of a wing in the Amazon rain forest can allegedly set off a
storm in California; but in his sense of the incremental significance

of individually trivial, unclassifiable details, Chekhov was philo-
sophically much in advance of his time. The traditional war between science and the arts, based on the claims of rival system-
builders to have organized the totality of things into a single
pattern, seemed absurd to him:

> Both anatomy and belles-lettres are of equally noble de-
> scent; they have identical goals and an identical enemy—
> the devil—and there is absolutely no reason for them to
> fight. . . . If a man knows the theory of the circulatory
> system he is rich. If he learns the history of religion and
> the song "I Remember a Marvelous Moment" in addition,
> he is the richer, not the poorer, for it. We are conse-
> quently dealing entirely in pluses. It is for this reason that
> geniuses have never fought among themselves and Goethe
> the poet coexisted splendidly with Goethe the naturalist.
>
> It is not branches of knowledge that war with one an-
> other, not poetry with anatomy; it is delusions, that is,
> people. When a person doesn't understand something, he
> feels discord within. Instead of looking for the causes of
> this discord within himself as he should, he looks outside.
> Hence the war with what he does not understand.[32]

Science and artistic intuition, he once wrote, have the same purposes and the same nature; "Perhaps with time, and with the per-
fecting of methods, they are destined to merge into one mighty and
prodigious power, which now it is difficult even to imagine."[33]

An attentive reader of Darwin, Chekhov had no difficulty in
accepting what many still find most unpalatable in the Darwinian
revolution: the proposition that unscripted events of the kind that
concern the artist play as powerful a role as general laws in the
evolution of life, and that the human race has no special destiny
exempting it from the vicissitudes of that process. He compares the
famine and cholera threatening his region at the beginning of the
1890s with an influenza epidemic then affecting horses in central
Russia: "It is obvious that nature is doing everything in her power
to rid herself of all weaklings and organisms for which she has no

use." He notes that Tolstoy is prepared to deny that human beings are immortal, "but good God, how much personal animosity there is in his attitude!" Chekhov viewed life's evanescence and unpredictability without resentment. As he observes to Suvorin, nature "gives a person equanimity. And you need equanimity in this world. Only people with equanimity can see things clearly, be fair and work."[34]

There was nothing gloomy in this acceptance of the way things are. The same letter contains a marvelous, precisely observed description of spring in a Ukrainian garden exuberant with myriad new life, where "every hour of the day and night has its own specialty. . . . Between eight and nine in the evening for instance, the garden is filled with what is literally the roar of maybugs." Chekhov believed that the romantic yearning for a world modeled on religious or rational ideals of perfection had blinded human beings to the beauty and rich potential of the world they actually lived in. The history of the feats of Russian explorers in the Far East, which he read in preparation for his trip to Sakhalin, was "enough to make you want to deify man, but we have no use for it, we don't even know who those people were, and all we do is sit within our four walls and complain what a mess God has made of creating man."[35]

The letters Chekhov wrote during his travels in the Amur region reveal an intense love of the natural world and a prescient concern for its survival. A central theme of *Uncle Vania* is Dr. Astrov's passionate denunciation of the thoughtless destruction of the Russian landscape: "There are fewer and fewer forests, the rivers dry up, wild animals are dying out, the climate is getting worse, and with each passing day the earth is becoming poorer and uglier."[36] The beauty of the natural world is the subject of one of Chekhov's most innovative works: the long story "The Steppe," which describes the journey through southern Russia of a nine-year-old boy whose perceptions of the constantly changing face of the Russian plain in summer merge with those of the author-narrator.

Describing the steppe's flora and fauna with a precision rarely matched by Chekhov's translators, the story is concerned with the marvels that the everyday world can reveal to an attentive observer. The keen-sighted carter Vania can see foxes playing in their burrows, hares washing their paws: "besides the world seen by everyone," Vania had "another world of his own, accessible to no-one else, and probably a very beautiful one: when he gazed with such delight it was hard not to envy him."[37] Another such world was revealed through the nightly transformation of the exhausted, parched landscape of the day:

> In the churring of insects . . . in the flight of the night-bird, in everything you see and hear, you begin to sense triumphant beauty, youth, the fulness of power, and the passionate thirst for life; the soul responds to the call of its lovely austere motherland and longs to fly over the steppes with the nightbird. And in the triumph of beauty, in the overabundance of happiness, you are conscious of yearning and sorrow, as though the steppe knows she is solitary, knows that her wealth and inspiration are wasted for the world, not celebrated in song . . . : and through the joyful cacophony one hears her mournful, hopeless call for singers, singers![38]

"Perhaps," Chekhov wrote, "['The Steppe'] will open the eyes of my contemporaries and show them what splendor and rich veins of beauty remain untapped, and how much leeway the Russian artist still has."[39] Behind this modest wish lay a deeply subversive intention: a challenge to the aesthetic and moral assumptions underlying traditional aspirations to beauty and good as changeless perfection, ideals beyond history and time.

Chekhov's insistence on the self-sufficient value of transient life is strikingly reminiscent of *From the Other Shore*, that great iconoclastic text in which Aleksandr Herzen attacks all religious and secular eschatologies that view the present as a mere staging-post in the progression to a future goal. In an age that had begun to look to science for all-embracing teleological explanations of the world and human behavior and a guarantee of endless progress, Herzen emphasized the slowness and unpredictability of change and the role of chance, heredity, and physiology in thwarting our attempts to impose a rational direction on history. To look at the end and not at the action itself is "the greatest of errors . . . nature is not so miserly, and does not disdain what is transient, what lives only in the present. At every point she attains all that she can attain." In history as in nature "all is improvisation . . . there are no itineraries."[40]

Herzen maintained that true morality was not faithfulness to a fixed set of principles but an "aesthetics of behavior," attained through the cultivation of an imaginative empathy with the demands and needs of particular individuals and situations. It is precisely such a model that the twenty-six-year-old Chekhov sets before his talented but loutish brother Nikolai, whom he exhorts to try to develop the qualities that characterize well-bred people. Such people "do not throw a tantrum over a hammer or a lost eraser. When they move in with somebody, they do not act as if they were doing him a favor, and when they move out, they do not say, 'How can anyone live with you!'" They do not seek to play on people's heartstrings by complaining "'No one understands me!' or 'I've squandered my talent on trifles!' . . . because this smacks of a cheap effect, and is vulgar, false and out-of-date." They respect the property of others and therefore pay their debts; they show their respect for others by gentleness and indulgence: "Their compassion extends beyond beggars and cats. They are hurt even by things the naked eye can't see . . . they know how to keep their mouths shut and they do not force uninvited confidences on people. . . . They do not lie even about the most trivial matters. A lie insults the listener and debases him in the liar's eyes." Such people "cultivate their aesthetic sensibilities. . . . They don't guzzle vodka on any old occasion. . . . They drink only when they are free, if the opportunity happens to present itself. For they require a *mens sana in corpore sano*."[41]

Korovin remarked that Chekhov seemed to have "his own special sense of measure." In one of his stories Chekhov speaks of "the tact, the delicacy that are so essential when you have to do with a fellow-creature's soul."[42] He was repelled by Tolstoy's ideal of moral perfection, which demanded the sacrifice of all the attachments and

desires that distract human beings from the pursuit of a narrowly
defined good. "Alas! I shall never be a Tolstoyan!" Chekhov wrote
to Suvorin. "In women what I like above all is beauty, and in the
history of humanity, culture, which is expressed in rugs, carriages
with springs, and keenness of thought." But he was no aesthete: he
was sometimes accused of being too crudely naturalistic in his writing, to which he retorted that "manure piles play a highly respectable role in the landscape."[43]

This all-embracing view of the concerns of art was at odds with
the reigning orthodoxies of his time. As he wryly admitted, of all
contemporary Russian writers, "I'm the least serious and most frivolous. . . . I loved my pure muse, but lacked the proper respect,
betrayed her, and all too often led her into realms unbefitting
her."[44] He had an unbounded curiosity. In his correspondence with
his family he enquires tenderly after the health of an evil-tempered
mongoose that he had brought back from his travels in the Far
East: as Karlinsky observes, it is hard to imagine Dostoevsky even
noticing that such things existed. It is equally difficult to conceive
of either Dostoevsky or Tolstoy as author of the following phrase
(in a letter in which Chekhov bewails the financial pressures that
forced him to keep writing): "My ideal: to be idle and love a plump
girl." To be idle, he wrote in a notebook, "involuntarily means to
listen to what is being said, to see what is being done; but he who
works and is occupied hears little and sees little."[45]

He indulged his passion for creative idleness. His trip to Sakhalin
ended with a leisurely sea voyage through the Indian Ocean and
was followed the next year by an extended tour of western Europe.
His letters from abroad have none of the xenophobia characteristic
of most great Russian writers. He was equally fascinated by the
native peoples of Siberia and the dandyism of the cabbies in Vienna.
The great European capitals delighted him with their art and architecture, the elegance of their women, and the opulence of their
stores. The sight of two Dutch girls in Rome makes him picture "a
neat little white turreted house, excellent butter, superb Dutch
cheese, Dutch herring, a dignified pastor, a staid schoolmaster . . .
and it makes me want to marry a sweet little Dutch girl and have

her and me and our neat little house become a picture on a tray."[46]
The narrator of "An Anonymous Story," one of Chekhov's most
profound works, knows he will soon die from tuberculosis and is
obsessed with the urge to live the time left to him to the full: "I
was ready to embrace and include in my short life every possibility
open to man. I wanted to speak, to read, and to hammer in some
big factory, to stand on watch, to plough. I yearned for the Nevsky
Prospekt, for the fields, for the sea; for every place to which my
imagination could stretch."[47]

This was not the escapism of some Chekhov characters. His narrator, a disillusioned revolutionary whom he endows with many of
his own views, is consumed by "a passionate, irritated longing for
ordinary, everyday life"; he dreams of how it would feel to have "a
wife, a nursery, a little house with garden paths," to be a country
gentleman, a university professor, a retired navy lieutenant, a trav-
eler, an explorer.[48] A character in the story "Three Years" explains
in the course of a midnight discussion on the meaning of life,

> I'm a chemist, I think in chemical terms, and I shall die a
> chemist. . . . But I am greedy, and I am afraid of dying un-
> satisfied; and chemistry is not enough for me, and I seize
> upon Russian history, history of art, the science of teach-
> ing, music. . . . I am worn out with ideas and images—my
> head is crowded with them, and I can feel a pulse throb-
> bing in my brain. I have absolutely no desire to become
> anything special, to create something great. I simply want
> to live, to dream, to hope, to keep pace with everything.
> . . . Life is short, my dear fellow, and one must live it to
> the full.[49]

Chekhov was fascinated by lives that were utterly removed from
his own experience, although he managed to combine a formidable
number of parallel existences in his forty-four years—writer, physician, civic activist, farmer, gardener much admired for his skill in
pruning roses, and, for the last four years of his life, the husband
of the actress Olga Knipper. Although her stage career in the Moscow Art Theater condemned the couple to long periods apart, their

correspondence leaves no doubt of the depth of their feeling for each other. When in 1897 Chekhov was diagnosed as suffering from advanced tuberculosis, Tolstoy arrived at his hospital bed to discuss death and immortality, but Chekhov remained unpreoccupied by ultimate questions. (He had had all the symptoms of the disease for about ten years but chose to ignore them.) A year after the diagnosis he writes to a woman friend, "The older I get, the faster and stronger the pulse of life beats in me."[50] He never gave up hope of recovery and resumed as many of his multifarious activities as he could: in the last months of his life he frequently expressed his intention to enlist as a military doctor in the Russian Far East. His last letter, written from Badenweiler, where he died on 2 July 1904, contained the following judgment: "There's not a single well-dressed German woman; their lack of taste is depressing."[51] His wife describes his final moments in a scene that sounds like pure Chekhovian theater. The doctor ordered champagne to ease his breathing. Chekhov sat up, announced to the doctor in German, *"Ich sterbe"* (I'm dying): "Then he picked up his glass, turned to me, smiled his wonderful smile and said: 'It's been such a long time since I've had champagne'. He drank it all to the last drop, lay quietly on his left side and was soon silent forever. The . . . stillness . . . was broken only by a huge nocturnal moth which kept crashing painfully into the light bulbs and darting about the room. . . . [Then] the cork flew out of the half-empty champagne bottle with a tremendous noise."[52]

In an essay written immediately after Chekhov's death, the Russian philosopher Lev Shestov asserts that throughout his entire literary career, Chekhov was doing only one thing: "Stubbornly, sadly, monotonously, . . . he was killing human hopes"; *The Seagull* was typical of his work in that sovereign chance reigns everywhere and in everything, boldly issuing a challenge to all ordered models of the world.[53]

From a much longer perspective, however, Chekhov appears not as a pessimist but as a precursor of twentieth-century attempts to find new grounds for moral values. He was familiar with Nietzsche's thought, telling Suvorin that although he disliked his bravura, he would like to meet him on a train or a steamer and spend the whole night talking to him.[54] His art can be seen as presenting a more measured alternative to Nietzsche's electrifying message that there are "neither eternal facts nor indeed eternal values": we are "*historical* through and through."[55] In the last years of Chekhov's life the Russian literary avant-garde became infatuated with Nietzsche's irrationalist vision of the will to power as the sole creator of values: Chekhov's scientific training led him to a more sober but by no means pessimistic view of the nature and limits of human freedom in a world in which "everything . . . is relative and approximate."[56] This aspect of his work has yet to receive its due attention. His stories, even more than his plays, are remarkable for combining the insights of an artist and a Darwinian scientist into what it means to be creatures shaped by time and chance.

The weight of past time presses on Chekhov's characters in the form of heredity, environment, memory, and habit, preventing the personal or social transformation to which they aspire. Chekhov's own family history is reflected in "Three Years," in which the young merchant Laptev, the grandson of a serf, feels crushed by the burden of the past. His wealth cannot compensate for his lack of a sense of personal worth; when his brother boasts of their distinguished merchant family he retorts, "The landowners thrashed our grandfather and every low little government official punched him in the face. Our grandfather thrashed our father, and our father thrashed us. . . . What sort of nerves, what sort of blood, have we inherited?"[57] Those characters whose talents and insights have outstripped their milieu tend to suffer from what (in a letter to the director Vsevolod Meyerhold) Chekhov described as "the sort of loneliness that only lofty . . . personalities experience," expressed in a state of chronic irritability.[58]

The isolation and unrequited love that afflict so many of Chekhov's characters are frequently a consequence of the differing speeds and trajectories of their intellectual and emotional growth. Laptev's life is slowly poisoned by the knowledge that his wife married him only to escape loneliness and poverty. After years pass she begins to love him, by which time he has ceased to be able to respond. The disenchanted revolutionary who narrates "An Anonymous Story" falls in love with a woman who wants from him only what he has ceased to be able to offer: a faith to restore meaning to her life.

The shaping of character through time was much harder to present on the stage, as Chekhov discovered through his portrayal of the world-weary nobleman in *Ivanov*. He points out to Suvorin that the relationship between the thirty-five-year-old Ivanov and his twenty-year-old neighbor Sasha was intended to reflect the clash between real life and romantic illusions. The critics saw Ivanov as a scoundrel, not recognizing that his inertia, punctuated by brief fits of enthusiasm, had become a chronic condition and that Sasha's desire to set him on his feet was based on literary notions about the redeeming power of love. "She doesn't realize," Chekhov wrote, "that for Ivanov love is merely an additional complication, another stab in the back. And what happens? Sasha works on him for a whole year, yet instead of reviving he sinks lower and lower. . . . Of course, I don't use terms like . . . excitability, weariness, etc., in the play; I'd hoped that the reader and the spectator would be attentive and not need a sign saying, 'This is a plum, not a pumpkin.'"[59]

A contemporary recalls Chekhov observing that the stage should portray how things really happen: "People eat their dinner, just eat their dinner, and meanwhile their happiness is taking shape or their lives are being destroyed."[60] Chance may seem sometimes to alter the course of a life—as in *The Cherry Orchard*, when a voice calling from offstage prevents Lopakhin from proposing to Varia; but whether or not a character bows to fate at such points is shown to depend in part on an outlook and values shaped by past choices. The eponymous hero of the story "Ionich" is a provincial doctor who is attracted by a young woman with whom he can discuss literature and art. She leaves the town to study while he sinks further into the selfishness and inertia of his milieu; when she returns after four years he is disconcerted by the reminder of his former idealism and begins to avoid her until, passing her house, he resolves to go in "for a moment but on second thoughts did not.

And he never went to the Turkins' again."[61] The story ends some years later, with the outcome of his succession of choices: a dreary, ruined life.

The fatalism of some Chekhov characters is a pretext for avoiding the responsibility of moral freedom: he wants us to see that the past does not necessarily foreclose the possibility of real choice or predetermine the potential of the present. The stories, like the plays, remind us of the openness of time and the reality of choice through the variety of perspectives from which characters approach a given individual or situation. The vision of some characters is distorted by romantic yearning or by nostalgia for an idealized past—"Russians love recalling life, not living it," Chekhov observed[62]—but others, like the carter Vania, are able to perceive hidden depths in the seemingly banal. Laptev is oppressed by the cheerless monotony of Moscow winters; his friend, whose view of the present is enriched by a love of Russian history, is agreeably excited by the drab gray buildings lashed by rain.

At the end of act 4 of *The Seagull* Nina recalls the shot gull that had been laid at her feet years before: "I'm a seagull! . . . No, that's not right. . . . I've changed . . . I've become a real actress."[63] Discarding the romantic image of a victim, she denies the power of the past to determine the future. A range of characters in the plays, from the oldest sister, Olga, in her twenties, to *The Seagull's* Dr. Dorn at fifty-five, feel prematurely old, a way of expressing their sense of being trapped by circumstances. In the stories men visibly age, women become plainer, as the result of some emotional loss. But others, if only briefly, are able to cheat time through a transformed attitude to experience: the twice-widowed, prematurely aged Darling in the story of that name is rejuvenated by being able to care for a motherless child.

Chekhov protested against the critics' tendency to call his characters failures: "Classifying people as successes and failures is looking at human nature from a narrow, biased vantage point. Are you a success or not? Am I? What about Napoleon? . . . Where is the criterion? You have to be a god to distinguish the successes from the failures without making a mistake."[64] His characters possess the quality of "unfinalizability" that Mikhail Bakhtin discerned in Dostoevsky's heroes; they express their freedom through their capacity to surprise: a vulgar, cynical government clerk sits down at a piano and plays with astonishing depth and nobility of feeling—before reverting to his usual persona. Chekhov's "anonymous hero" tells a world-weary intellectual that it is never too late to reshape one's life: "The thief hanging on the Cross was able to regain the joy of life and boldly confident hope, although perhaps he had no more than an hour to live." Life "is given only once and one wants to live it boldly, with full consciousness and beauty."[65]

This, surely, is "what Chekhov meant."

The Flesh of Time:
Mikhail Bakhtin
CHAPTER SEVEN

I n June 1995 an international conference was held in Moscow
to celebrate the centenary of one of Russia's best-known intellectuals—the philosopher and critic Mikhail Bakhtin. Participants from twenty countries came together to discuss the
legacy of a thinker who had emerged from obscurity in his old age
to become the object of a cult, first in his own country and then
in the West. His influence on literary and linguistic studies and the
human sciences has grown steadily from the mid-1970s, creating a
Bakhtin industry of monumental proportions; as the commentaries
on his work pile up, Bakhtin centers are beginning to dot the globe
from Saransk to Sheffield. But as Caryl Emerson's study of Bakhtin's first hundred years reveals, no clear sense of his place in
twentieth-century thought has yet emerged from these labors.[1] On
the contrary, his heritage has become ever more fiercely contested
by rival claimants. In the West his ideas have been appropriated by
structuralists and poststructuralists, Marxists and post-Marxists,
liberals, Christians, materialists, sociolinguists, and postmodern
pragmatists. In post-Soviet Russia attempts to place Bakhtin are
part of the revaluation of an entire intellectual heritage that was
distorted or suppressed under communism. His ideas are now a
focus of contention among Russian nationalists, neohumanists, and
religious revivalists, all of whom have sought to claim him as a
precursor, while others maintain that his true significance for the
new Russia lies in his nonconformism and his independence from
all schools of thought: V. L. Makhlin describes him as a non-
Marxist, a nonformalist, a nonstructuralist, a non-Freudian, a non-

existentialist, a noncollectivist, a nonutopian, a nontheologian, and a nonmodernist.[2]

Bakhtin's most searching critics in the West have approached him in a similar spirit, citing his consistent opposition to systematizing theories of literature, culture, and the self. Emerson and G. S. Morson argue that Bakhtin's suspicion of what he called theoretism or monologism places him among the minority of Russian thinkers who resisted the ideological intransigence of the majority tradition, defending the claims of the individual and the particular against the tyranny of systems, maintaining that not all values could or should be harmonized, and warning of the dangers of seeking final solutions to open problems. In his rejection of absolutist approaches to ethics Bakhtin was, as Morson and Emerson show, particularly close to Tolstoy.[3] But his position was more consistent than that of Tolstoy, Dostoevsky, and many other Russian writers and thinkers who were torn between their pluralistic vision and their yearning to uncover a single unitary pattern which would resolve all the contradictions of experience and give a firm sense and direction to their lives. Bakhtin was not immune to the attractions of utopian thought but was more aware of its dangers than most. He began very early in his career to meditate on the ways in which language, culture, and intellectual habits lead human beings to idealize abstractions and to devalue the world of immediate experience. In this he was covering ground explored in the previous century by the greatest of Russian philosophers of freedom, Aleksandr Herzen. By focusing on certain congruences in their thought, I intend to situate Bakhtin more precisely in his Russian context, as a representative of a tenuous but robust strand of anti-ideological thought which has survived in Russia from the early nineteenth through all of the twentieth century and has much potential for the twenty-first.

The story of Bakhtin's astonishing career is too well known to need detailed retelling here. Born in 1895 to a cultivated gentry family in the south Russian city of Oryol, he studied philosophy and classics at Petrograd University, where he developed a strong interest in German philosophy from Kant to the Marburg school of neo-Kantians. After the Revolution, plagued by ill health, he supported himself with intermittent teaching and lecturing, while developing his ideas within a small group of similarly gifted intellectuals who met to discuss literature and philosophy. In 1924 he settled in the newly renamed Leningrad, where his circle included the biologist I. I. Kanaev, the poet N. A. Kliuev, and the experimental writers Konstantin Vaginov and Daniil Kharms. The climate of the time made publication difficult. Bakhtin's first major work, *Problems of Dostoevsky's Poetics,* which expounded his theory of dialogism, appeared only in 1929, shortly after his arrest in one of the roundups of intellectuals that accompanied the launching of Stalin's "cultural revolution." A favorable review of the book by Anatoly Lunacharsky, the commissar of enlightenment, helped get his sentence reduced: he was exiled to Kazakhstan, where among other odd jobs he taught bookkeeping to collective farm members while working on the theory of the novel. In 1946 he submitted a doctoral dissertation on François Rabelais, which was rejected as ideologically unsound. After the war he taught literature at the Teachers' College (later University) of Saransk, a remote town east of Moscow. He emerged from obscurity in the early 1960s when a group of young Moscow scholars who admired his book on Dostoevsky were amazed to discover that he was still alive. That book was republished in an expanded edition in 1963, followed two years later by his reworked dissertation, *Rabelais and Folk Culture of the Middle Ages and Renaissance.* Both books caused a sensation in Russian literary circles unaccustomed to original, independent thought. Brought back to Moscow, Bakhtin was treated as a celebrity by literary scholars. Confined by illness to his apartment in his last years, he continued to write until his death in 1975; meanwhile, his work had become well known in the West through the translations of his two books and his essays on the historical poetics of the novel, published collectively in 1981 as *The Dialogic Imagination.*

Academic excitement over Bakhtin grew as it became evident that his key concepts, including heteroglossia, chronotope, polyphony, unfinalizability (*nezavershennost*), outsideness (*vnenakhodi-most*), dialogue, and carnival, challenged systematic thought across a range of disciplines, offering new and fruitful approaches not merely to language and literature, but to human experience in general. But assessments of his work have become more discriminating, and the last two concepts (buzzwords throughout the humanities in the 1980s) have come to be seen as the most problematic in an oeuvre whose originality and scholarly precision are now widely held to have been overvalued.

Certainly, Bakhtin's admirers have tended to inflate the philosophical importance of his analysis of self–other relations. Although aspects of it anticipate later theories of intersubjectivity, it lacks philosophical rigor. Its value lies in the way in which, by challenging conventional thinking about language, psychology, and cultural history, it encourages the reader to reconsider the question of his or her moral responsibility in the everyday world. Referring to the widespread tendency to approach Dostoevsky's novels as the vehicles of a single authorial ideology, Bakhtin observed, "The *scientific* consciousness of contemporary humanity has learned to orient itself in the complex circumstances of 'the probability of the universe'; no 'uncertainties' are capable of confusing this scientific consciousness, for it knows how to allow for them and to calculate them. It has long since grown accustomed to the Einsteinian world with its multitudinous systems of measurement, etc. But in the realm of *artistic* cognition people sometimes continue to demand the crudest, most primitive certainty, which is self-evidently not true."[4]

In the best tradition of Russian thinkers, Bakhtin was preoccupied with questions of practical ethics.[5] He believed that human beings could be morally coherent and maximally creative only if they learned to live without the traditional props of faith in absolutes and final certainties. He argued that, like all phenomenal being, the self is intrinsically dialogical: its viability depends on the quality of its responses to its environment. It cannot be understood or expressed except in relation to an audience whose real or imagined responses continually shape the way in which we define ourselves. Bakhtin diverged from traditional and Saussurian linguistics in approaching language not as a formal system, but as utterances whose meaning is contingent on relationships of "intense interaction and struggle" between the points of view of speakers, readers, and writers in socially specific circumstances at particular historical moments. Each word, he wrote, "tastes of the . . . contexts in which it has lived its socially charged life." The dialogical nature of our relationship with an evolving environment invalidates the notion of fixed and final truths. The more highly differentiated a society becomes, the greater importance its members attach to each others' values as the subject of "interpretation, discussion, evaluation, rebuttal, support, further development." There are no limits to the dialogic context: it embraces the remote past as well as the present. Novelistic images (for example, Cervantes's Don Quixote) live different lives in different epochs, "reaccentuated" in a variety of ways which are a continuation of the unresolved argument embodied in them: "Nothing definitive has yet taken place in the world, the final word of the world and about the world has not yet been said, the world is open and free."[6]

In *Rabelais* and in a chapter added to the second edition of his book on Dostoevsky, Bakhtin explores the way in which "official monologism" with its claim to possession of a ready-made truth has been subverted throughout history by a carnival sense of the world: a grasp of the primal realities of existence—birth, decay, metamorphosis, rebirth, and the impermanence of all human structures and powers. Traditionally expressed in folkloric humor and the rituals of the common people, this sense of truth was acted out on streets and squares in the spectacles of carnival, in which institutions were travestied, authorities mocked, and divinities profaned. During the carnival the population lived a "life turned inside out," their costumes and actions depicting grotesque contrasts and pairings of opposites: youth and age, noble and lowly, sacred and blasphemous.[7] The laws and hierarchies governing everyday existence were temporarily suspended and symbolically overturned, as in the ritual performance of the mock crowning and subsequent uncrowning and beating of the carnival king. Bakhtin traced carnival ambivalence in literature from its beginnings in the Menippean satires of antiquity to the Renaissance, when in the hands of Boccaccio, Shakespeare, Cervantes, and Rabelais it became the vehicle of a new humanism, rehabilitating the world which medieval eschatology had taught humanity to despise. Gargantua and Pantagruel are carnival heroes; the gigantic scale of their physical functions mocked medieval asceticism and celebrated the earthy realities of life.

In his writings on the novel Bakhtin tracks the seepage of the carnival attitude into modern literature through the picaresque novel and the techniques of parody and the grotesque, which presented life "drawn out of its usual rut," approaching the established order of things in a spirit of play. Through this "muted laughter" such writers as Dostoevsky had explored the subterranean processes whereby traditional beliefs and dogmas begin to lose their hold on minds, accepted categories and distinctions break down, and new ways of perceiving the world evolve. Mid-nineteenth-century Russia had experienced such a revolution in consciousness when profound economic and social changes had shattered old institutions and certainties. At that time "not only people and their actions, but also *ideas* broke out of their self-enclosed hierarchical nests and began to collide."[8] Bakhtin argued that Dostoevsky conveyed this phenomenon with exceptional power through the carnivalistically scandalous scenes in his novels and through their polyphonic structure, which presented characters as a plurality of independent voices, points of view on the world that engage in a genuine open-ended dialogue. Refusing to be finalized by others' definitions of them, their every thought a rejoinder in a debate with themselves and others on the values by which they live, Dostoevsky's characters embody that capacity to surprise which frustrates all attempts to enclose human beings within the confines of systems.

Ironically, the analysis of Dostoevsky that brought Bakhtin to world attention is now widely considered to be the most flawed aspect of his work. His interpretation of the novels as polyphonic has been judged a misreading of Dostoevsky's intentions and an oversimplification of his technique, while his view of dialogism as

open-ended and liberating exchange does not take us far in understanding Dostoevsky's most self-obsessed and tragic heroes, who
experience the utterances of others as entrapment or use them to
consolidate a prior vision of the world. Bakhtin's historical account
of folk carnival has attracted equally severe criticism as a utopian
fantasy which opposes an idealized common people to an alien
"official culture" and lends itself to distorted and schematized read-
ings of literary texts and historical periods.[9]

Bakhtin addressed this last charge in 1946 in his defense of his
doctoral dissertation on Rabelais. The transcript of the discussion
records that he accepted his examiners' view that his interpretation
of medieval and Renaissance society was selective and simplistic and
that he had exaggerated the joyous aspects of popular life; but he
maintains that he had not intended the work to be a compilation
of the facts that historical research had already made widely available. He was well aware of the dark side of the people's life and of
carnival revolt; but his aim had been to reveal the role that laughter
could play in transforming human consciousness and in liberating
people from fear.[10] This may sound suspiciously like the forcing of
fact to conform to theory, but unlike some of his Western neo-
Marxist interpreters, he never presented carnival as a manifestation
of the dialectical movement of history toward the overcoming of
self-alienation.[11] He observes that laughter is "essentially not an
external but an interior form of truth"; its insights were ephemeral
and followed by a reversion to old beliefs and fears.[12] But these
brief moments, by revealing the world in a new light, opened the
way to investigation and experiment. As a mode of literary creation,
carnivalization was "a sort of heuristic principle" that made new
discoveries possible. In European literature it had performed the
momentous function of breaking down boundaries between styles,
genres, and self-enclosed systems of thought: "It destroyed all kinds
of isolation and mutual neglect, it brought together things that were
far apart, and united things that were separated." In the works of
the great Renaissance writers the carnival sense was expressed as a
"truly *divine freedom*" of approach to the world and the human
being. In the scandalous scenes in Dostoevsky's novels, full of car-

nivalized contrasts, "the 'rotten strings' of the official and personal lie are snapped (or at least weakened for an instant) and human souls are laid bare. . . . A different—more authentic—sense of themselves and their relationships to one another is revealed."[13]

In the course of an interview in 1973, when asked whether in the twenties he had considered himself "more of a philosopher than a philologist," Bakhtin replied, "More of a philosopher, and such I have remained until the present day."[14] His brand of philosophy was distinctively Russian in its concern with applied ethics: his writings on the carnivalesque are best approached not as contributions to literary criticism, cultural history, or political theory but rather as reflections on the phenomenology of fear and the spiritual resources that can defeat it.[15] Bakhtin's study of carnival was modest in compass but vastly ambitious in purpose: by tracking successive incarnations in history and literature of one aspect of human potential, he hoped to contribute to a transformation of our inner relationship with the world.

"I am an obsessed innovator," Bakhtin told his examiners in 1946; such people "are very rarely understood."[16] In the search to understand Bakhtin the emphasis has recently shifted from his studies of genre to their philosophical grounding. Scholars have found this exceptionally difficult to define: the relevant source material is frustratingly scrappy, consisting of essays and larger fragments written in the 1920s and published posthumously, and Bakhtin's often gnomic responses to his questioners in interviews given in the 1970s. This material has been heavily annotated by commentators searching for parallels between Bakhtin's insights and those of philosophical heavyweights from Henri-Louis Bergson and Martin Buber to Edmund Husserl and Martin Heidegger;[17] but very few either in Russia or the West have pointed to the remarkable parallels between his thought and that of another misunderstood innovator, Aleksandr Herzen.[18] I believe that a comparison of their respective obsessions will lead us to the elusive essence of Bakhtin's philosophical enterprise.

The first chapter of Bakhtin's book on Rabelais starts with a

quotation from Herzen: "It would be extremely interesting to write
the history of laughter." In a long footnote Bakhtin includes the
passage from which this quotation is taken—Herzen's response to
criticism of the satirical tone used by his paper the *Bell* in discussing
the attitudes of the Russian nobility and tsarist officialdom. "Laughter is no joke," Herzen declared, and he had no intention of de-
sisting from it. "No one laughs in church, in palaces, when waging
war, in front of the office chief, or the commissioner of police. . . .
Domestic serfs have not the right to smile in the master's presence.
Only equals laugh among themselves [Bakhtin's italics]."[19] Authority
has always feared laughter's subversive force, and with reason: to
smile before the ancient bull-god Apis would have been to demote
him to the status of a common farmyard animal. "Truly, there is
something revolutionary in laughter. . . . The laughter of Voltaire
destroyed more than the tears of Rousseau": Bakhtin cites these
words from another article in which Herzen responds to Russian
liberals who had attacked him for an irreverent approach to the
culture and institutions of their "elder brothers"—the advanced
democracies of the West. Herzen saw no reason to apologize: "A
person looks freely at an object only when he does not bend it to
his theory and does not himself bow before it. . . . An object about
which one cannot speak smilingly without falling into blasphemy,
without fearing pangs of conscience, is a fetish. People are crushed
by it, they fear to mix it with *ordinary* life. Thus Egyptian sculpture
and our primitive iconography gave idols unnatural poses and unnatural coloring in order to distinguish them from the despised
world of earthly beauty and the color of warm, living flesh."[20]

Bakhtin may seem excessively reverent in his praise of the profundity of Herzen's reflections on the historical function of laughter; but he rightly perceived that he and Herzen were engaged in
the same serious philosophical project. Both of them used *laughter*
as a shorthand term for what Bakhtin described as "a specific
aesthetic attitude to reality . . . untranslatable into logical language
. . . , a specific means of artistic perception and cognition." Using
Dostoevsky as his example, Bakhtin calls it "an unusually flexible"
form of artistic vision that "makes possible new things" through

its capacity to grasp the many-sidedness and potential of the fleeting moment and of the most commonplace individuals and events.[21] Herzen had described a similar approach, which did not impoverish the world by forcing it into systems, as "artistic thinking."[22] Such a vision, Bakhtin explains, is able to capture phenomena in the process of change and transition, "in their continuous, creative, renewing changeability; death is foreseen in birth and birth in death, defeat in victory and victory in defeat, discrowning in coronation." Its world is one of "birth, renewal, fertility, abundance"—the untidy world of everyday reality that cannot be encompassed by fixed concepts or reduced to single meanings. Laughter "does not deny seriousness but purifies and completes it. . . . it liberates from fanaticism and pedantry, from fear and intimidation, from didacticism, naiveté and illusion, from the single meaning, the single level, from sentimentality." It does not permit seriousness to atrophy and break away from the unfinished wholeness of everyday existence: "It restores this ambivalent wholeness."[23]

The last two words encapsulate the approach to the world that Herzen had preached in opposition to the idealists of his age: every historical moment, every action, is both aesthetically and ethically open—full of unrealized possibilities and yet complete in itself, independently of its hypothetical place in any larger scheme of things. Both thinkers believed that such an understanding of the world must become general if humanity's creative powers were to be maximally developed: hence their attack on what Bakhtin refers to as "the great *interior censor*":[24] the deference to authorities and norms anchored in our cultural past that fetters thought and circumscribes our actions in the present. They believed that in order to make new things possible, we have to change the way we think and speak about the everyday world.

Bakhtin and Herzen had both begun their rehabilitation of that despised sphere with critiques of the great utopian systems that dominated progressive thought in their respective ages. Herzen witnessed the transformation of Hegel's schema of rational progress into the revolutionary messianism of the Left Hegelians and Karl Marx, while Bakhtin's early development as a philosopher took place in the context of the religious and neo-Kantian idealism that shaped much of Russian thought and literature in the two decades before the Revolution, before it was swept away by the new orthodoxy of Marxist dialectical materialism. His first surviving philosophical work, written in 1919–21 and published for the first time in 1986 under the title *Toward a Philosophy of the Act*, is a fragment of a never-completed project on the phenomenology of the individual deed and is centrally concerned with the theme that inspired some of Herzen's finest passages—the way in which teleological systems and doctrines of progress distort the reality of human participation in the historical process and the nature of moral responsibility. Bakhtin contends that all modern philosophy is guilty of this sin:

> We are presented as it were with two value-contexts, two kinds of life: the life of the whole boundless world . . . and my small personal life. . . .
>
> Instead of bringing all theoretical (possible) knowledge [*poznanie*] of the world into communion with our actual life-from-within as answerable cognition [*uznanie*], we attempt to bring our actual life into communion with a possible, theoretical context, either by identifying as essential only the universal moments in our actual life, or by understanding our actual life in the sense of its being a small scrap of the space and time of the large spatial and temporal whole, or by giving it a symbolic interpretation.
>
> What happens in all these cases is that the living, compellent, and inescapable uniqueness of our actual life is diluted with the water of merely thinkable empty possibility . . . , is declared to be valid only as a moment of infinite matter, toward which we are indifferent, or as an exemplar of *Homo sapiens*, or as a representative of his own ethics, or as an embodiment of the abstract principle of the Eternal Feminine [a reference to the "sophiology" of Vladimir Solovyov]. That which has actual validity always turns out to be a moment of that which is possible: my own life

turns out to be the life of man in general, and this latter
life turns out to be one of the manifestations of the
world's life.[25]

As Herzen had done in his early reflections on the nature of
moral freedom, Bakhtin homed in on Kant's reliance on moral
norms as exemplifying the approach to the self characteristic of
Western philosophy since Descartes. He studied and lectured on
Kant intensively in the early 1920s and later wrote that while using
Kant's ideas of the importance of space and time in the cognitive
process, he differed from Kant "in taking them not as 'transcendental' but as forms of the most immediate reality."[26] As he explains
in his attempt to sketch out a philosophy of the act, Kant's moral
doctrine was a system of generalizations based on theoretical transcriptions of moral acts that was of limited use as a guide to how
to perform such acts in real-life situations, which could not be
precisely predicted or replicated. There are no moral norms that
are determinate and valid in themselves, "but there *is* a moral *su-
biectum* with a determinate structure . . . and it is upon him that
we have to rely." Our moral responsibility derives from our "*non-
alibi in Being*," an acknowledgment of the fact that we each occupy
a unique and unrepeatable place in time and space: "That which
can be done by me can never be done by anyone else." Moral
consciousness is the acceptance of answerability for one's irreplaceable participation in Being: "My uniqueness is given yet at the same
time only exists to the extent to which it is really actualized by me
. . . . I *am* actual and irreplaceable, and therefore *must* actualize my
uniqueness." We may seek to prove our alibi in Being by representing our lives as the ritualistic acting out of some universal principle, but if we are no more than embodiments of eternal truth
whose validity is independent of our acts, these acts would be rendered superfluous. By attempting to shift our personal responsibility onto ideologies and systems, we become "imposters and pre-
tenders."[27]

In "Robert Owen" Herzen mocks the notion of a historical
arrière-pensée which "becomes incarnate whatever the cost, and at-

tains its ends by means of kings and peoples, wars and revolutions. ... With what purpose, if it exists already, does it constitute itself again?" The moral value and the dignity of our lives lie not in the incarnation of some universal principle but in the fact that each one of us can be "an *irreplaceable reality,*" able to do what no one else can do.[28]

Both men were intensely aware that their insistence on the primacy of individual and concrete manifestations of being ran counter to assumptions deeply embedded in European culture. Herzen observed that all our ways of thinking about human beings and morality, all our images and metaphors, tend to privilege the universal and eternal over the particular and the transient, and he regretted that philosophy had not yet mastered the concept of individuality. Bakhtin argues that even philosophers who have consciously attempted to free themselves from the legacy of rationalism have succumbed to a "fatal theoreticism" based on the belief that "the truth of a situation is precisely what is repeatable and constant in it. Moreover, that which is universal and identical ... is fundamental and essential, whereas individual truth [*pravda*] is artistic and irresponsible." He continued to meditate on this tendency of the intellect throughout his life, observing (in a note made at the beginning of the 1970s) that in explaining a phenomenon "what we foreground is the *ready-made* and *finalized.* Even in antiquity we seek out what is ready-made and finalized, not what has originated and is developing."[29]

Toward a Philosophy of the Act was intended as a master plan in four parts—only one of which has survived—for a "first philosophy" (Aristotle's term for a fundamental ontology that lays the foundations for all further philosophizing).[30] Bakhtin argues that as theoretical transcriptions from concretely historical being-as-event, modern philosophies (up to and including neo-Kantianism) were all inadequate in this respect. The need of the "striving and action-performing consciousness" to orient itself in the world of events had given rise to historical materialism, but that doctrine committed the common methodological sin of failing to distinguish between what is and what ought to be. A first philosophy could not

proceed by constructing general propositions about the world. The
subject of moral philosophy is "a world of proper names, a world
of *these* objects and of particular dates of life"; it can be approached
only "participatively," in the way we experience the world through
our actions:

> The ongoing event can be clear and distinct, in all its con-
> stituent moments, to a participant in the act or deed he
> himself performs. Does this mean that he understands it
> logically? That is, that what is clear to him are only the
> universal moments and relations transcribed in the form of
> concepts? Not at all: he sees clearly *these* individual,
> unique persons whom he loves, *this* sky and *this* earth and
> *these* trees . . . ; and what is also given to him simultane-
> ously is the value, the actually and concretely affirmed
> value of these persons and these objects. He intuits their
> inner lives as well as desires . . . and he understands . . .
> *not* the abstract law of his act, but the actual, concrete
> ought conditioned by his unique place in the given con-
> text of the ongoing event. And all these moments, which
> make up the event in its totality, are present to him as
> something given and as something-to-be-achieved in a
> unitary light, in a unitary and unique answerable con-
> sciousness. . . . And this event as a whole cannot be tran-
> scribed in theoretical terms if it is not to lose the very
> sense of its being an event, that is, precisely that . . . with
> reference to which [the performed act] orients itself.[31]

Bakhtin contends that while we should not exaggerate the power
of language to express the experience of the "concrete truth" of
being-as-event, we should also not regard that truth as something
ineffable which cannot be clearly articulated. Language developed
historically in the service of participative thinking and performed
acts, and while lived experience could never be conceptually represented in any fully adequate form, the task "is always present as
that which is to *be* achieved."[32] Herzen had expressed a similar
cautious hope that after many false starts and confusions, humanity

would be cured of the worship of abstractions, "as they have been of other historical diseases." Both men focused their critique on the habits of thought inculcated by more than two millennia of Western civilization which, as Herzen put it, had advanced under the twin banners of "Romanticism for the heart" and "Idealism for the mind,"[33] leading human beings to seek self-realization in some transcendent sphere cut off from humdrum daily existence. In a short essay of 1919, "Art and Responsibility," Bakhtin attacks the notion (exemplifed in the romantic image of the alienated artist) of a divorce between aesthetic creativity and everyday life, as a pernicious fiction that blinds us to the fact that our every response to our environment is a creative act. He suggests that the real motive behind attempts to contrast the exalted concerns of art with the humble prose of daily life "is nothing more than the mutual striving of both art and life to make their own tasks easier, to relieve themselves of their own answerability. For it is certainly easier to create without answering for life, and easier to live without any consideration for art."[34]

Bakhtin and Herzen both argue that one should speak not of moral norms or systems but of moral creativity—in Bakhtin's words, "the process of creating the ethical deed"; his term for this is "architectonics"—the shaping of a relationship between the individual and his or her constantly changing natural and cultural environment: "It is this concrete architectonic of the actual world of the performed act that moral philosophy has to describe, that is, *not* the abstract scheme but the concrete plan or design of the world of a unitary and once-occurrent act or deed, the basic concrete moments of its construction and their mutual disposition. These basic moments are I-for-myself, the other-for-me and I-for-the-other. All the values of actual life and culture are arranged around the basic architectonic points of the actual world of the performed act or deed; scientific values, aesthetic values, political values (including both ethical and social values), and finally, religious values."[35]

The architectonics of responsibility that Bakhtin attempted to work out in the early 1920s have been described as not a theory, but rather an agenda of topics so complex that one lifetime would not have sufficed to think them through.[36] He made a start in that direction through his work on the novel form. He argued that the very characteristics of the novel which have led it to be widely regarded as artistically inferior to other genres—its structural and stylistic openness and its diversity of voices—constitute its unique virtue as a source of moral understanding. Above all, it sharpens our sense of the particular. Characters make choices in situations that cannot be represented in neat formulas. They express their beliefs and values in their individual styles and in "heteroglot" social environments in which no view is incontestable. Some, like Konstantin Levin in *Anna Karenina*, are obsessed with the search for timeless truth; but their moral stature emerges through their ability to respond meaningfully to the unfinished ambivalence of quotidian existence. Hence Bakhtin's term for the distinguishing feature of the novel form: "prosaic wisdom."[37] The "living discourse" of the novel, "still warm" from the passions and struggles of everyday life, the genre's ability to convey the "density and concreteness of time" with such markers as a human life, provide an education in moral discrimination which no system of universal norms can furnish. By situating actions and events in well-determined temporal frames and spatial areas, the novel "makes narrative events concrete . . . causes blood to flow in their veins." Time "thickens, takes on flesh, becomes artistically visible."[38]

Thought must "take on flesh, descend into the marketplace of life, unfold in all the splendor and beauty of transient existence": this was Herzen's advice to those who sought to understand and influence historical processes. In their search for methods and approaches that would convey the "ambivalent wholeness" of the contingent world, both thinkers turned to the natural sciences. Herzen recommended their experimental methods for the training of historians. Bakhtin was intensely interested in physical and biological science: critics have pointed to the way in which his notions of dialogism and addressivity mirror the interdependence of organisms and their physical environments.[39] Great novelists, he believed, possessed a "relativized, Galilean linguistic consciousness" which could represent a wide diversity of voices, worldviews, meanings, and values engaged in open-ended struggle and evolution.[40] Like Herzen, he paid especially close attention to the discoveries that were progressively replacing linear thinking with multiperspectivism in the human and natural sciences. He records that a lecture in 1925 by the eminent physiologist A. A. Ukhtomsky on the interconnectedness of spatial and temporal relations in biology inspired his own study of the chronotope, or space-time (a term he adopts from Einstein's theory of relativity), in the novel.[41]

True "artistic thinking," as defined by Bakhtin and Herzen, shares the scientist's fascination with the evolving forms of an unpredictable and unfinalizable world. They each cite the example of Goethe, who was engrossed both as artist and scientist in the study of existence as process. Bakhtin admired Goethe's "heroic" struggle to introduce ideas of emergence and development into the natural sciences. He devotes much of an unfinished work on the Bildungsroman to a discussion of the feeling for historical time that enabled Goethe to perceive in the concretely visible not static existence but emergence, development, and history: "For [Goethe] contemporaneity—both in nature and in human life—is revealed as an essential multitemporality: as remnants and relics of various stages and formations of the past and as rudiments of stages in the more or less distant future."[42] Bakhtin's work on Goethe in the late 1930s coincided with and evidently influenced the writing of his doctoral thesis on Rabelais and the carnival vision of the world. As the misunderstood innovator explained to his examiners, he had aimed in his study "to catch existence in the process of becoming."[43]

This emphasis on the unfinalizability of history and human beings stood in radical opposition to the dominant eschatological tendency of Russian thought which looked to some formula—whether sobornost or socialism—for a final resolution of all conflicts between essence and existence, the part and the whole. Herzen insisted that social and political forms must, like uniforms, "adapt willy-nilly to a living content"; if they do not, that is a sign that the given society lacks the freedom or the creative vitality to shape its own existence.[44] Bakhtin writes in similar vein,

> An individual cannot be completely incarnated into the
> flesh of existing sociohistorical categories. There is no
> mere form that would be able to incarnate once and for-
> ever all of his human possibilities and needs, no form in
> which he could exhaust himself down to the last word,
> like the tragic or epic hero; no form that he could fill to
> the very brim, and yet at the same time not splash over
> the brim. There always remains an unrealized surplus of
> humanness; there always remains a need for the future,
> and a place for this future must be found. All existing
> clothes are always too tight, and thus comical, on a man.[45]

Herzen had argued that we should be comforted, not distressed, by the empirical evidence that humanity was not programmed to reach a final state of harmony. If such a future could be predicted confidently, our lives would come to seem no more than shadowy anticipations of the fulfillment promised to future generations. The romantic longing for wholeness was equally foreign to Bakhtin's thought. He spoke not of alienation but of alterity (*drugost*)—not a fall from some Eden that would one day be regained, but an empirical state which had both limitations and advantages. No two bodies can simultaneously occupy the same place or see the same thing, nor can we ever see ourselves entirely; each of us in any given context has an "excess of seeing" with regard to others, whose perspectives can in turn supplement our view of ourselves. Bakhtin believed that this is a condition whose creative potential is to be celebrated. He deplores "the false tendency toward reducing every-thing to a single consciousness, toward dissolving in it the other's consciousness."[46] The overcoming of all tension and struggle, even if it were possible, would result in the creative impoverishment of humanity: "In what way would it enrich the event if I merged with the other, and instead of *two* there would now be only *one*? And what would I myself gain by the other's merging with me? If he did, he would see and know no more than what I see and know myself. . . . Let him rather remain outside of me, for in that position he can see and know what I myself do not see and do not know from my own place, and he can essentially enrich the event of my own life."[47]

Human creative fulfillment does not come about through the synthesizing of points of view: "On the contrary, it consists in the intensification of one's own outsideness [vnenakhodimost] with respect to others, one's own *distinctness* from others: it consists in fully exploiting the privilege of one's own unique place outside other human beings." This outsideness must be preserved if solidarity with others, expressed in ethical actions, is to be fruitful. A pure projection of myself into the other would represent no more than an infection with another's suffering. Aesthetic and ethical activity begins only when what we receive through our empathy with others is completed with elements of our own perspective. "Sympathetic understanding is not a mirroring, but a fundamentally and essentially new valuation, a utilization of my own architectonic position in being outside another's inner life."[48]

Bakhtin rejected the claim that in order to understand a foreign culture one should seek to view the world wholly from its perspective: on the contrary, one's location outside a given culture permits one to uncover meanings and potential hidden from those within: "For one cannot really even see one's own exterior and comprehend it as a whole, and no mirrors or photographs can help; our real exterior can be seen and understood only by other people, because they are located outside us in space and because they are *others*."[49] Through this process both the foreign culture and one's own are enriched in new and unexpected ways.

Bakhtin and Herzen both vigorously exploited the advantages of their outsideness in relation to Western culture. Herzen was equally opposed to the Slavophiles' belief that Russian culture should seal itself off from foreign influences and to the Russian Westernizers' demand that their country abandon its native institutions and merge culturally with the West. He believed that the great unsolved problem of the modern age—to discover a form of social organization that would combine the values of individual autonomy with social solidarity—could best be approached if Russia, with its still existing peasant communes, and the West, with its tradition of the defense of individual freedom, brought their differing perspectives to bear on each other's values and experience. His own outsider's reflections on the strengths and weaknesses of European political culture contain some profound perceptions, but he has had few listeners. In contrast, Bakhtin's studies of European literary genres and folk culture have become milestones in Western literary and cultural theory. He owed some of his most significant insights to his perspective as a thinker on the margins of his own society, who had lived through one of the two greatest revolutions of the modern age. Hence his affinities with another historical turning point, the early Renaissance, which he celebrates as a time when a creative thinker could exist simultaneously in different cultures and value systems, approaching each from the perspective of an outsider. He was fascinated with such thresholds and border zones, where norms and canons lose their force and language sheds that "hidden dogmatism" which follows from the strict demarcation of vocabularies. At such points in history, he maintained, creative freedom and inventiveness reach their height, expressed in images that are "completely new, self-criticizing, absolutely sober, fearless."[50]

This last phrase signals a significant difference between the two thinkers. When Herzen writes of the fight against stultifying dogma and repressive authority, it is usually with specific reference to the contemporary situation in Russia or Europe, and he warns the reader not to believe that there are any easy solutions to real conflicts. When Bakhtin writes on the same theme it is often unclear whether he is talking about literature, life, or both, and this indeterminacy allows him to indulge in a degree of wishful thinking that Herzen would have dismissed as pure utopianism. The implied other in Bakhtin's dialogues has been described as being "as a rule benignly active, always at work to define us in ways we can live with and profit from."[51] Herzen's analysis of social struggle in France in 1848 and peasant revolts in Russia led him to question the realism of those who believed that any genuine dialogue was possible between the ideals of a cultured minority and the demands of a desperate, vengeful mass movement. We have seen that Bakhtin admitted that his benevolent depiction of carnival revolt had been deliberately one-sided in order to force home a philosophical point, but it can be argued that even on the level of theory his discussion would have benefited from a clear distinction between two fundamentally different ways in which humans have historically sought to free themselves from repressive authorities and norms. As Tzvetan Todorov puts it, "Dialogue favours the establishment of the individual, of the 'Thou' as much as the 'I'; carnival dissolves the individual into the collective action of the crowd. Dialogue is choice and freedom, carnival demands submission to the group. Dialogue is order and sense, carnival chaos and orgy: dialogue is Apollo, carnival Dionysus."[52]

Dialogue is Bakhtinian: Rabelaisian carnival is Bakuninist in its celebration of the creative force of the passion for destruction—a principle which (as Herzen often reminded Bakunin) was attractive in theory but usually catastrophic in historical application. Some Russian scholars have explained Bakhtin's apparent blindness to the violence of mass movements and their potential for abuse as the result of conditioning by the rhetoric of Stalinism.[53] Certainly, it cannot easily be reconciled with his belief in the inalienable responsibility of individuals for their actions; but by far the greater part of his work is a consistent articulation of that belief. Despite his utopian propensities, Bakhtin's rejection of an alibi in Being set him squarely against the forms of imposture on which Stalin's tyranny relied.

As Caryl Emerson has observed, "Discrediting the absurd dichotomy between 'system or nothing'" was Bakhtin's single major task.[54] He distanced himself equally from relativism and dogmatism, pointing out that relativism made authentic dialogue about meanings and values unnecessary, while dogmatism made it impossible. But most commentaries on his work have tended to ignore his warnings about how not to categorize him. On the one hand, his ideas have been compared with those of relativists and neopragmatists like Richard Rorty;[55] on the other, his thought is frequently approached as a coherent ideological system. On the basis of texts whose authorship remains disputed, he has been represented as a Marxist, a Freudian, a formalist, and a semiotician;[56] while because he was a believer and associated with religious circles in the 1920s, his work is often approached as a coded theology. Parallels have been drawn between his thought and Orthodox religious philosophers, and with Buber, whom he is known to have admired. But the I-thou relationship in Buber's thought is grounded in an absolute Thou, whereas Bakhtin avoided discussion of ends and essences, focusing exclusively on processes in time and space. His concept of moral responsibility did not exclude the possibility of God but did not require a deity as the source of moral norms. For the same reason, attempts to interpret *dialogism* and even *carnival* as expressions of the traditional concept of sobornost, while impressively ingenious, do not carry conviction.[57] We long to believe that the meaning of our lives will not end with their factual existence, but "in being there are no guarantees of the ought-to-be," he wrote in the 1920s.[58]

Herzen frequently complained of being identified with systems that he opposed or, alternatively, of being represented as a pessimistic nihilist. He attributed these misunderstandings to his critics' persistence in interpreting his thought with the aid of the very categories that it was intended to subvert. Bakhtin, as we have seen, was engaged in a similar form of subversion, attempting to articulate a new way of describing the world—to which (as the most probing studies of his work have recognized) familiar dichotomies, such as rationalism/irrationalism, do not apply. The philosopher G. L. Tulchinsky describes Bakhtin's thought as a fundamentally other approach to reason and logic *(inoratsionalnost)* which rejects the teleological and programmatic interpretation of rationality as optimal effectiveness in the realization of preset goals; Bakhtin, he argues, is rational according to different criteria of effectiveness, rooted in the ancient idea of the harmonious wholeness of the Cosmos, which approach the world as "the reciprocal supplementarity of unrepeatable individualities."[59] In an article of 1976 the eminent classicist and philosopher S. S. Averintsev described Bakhtin as a "wisdom-lover among the specialists," who resisted the dehumanizing effects of the obsession with methodology in the humanities, offering instead "philosophical anthropology," the "ability to see the literary word as a human word."[60]

Bakhtin admired Averintsev, whose description of the study of symbols he cites in support of his own approach to methodology in the humanities: "not an unscientific, but a *differently scientific* [*inonauchnaia*] form of knowledge that has its own internal laws and criteria for precision"—a description that has been greeted as particularly appropriate to Bakhtin's own thinking.[61]

Herzen had the same kind of inoratsionalnost and inonauka in mind when he wrote in 1859, "There is not *one* kind of reason, there are *two:* the reason of the world *that is going down like the evening sun* does not coincide with the reason of the world *that is rising like the dawn*."[62] He and Bakhtin were among that avant-garde of thinkers who since the mid-nineteenth century have focused their attention on the erosion of faith in teleological systems and the ways it must affect our understanding of the world and of human relations. They both belonged to an even more select subset who were undismayed by the challenge of having to justify contingent existence without reference to first causes or final ends. Schopenhauer reacted to the role of chance in history by declaring all phenomenal existence worthless, while Nietzsche responded to it with his tragic "pessimism of *strength*."[63] But Herzen and Bakhtin wholeheartedly welcomed the discrediting of teleological thinking as a belated rehabilitation of the "world of earthly beauty" which idealists had disfigured, devalued, and despised for so many centuries. They did not believe that a genuinely scientific approach to the human personality would deny or diminish its value. To the narrow dogmatists among the Russian Left, who appealed to scientific method to justify their contempt for people and ideas that did not conform to their a priori systems, Herzen retorted that true science "even more than the Gospel teaches us humility. She cannot look down on anything, she does not know what superiority means, she despises nothing, never lies for the sake of a pose. . . . Science is love." Instead of seeking to impose their political recipes on the masses, the Left should attentively study the existing values and aspirations of those whose lives they sought to improve: "Manna does not fall from the sky, as it does in children's fairy tales; it grows up from the soil. . . . Learn to listen to the grass growing and don't lecture it on how to form ears of wheat."[64]

"Lovelessness, indifference," Bakhtin wrote, "will never be able to generate sufficient power to slow down and *linger intently* over an object, to hold and sculpt every detail and particular in it, however minute. Only love is capable of being aesthetically productive."[65] Aesthetic love was the defining characteristic of his and Herzen's approach to the world—as is also true of the third great innovator treated in this book: Chekhov, who, like the character in his story who aspired to "keep pace with everything," was lovingly attentive to the inexhaustible diversity of natural phenomena and human character. Bakhtin wrote in his old age of his "love for variations and for a diversity of terms for a single phenomenon. The multiplicity of focuses."[66] Apart from occasional excursions into utopian optimism, he remained faithful throughout his life to the views expressed in his early essay on art and answerability: "Inspiration that ignores life and is itself ignored by life is not inspiration but a state of possession," while on the other hand the person who complains that great art has no relevance to his humdrum daily existence "ought to know that the fruitlessness of art is due to his unwillingness to be exacting and to the unseriousness of the concerns in his life."[67]

Bakhtin's, Herzen's, and Chekhov's aesthetic approach to life was no hazy, all-embracing benevolence: it demanded an attention to the "humble prose of living"[68] (Bakhtin's term) that was far more exacting and serious than the attitude of those who relied on ready-made rules to guide their actions. Herzen often remarked on the depth of the human fear of freedom: the last thing we rely on is ourselves. The absence of universal norms opens up terrifying vistas: we can advance in any direction or remain stationary, with no certainty as to the outcome of any of our choices, knowing only that they will matter. Science has shown the world to be neither system nor chaos: open and largely unpredictable but not a directionless flux. Our every act has consequences that will affect the unitary texture of existence. It is therefore our moral responsibility to develop a sense of aesthetic measure and balance that will allow us to combine a coherence in our responses with an openness to the specific contours of individual situations and human personalities that will elicit their potential without demanding of them what they cannot give.

According to the testimony of their contemporaries, Herzen, Chekhov, and Bakhtin each possessed this sense of measure to a remarkable degree. It was expressed most clearly in their dislike of all forms of bullying and of the doctrinaire intolerance that seeks to force life down one path rather than considering the value of alternative ways of living and seeing. Chekhov speaks for all three when he reserves his most severe criticism for the "lazy, philosophizing, cold" type of intellectuals who "are ready to deny *everything*, because it is easier for a lazy brain to deny than to affirm."[69]

Conclusion:
A New-Style Russian Idea

A notable feature of Russian intellectual life since the fall of communism has been the proliferation of conferences and round tables whose aim is to identify and evaluate the distinctive characteristics of Russian thought and culture. Two topics have predominated: the nature of Russian thought and the "Russian mentality," and the relation of Russian and Western culture.[1] Attended by a mixture of historians, anthropologists, political scientists, writers, and philosophers, with an occasional sprinkling of invited delegates from the West, these debates, together with their echoes in the periodical press, reveal the post-Soviet intelligentsia to be deeply divided on the question of its self-image and values. The division tends to center on the interpretation of the past and future role of the messianic tendency commonly known as the Russian Idea.

Many commentators, while distancing themselves from the crude xenophobia of much contemporary Russian nationalism, argue that postcommunist society is in desperate need of a cohesive principle to counter its fragmentation and moral disorientation, "an integrating ideology . . . a new Idea," as one writer puts it, which will harmonize traditional Russian spiritual values with the country's changed role in the world.[2] The new idea most popular among religious nationalists seems no more than an updating of the old—the social and spiritual ideal of sobornost as preached by successive Russian religious philosophers. Its advocates echo the Slavophiles in lauding its advantages over liberal concepts of individual freedom, which they hold responsible for the social fragmentation and spiritual malaise in the West. As one contributor to the debate claims, such Western "liberal inventions" as legal guarantees of rights would be superfluous in a society grounded in the spiritual values of sobornost.[3]

This view is vigorously contested by a number of writers who argue that, far from transcending the liberal ideal of individual autonomy, the notion of sobornost reflects a tribal mentality that is incapable of grasping such a concept. Several commentators have pointed out that the community of faith and purpose that sobornost denotes never had a historical existence in Russia.[4] G. L. Tulchinsky, a philosophy professor at St. Petersburg University and a leading participant in the debate on Russia's philosophical heritage, has remarked on the strange evolution of this concept of spiritual togetherness from the theocratic idyll of a dissident minority into an ideological justification for despotism. Lenin's brand of political messianism skillfully manipulated the Russian dream of a monolithic society welded together by selfless dedication to a transcendent goal. The Soviet version of sobornost reached its apotheosis in the blend of deception, intolerance, and arbitrary force that was Stalinist totalitarianism. The post-Soviet revival of the concept (often at the hands of an unholy alliance of communists and religious nationalists) has been linked with a movement to rehabilitate the image of the former communist state as a community whose self-sacrificing dedication to national tasks contrasted sharply with the selfish materialism of the capitalist West.[5]

Those who recommend a return to the old-style Russian Idea as a solution to the country's post-totalitarian identity crisis have been accused by critics sympathetic to the new Westernizing reforms of confusing unity with uniformity: they argue that Russian society needs to display much more unity and much less uniformity if the country's political and economic transformation is to succeed. As one commentator puts it, true unity is impossible without a healthy intellectual pluralism: "Only those who perceive themselves as separate, individual, unique, can unite."[6] At the round table meeting on the Russian mentality held in 1994 the fear was expressed that the search to define a national consciousness might have the negative effect of providing Russians with a new collective noun to replace the people, state, and party as a force onto which they could devolve responsibility for their actions and destinies.[7] Scholars seeking to apply the methods pioneered by the French *Annales* school to an analysis of Russian history and culture have protested at the hijacking of their project by groups whose definitions of the Russian national character coincide with the values contained in their political programs. As A. P. Ogurtsov put it, such groups attempt to force all the diversity and ambivalence of Russian culture into a single spiritual matrix, designed to have the same crowd appeal as their crude propaganda slogans.[8]

The ideological divisions in the new Russia emerged sharply in debates over the teaching of philosophy in institutions of higher education after the fall of communism. Should the history of philosophy be divided according to historical epochs, as is usual in the West, or geopolitically, into three categories: Eastern, Western, and Russian? The second approach, in which the emphasis is on the nature of each tradition's "spiritual enquiry," has reportedly proved the more popular[9] but has been fiercely criticized both as intrinsically absurd—why not a German, Swiss, or Danish national philosophy?—and as a vehicle for the propaganda of the New Right.[10] Academics have begun to express unease at the emergence of a new ideological orthodoxy, scarcely less blinkered and intolerant than the old. Tulchinsky noted in 1997 that candidates outlining their methodology in examinations for doctorates in philosophy and the human sciences now tend to cite the authority of Russian religious philosophers "with the same unanimous uniformity" as they once cited Marx and Lenin.[11] Just as once no thinker could be considered enlightened or significant if he could not be shown to be a precursor of Marxism, now those who are not seen to have contributed to the Russian Idea—or, worse, who have opposed it—tend to be marginalized, demonized, or reinterpreted to fit a prior schema.

Andrzej Walicki has urged Russian intellectuals not to repeat the history of antirational messianism in Poland, whose intelligentsia had traditionally compensated for national disasters by asserting their belief in their nation's spiritual superiority over its more materially successful neighbors.[12] But many Russians, while sharing Walicki's view that it is imperative to develop an intellectual tradition that is more consonant with the new liberalizing and Westernizing reforms, argue that Western liberals have been over-optimistic in their hope that their own traditions can be grafted easily onto the new Russia. Tulchinsky observes that the dissident culture of the Soviet period produced ample evidence to the contrary—for example, Solzhenitsyn's Harvard address of 1978, in which he pronounced Western-style freedoms an absurdity.[13] His Western admirers showed no signs of noticing that the eschatological flavor of his intellectual tradition was in direct contradiction with liberal concepts of individual autonomy. Russia had never possessed a legal culture and institutions favorable to the implantation of classical liberalism; it was significant that the dominant school of nineteenth-century Russian liberalism had preached a messianic Hegelian philosophy of progress. In the next century the moral ethos of dedication to a common task had led the Russian artistic and literary avant-garde to welcome and collaborate with the Bolshevik Revolution, and the eschatological ideal of the "new human being," skillfully manipulated by Stalin, set the tone of Soviet cultural politics. Tulchinsky echoes the view of the émigré art historian Boris Groys: the avant-garde's battle with Stalin at the beginning of his regime was not about freedom, but about authorial rights over the program for restructuring the world and humanity.

Nevertheless, Tulchinsky argues that Russian history is also rich in examples of individuals and communities who have resisted the centralizing pull of the state in the name of their right to assume responsibility for their fate—dissident sects such as the Old Believers, the self-governing peasant communes and the Cossack communities of the South, and the local government institutions (zemstva) set up in the second half of the nineteenth century, which had represented the beginnings of a civil society and for that reason had been swiftly suppressed by the Bolsheviks. Tulchinsky suggests that post-Soviet Russian society could learn from these examples how to combine the principle of individualism with forms of solidarity that are rooted in the national experience—a more fruitful alternative than seeking to implant Western classical liberalism in unpromising Russian soil or pursuing an anti-Western myth of spiritual togetherness. Another critic, V. I. Mildon, draws attention to a new-style Russian Idea articulated by émigré religious philosophers like Evgenii Trubetskoy, Georgii Fedotov, and Lev Karsavin, who were shocked at the ease with which the concept of sobornost had lent itself to manipulation by tyrants, resulting in a country "inhabited not by people but by '*the* people.'"[14] Mildon presents the religious personalism of such thinkers as an attempt to avoid the extremes of some Western individualist doctrines through the synthesis of traditional Russian concepts of community and solidarity with a respect for difference—an approach that had a tenuous existence even in nineteenth-century Russian thought (Mildon traces it back to the revolt of Dostoevsky's Underground Man against systems that claimed to predict or regulate his actions). He emphasizes the current importance of this strand of thought as a source of inspiration on how post-Soviet Russian culture can incorporate Western-style freedoms while retaining its own identity.

Such attempts by Russian critics to reclaim aspects of their intellectual heritage that are at variance with its dominant messianic ethos have much in common with past efforts by scholars in Europe and the United States to highlight a humanistic countertradition in Russian thought. Bakhtin's name is increasingly cited by both Russian and Western academics as evidence of the vitality of such a tradition. Tulchinsky compares Bakhtin's belief that humanity has "no alibi in Being" with the spiritual experience recorded in the memoirs of prisoners of Stalin's camps, who had witnessed the destruction of all the civilized norms in which rational concepts of freedom and responsibility are grounded.[15] In this world of the absurd, devoid of all the structures and collectives that are the customary custodians of values, only those who created their personal zone of freedom, conceived as the responsibility for making such small choices as whether to clean their teeth or to walk along a certain floorboard, survived. Tulchinsky contends that this metaphysical experience of the primacy of freedom among those who were stripped of all power over their lives and selves exemplifies Bakhtin's claim that the core of freedom as responsibility resides not in external forms or collectives, but in the individual human spirit.

Joseph Frank has remarked that Bakhtin's heritage has become a lodestar by which various factions of the Russian intelligentsia are seeking to orient themselves in the confusion of their new freedom.[16] Although some groups have sought to claim him for the new nationalism by proclaiming dialogism a variant of sobornost, others assert that his pluralism, together with his insistence on the inalienable responsibility of each individual, is a corrective both to the collectivistic emphasis in Russian thought and to the claims of Western postmodern thinkers that we live in a world of hyperreality in which it is no longer useful or even possible to distinguish between truth and untruth, science and ideology.

At the Moscow centennial conference on Bakhtin, Russians holding this view were able to establish common ground with Western scholars who find Bakhtin an inspiring model for a fresh approach to moral and cultural values, free from the fetters of ideological thinking and outworn stereotypes.[17] For many decades a committed handful of scholars has attempted to draw attention to the value of Herzen's and Chekhov's perceptions in this regard.[18] But despite their efforts, both of these thinkers remain victims of stereotypical interpretations which grossly distort their thought. The general view of Chekhov both in Russia and the West has changed little since Evgenii Zamiatin, writing in the early years of the Soviet state, observed that if you mentioned his name to the new generation, the usual replies would be, "Chekhov? He's about whining, pessimism, superfluous people. . . . Chekhov? You won't find anything there related to the new trends in literature . . . or to social questions."[19] Herzen's fate is more bizarre: attacked from all sides in his lifetime, he was subsequently canonized by Lenin as a revolutionary thinker, with the result that his works, while freely published in the Soviet Union, remained unread by the dissident intelligentsia, few of whom seem to have questioned his official designation as a pre-cursor of Bolshevism. In the mid-1950s Isaiah Berlin was moved to protest, "Russia is not so rich in first-rate thinkers that she can afford to ignore one of the three moral preachers of genius born upon her soil."[20]

Half a century on, it would seem that Herzen's moral message is equally needed in the West. In a postideological age we have to learn how to live with uncertainty, replacing the aspiration toward exclusive possession of the truth with the habit of pooling resources and combining perspectives in day-to-day attempts to cope with the common problems of humanity. Not all those who admire Bakhtin's efforts to replace ideological confrontation by dialogical encounter between cultures are aware that, like much else that is valuable in the Russian countertradition, this strand of thinking can be traced back to Herzen. In the mid-1850s he observed that neither Russia nor the West had found solutions to the most pressing prob-lems besetting humanity:

> Two extreme, one-sided developments have led to two ab-surdities: to the Englishman, independent and proud of his rights, whose independence is based on a form of polite cannibalism, and to the poor Russian peasant, impersonally swallowed up in the village commune, given over into serf-dom without rights. . . .
>
> How are these two developments to be reconciled? How is the contradiction between them to be resolved? How is the independence of the Englishman to be preserved with-out the cannibalism, how is the individuality of the [Rus-sian] peasant to be developed without the loss of the prin-ciple of the commune? Precisely in this [dilemma] lies the whole agonizing problem of our century.[21]

The twentieth century has modified the terms of the dilemma with-out resolving it. It is not surprising that many Russians prefer the one-sidedness of their communal traditions to what they see as the spiritually barren freedoms of the West. Herzen proposed another path: cross-fertilization on the basis of mutual respect. Europe, he told the French historian Jules Michelet, "has not resolved the antinomy between the individual and the state, but she has set herself the task of resolving it. Russia too has not found the solution. Before this question begins our equality."[22]

Notes

Abbreviations

MB   Mikhail Bakhtin
FB   Francis Bacon
AC   Anton Chekhov
CD   Charles Darwin
AH   Aleksandr Herzen
JSM   John Stuart Mill
PJP   Pierre-Joseph Proudhon
FS   Friedrich Schiller

ACL   *Anton Chekhov's Life and Thought: Selected Letters and Commentary,* trans. from the Russian by M. Heim in collaboration with S. Karlinsky. Selection, introduction, and commentary by S. Karlinsky (Evanston, Ill., 1997).

AE   Friedrich Schiller, *On the Aesthetic Education of Man, In a Series of Letters,* ed. and trans. by E. M. Wilkinson and L. A. Willoughby (Oxford, 1967).

Bacon   J. Spedding et al., eds., *The Works of Francis Bacon,* 4 vols. (London, 1858).

OS   A. I. Herzen, *From the Other Shore and The Russian People and Socialism,* trans. M. Budberg and R. Wollheim (Oxford, 1979).

SS   A. I. Herzen, *Sobranie sochinenii,* 30 vols. (Moscow, 1954–66).

TAS   A. Kelly, *Toward Another Shore: Russian Thinkers Between Necessity and Chance* (New Haven, 1998).

VF   *Voprosy filosofii*

INTRODUCTION
Two Russian Ideas

1. T. Colton, *The Dilemma of Reform in the Soviet Union* (New York, 1984), 99. Cited in A. Yanov, *The Russian Challenge,* trans. I. J. Rosenthal (Oxford, 1987), 70.

2. N. Berdiaev, *Russkaia ideia* (Paris, 1946), 249.

3. A. F. Zotov, "Sushchestvuet li mirovaia filosofiia?" *VF,* 1997, 4:21.

4. A. Walicki, "Po povodu 'russkoi idei' v russkoi filosofii," ibid., 1994, 1:68–71. Walicki observes that many Russian philosophers now

seem even proud to admit to a close link between totalitarianism and the Russian Idea, viewing the very possibility of the fall into totalitarianism as proof of the philosophical height attained by the "theocratic impulse" in Russian thought—on the Aristotelian principle that the very worst is usually a distortion of the very best. Ibid., 71.

5. See the use of this term by G. S. Morson in "Prosaic Bakhtin: 'Landmarks,' Anti-Intelligentsialism, and the Russian Counter-Tradition," *Common Knowledge* 2, no. 1 (1993): 35–74. See also my discussion of the countertradition in the Introduction to *TAS*.

7. V. S. Solovyov, *Sobranie sochinenii*, 10 vols., 2d ed. (St. Petersburg, n.d.), 5:387.

8. *Vekhi. Sbornik statei o russkoi intelligentsii*, 2d ed. (Moscow, 1910), 34; N. Berdiaev, *Novoe srednevekov'e. Razmyshlenie o sud'be Rossii i Evropy* (Berlin, 1924), 28; *Vekhi*, 21.

9. *Vekhi*, 7, 29.

10. Karl Marx, *Early Writings*, trans. and ed. T. Bottomore (London, 1963), 155; R. Tucker, "Lenin's Bolshevism as a Culture in the Making," in A. Gleason, P. Kenez, and R. Stites, eds., *Bolshevik Culture: Experiment and Order in the Russian Revolution* (Bloomington, Ind., 1985), 25.

11. On Nietzschean Marxism, see chap. 13 of *TAS*.

12. On Berdiaev's interpretation of the Bolshevik Revolution, see J. Burbank, *Intelligentsia and Revolution: Russian Views of Bolshevism 1917–1922* (Oxford, 1986), 193–208. On Eurasianism, see ibid., 215–22.

13. See Yanov, *The Russian Challenge*, chaps. 9–19. See also Yanov's analysis and prognostications about the post-Soviet development of these movements: *Posle Eltsyna: "Veimarskaia" Rossiia* (Moscow, 1995).

14. Walicki, "Po povodu 'Russkoi idei,'" 69–71. See also the paper given at the same conference by the American scholar James Scanlan: "Does Russia Need Russian Philosophy?" Scanlan suggests that the study of the Russian Idea is more of a luxury than a necessity in the current atmosphere of political and economic uncertainty and urges Russian academics to give greater emphasis to those strands of Russian thought that could form a counterweight to corporatist tendencies in Russian society (*VF*, 1994, 1:62–64), a view that one participant in the conference ascribed to "theological color-blindness"—the incapacity of a foreigner to recognize the uniqueness of the Russian Orthodox tradition and its centrality in Russian history. N. K. Gavriushin, "Russkaia filosofiia i religioznoe soznanie," ibid., 68.

15. On the ambivalence of Dostoevsky, Tolstoy, and the populist movement, see *TAS*, part 2. On Struve's thought, see ibid., 173–86.

16. On Herzen's attack on Schopenhauerian pessimism, see ibid., chap. 16.

17. S. J. Gould, *Wonderful Life: The Burgess Shale and the Nature of History* (London, 1989), 44.

18. For Herzen's first use of this metaphor, see *TAS*, 1; see also my discussion of his work *From the Other Shore* in ibid., chap. 15.

19. *OS*, 128.

CHAPTER ONE
Herzen and Francis Bacon

1. I. Berlin, *Russian Thinkers* (London, 1978), 207. Berlin's first two essays on Herzen, "Herzen and Bakunin on Individual Liberty" and "Alexander Herzen," were first published in 1955 and 1956, respectively, and are included in *Russian Thinkers*. In 1956 Herzen's work *From the Other Shore* was published in London with Berlin's introduction.

2. On the resemblance between Herzen's defense of egoism and Stirner's book, see A. Walicki, *The Slavophile Controversy*, trans. H. Andrews-Rusiecka (Oxford, 1975), 387–88.

3. M. Malia's detailed study of Herzen's early intellectual development contains only one reference to Bacon, in a summary of one of Herzen's articles. See *Alexander Herzen and the Birth of Russian Socialism 1812–1855* (Cambridge, Mass., 1961), 91, 315. Another biographer, R. Labry, notes that it would be interesting to look more closely at the study that Herzen made of Bacon and Descartes before he wrote his *Letters on the Study of Nature*. "Mais cet examen nous entraînerait hors des limites de notre travail" (But such an analysis would go beyond the scope of our work): *Alexandre Ivanovič Herzen 1812–1870* (Paris, 1928), 257.

4. See Malia, *Herzen*, chap. 10; and Walicki, *The Slavophile Controversy*, 377–89.

5. *Bacon*, 4:19.

6. See C. D. Broad, *The Philosophy of Francis Bacon* (Cambridge, 1962), 63.

7. AH to Ogaryov, 1–2 August 1833. *SS*, 21:21.

8. Ibid., 8:114.

9. Ibid., 1:22, 24, 22, 24–25.

10. Ibid., 24–25.

11. AH to Ogaryov, 7 or 8 August 1833. *SS*, 21:23–24. Such triadic schemas were much in fashion at the time. Herzen refers to an article by a French writer which has parallels with his own ideas. See C. Di-

dier, "Les trois principes: Rome, Vienne, Paris," *Revue Encyclopédique* 53 (1832): 37–66.

12. L. Feuerbach, *Kleine philosophische Schriften* (Leipzig, 1950), 36.

13. AH to Ogaryov, 14 November to 4 December 1839. *SS*, 21:55.

14. *SS*, 9:27.

15. M. Bakunin, "Reaktsiia v Germanii," *Sobranie sochinenii i pisem 1828–76*, ed. Iu. Steklov, 4 vols. (Moscow, 1934–35), 3:130.

16. *SS*, 3:66.

17. AH to N. Ketcher, 2 March 1845. *SS*, 22:233.

18. Ibid.

19. *SS*, 3:86, 75.

20. *SS*, 2:303–04. Bacon, 4:69. (Herzen cites Bacon in the original Latin.)

21. *SS*, 2:304, 305.

22. Ibid., 306, 372, 412.

23. Ibid., 2:140, 141.

24. ooMalia, *Herzen*, 312. See *SS*, 3:146.

25. G. W. F. Hegel, *Lectures on the History of Philosophy*, 3 vols. (London, 1896), 3:172–73.

26. Hegel, *Political Writings*, trans. T. M. Knox (Oxford, 1964), 325.

27. Hegel, *History of Philosophy*, 3:172.

28. *SS*, 3:267, 254.

29. AH to A. Kraevsky, 23 June 1845. *SS*, 22:240, 3:251. Elsewhere, however, Herzen accuses Bacon of "some one-sidedness" while emphasizing that he was "far removed from vulgar empiricism" (ibid., 260). He notes that even Bacon was not entirely free from the superstitions of his time—notably, belief in astrology and magic (ibid., 228n1). Herzen's only other criticism of Bacon in the *Letters* is in connection with what he sees as innate English conservatism: "The Englishman considers it indelicate to step over certain limits, to touch on certain questions: he is a pedantically strict observer of proprieties.... Bacon, Locke, England's moralists and political economists, the parliament which sent Charles the First to the scaffold, Stafford, who wished to overthrow the power of parliament—all try above all to present themselves as conservatives: they all march forward looking backwards and do not wish to recognize that they are moving onto new, uncultivated ground" (ibid., 309–10).

30. *SS*, 3:260–61; Bacon, 4:59–60, 66–68.

31. *SS*, 3:264, 265–66.

32. Ibid., 262, 69–70.

33. Ibid., 254, 314–15, 119, 75–76.

34. Ibid., 114. See also his description of Goethe's method in 2:148.

35. Ibid., 3:211.

36. Ibid., 2:298.

37. *OS*, 3, 135.

38. A variant of the manuscript contains the following passage, omitted from the final edition: "All philosophers, with the exception of Bacon and Hume, have been priests and not people: they all . . . contemplated history and nature in the firm conviction that they alone possessed the key—that all they had to do was to express the wish, and mankind would follow the path which they indicated: they all acted like the powers that be, participated in secret rites instead of denouncing them. . . . The time has finally come for us to take stock of the extent of our power, to recognize that neither nature nor peoples (which are also a more advanced stage of nature) are in any way resistant to reason. . . . Everything obeys man to the extent to which it is understood by man" (*SS*, 6:449). The last sentence echoes the first aphorism of the *Novum Organum* (see below, n. 51). In the final version, although Herzen describes Bacon as the first sober thinker since Aristotle, he also criticizes him: "What hairsplitting, what rhetoric, what circumlocution, what sugaring of the pill the best minds like Bacon or Hegel had to resort to in order to avoid plain speaking, fearful of the indignation of fools or the catcalls of the vulgar!" (*OS*, 112, 115).

39. Bacon, 4:54.

40. *OS*, 90, 40, 31, 159, 23, 75, 24, 93–94, 76, 92.

41. Ibid., 117.

42. Ibid., 115, 109–10.

43. Ibid., 103, 104, 83.

44. See chap. 5 of this volume.

45. *OS*, 106, 159.

46. Bacon, 4:59.

47. *SS*, 11:70, 18:458, 19, 191.

48. Bacon, 4:92–93. Herzen's recollection of the aphorism is defective: he asserts that Bacon "divided scholars into *spiders and bees*." (*SS*, 16: 162).

49. *SS*, 16:163.

50. Ibid., 162.

51. Ibid., 11:247; see also *OS*, 25: "Nature and life go their ways indifferent, submitting to man only to the extent to which he has learnt to work by their very methods." Herzen probably had in mind the first aphorism of the *Novum Organum*: "Man, being the servant and interpreter of Nature, can do and understand so much and so much only as

he has observed in fact or in thought of the course of nature: beyond
this he neither knows anything nor can do anything" (Bacon, 4:47).

52. *SS*, 11:249.

53. Ibid., 248.

54. AH to A. A. Herzen, 1 December 1859. *SS*, 26:314.

55. *SS*, 20:438.

56. Ibid., 19:198, 20:345.

57. See, for example, the following articles published in *The Bell:*
"Miaso osvobozhdeniia," "Molodaia i staraia Rossiia," and "Zhurnalisty
i terroristy." *SS*, 16:25–29, 199–205, 220–26.

58. Ibid., 20:579, 577, 586.

59. Marx, *Early Writings*, 594.

60. *OS*, 147.

61. Berlin, *Russian Thinkers*, 209.

62. *SS*, 20:348.

63. Bacon, 3:406, 4:52.

64. *SS*, 14:107, 18:369, 16:160, 18:454, 16:160.

65. The Russian liberal thinker P. B. Struve saw in Herzen a precursor of his own brand of conservative liberalism. See P. Struve, "Gertsen," *Russkaia mysl'* 4 (1912): 131–39. See also V. I. Lenin, "Pamiati Gertsena," *Polnoe sobranie sochinenii*, 5th ed. (Moscow, 1967–70), 21:255–66.

66. Bacon, 4:106; *SS*, 2:60.

67. Bacon, 4:450–51.

68. *OS*, 51, 141, 121, 3.

69. Bacon, 4:94.

70. *SS*, 24:184.

CHAPTER TWO
Herzen, Schiller, and the Aesthetic Education of Man

1. There is considerable literature on this theme, in particular on
Schiller's influence on Dostoevsky. Two general surveys on the subject
are E. Kostka, *Schiller in Russian Literature* (Philadelphia, 1965); D. Čizevski, "Shiller v Rossii," *Novyi zhurnal* 45 (1956): 109–35.

2. Malia, *Herzen*, 55.

3. See Dostoevsky's remarks, quoted in G. Florovskii, "Iskaniia molo-
dogo Gertsena (II)," *Sovremennye zapiski* 40 (Paris, 1929): 342; and the
assessments by Florovsky himself (ibid., 364) and V. Zenkovskii, *Istoriia
russkoi filosofii*, vol. 1 (Paris, 1948), 278.

4. See Malia, *Herzen*, chap. 3; and "Schiller and the Early Russian
Left," *Harvard Slavic Studies* 4 (The Hague, 1957), 169–200.

5. See, for example, F. Neumann, *The Democratic and the Authoritarian State: Essays in Political and Legal Theory* (Glencoe, Ill., 1957), 271–72; D. Regin, *Freedom and Dignity: The Historical and Philosophical Thought of Schiller* (The Hague, 1965). For a survey of the changing reactions to Schiller's treatise in Germany, France, and England over the past two centuries, see the Introduction by E. Wilkinson and L. Willoughby to *AE*, cxxxiii–cxcvi. They assert that in England it was not realized that the *Letters* had political implications at all until this was pointed out by the philosopher Stuart Hampshire in articles in *The Listener* (1960) and *The New Statesman and Nation* (1962).

6. R. Miller, *Schiller and the Idea of Freedom: A Study of Schiller's Philosophical Works with Chapters on Kant* (Oxford, 1970), 67.

7. "Xenien," *Schillers Werke. Erster Band. Gedichte 1776–1779* (Weimar, 1943), 357.

8. "Ueber Anmuth und Würde," *Schillers Werke. Zwanzigster Band. Philosophische Schriften. Erster Teil* (Weimar, 1962), 286, 283.

9. See ibid., 289, 292–94. The "beautiful soul" is only an idea, "to which . . . with all his efforts, [man] can never wholly attain. The reason is the unchangeable constitution of his nature: the physical conditions of his existence themselves prevent him," On occasions when instinct, without waiting for the pronouncement of reason, seeks to draw the will along with it by the blind force of passion, man must break the violence of his desires by an act of will: "And as nature never withdraws its demands for moral reasons, it follows . . . that there is no possible accord between inclination and duty, reason and sense, so that man can not act here with the whole harmony of his nature, but exclusively with his rational nature. In such cases actions have not moral beauty, but moral grandeur." By such an act against nature, man reveals his autonomy "as a moral being, who does not merely detest and desire, but at all times must will his aversions and desires." The relation of Schiller's ethics to Kant's is still a matter of debate. See, for example, H. Reiner, *Duty and Inclination: The Fundamentals of Morality Discussed and Redefined with Special Regard to Kant and Schiller* (The Hague, 1983).

10. Schiller, "Anmuth und Würde," 286.

11. D. Regin expresses a general view in describing this essay as marking Schiller's retreat from the real world into an "ivory tower of sublimity." *Freedom and Dignity*, 193–95.

12. See Neumann, *The Democratic and the Authoritarian State*, 271; Regin, *Freedom and Dignity*, 1.

13. *AE*, 35.

14. Ibid., 51.
15. Ibid., 21, 23.
16. Ibid., 85n.
17. Ibid., 19.
18. Ibid., 91n3.
19. Ibid., 19.
20. Ibid., 189.
21. Ibid., 153.
22. Ibid., 63, 141.
23. Ibid., 9.
24. Ibid., xciv.
25. Ibid., 173.
26. See ibid., clxivff.
27. Ibid., 163.
28. An analysis of Schiller's use of the word "aesthetic" in his treatise, and his distinction between "energising" and "melting" beauty (Letters 16 and 17), is beyond the scope of this study. See, however, *AE*, clviii, on the confusion over Schiller's use of the word, in particular its identification with the doctrine of art for art's sake. Claiming that this doctrine has had a detrimental effect on the proper evaluation of Schiller's aesthetic theories, D. Regin argues cogently that "aesthetic" for Schiller "meant reconciliation, unity. It presented a synthesis suspending the polarity of the sensate and the intellectual forces in man's mind." *Freedom and Dignity*, 18.
29. Letter to C. Garve, quoted in *AE*, xviii.
30. Ibid., 7.
31. See ibid., xvff.
32. Ibid., 29, 23.
33. Regin, *Freedom and Dignity*, 140. For a postmodern view, see Paul de Man's interpretation of the *Letters* in *The Rhetoric of Romanticism* (New York, 1984), 263. See also C. Norris on debates over the postmodern trend of using aesthetic models and analogues to raise questions in sociopolitical theory: *What's Wrong with Postmodernism? Critical Theory and the Ends of Philosophy* (London, 1990), 16ff. Discussion of the *Aesthetic Education* in this context tends to be based on familiar misinterpretations of Schiller's thought.
34. *AE*, 47, 91n3.
35. Ibid., 47.
36. Malia, *Herzen*, 38.
37. *SS*, 1:13–25. See chap. 1, above.
38. AH to N. Ogaryov, 14 November 1839. *SS*, 22:53, 54, 55.

39. *SS*, 2:217.

40. Ibid., 1:278–79.

41. Ibid., 3:38.

42. Ibid., 2:93.

43. Ibid., 92.

44. Ibid., 90, 98.

45. Ibid., 60–61.

46. Ibid., 3:195–96.

47. Ibid., 2:60–64.

48. Ibid., 4:190.

49. Ibid., 5:176, 10:202, 208.

50. Ibid., 10:203, 206, 205, 198.

51. Ibid., 2:298, 114.

52. Ibid., 3:77.

53. *AE*, 89.

54. *SS*, 2:412.

55. Ibid., 3:236, 237, 144.

56. Ibid., 144–15.

57. Ibid., 146; 2:388.

58. "Bedeutende Fördernis durch ein einziges geistreiches Wort," Goethe, *Werke* (Hamburg, 1948–69), 13:37–41. Compare Schiller's concept: *darstellend denken;* see *AE*, cxivff.

59. *SS*, 3:114–15

60. Ibid., 138.

61. Ibid., 75–76, 77, 85.

62. Ibid., 68.

63. *AE*, 101.

64. *SS*, 3:86, 87.

65. *AE*, 43.

66. *SS*, 3:74–75, 87.

67. Ibid., 77. See *Schillers Briefwechsel mit Körner von 1784 bis zum Tode Schillers,* 4 vols. (Leipzig, 1859), 2:75.

68. *SS*, 86, 142.

69. Bakunin, *Sobranie sochinenii,* 3:129–30.

70. See, for example, Malia, *Herzen,* 422, and J. Zimmerman, *Midpassage: Alexander Herzen and European Revolution 1847–1852* (Pittsburgh, 1989), 228.

71. Malia, *Herzen,* 421, 423. For a discussion of the influence of Marxist historicism on scholarly interpretations of utopian socialism, see K. Steven Vincent, *Pierre-Joseph Proudhon and the Rise of French Republican Socialism* (Oxford, 1984), 121–26.

72. *OS*, 92; *SS*, 11:48; *OS*, 140, 136.

73. *SS*, 16:203.

74. *OS*, 128.

75. Ibid., 38, 141; *SS*, 19:148.

76. See D. Čizevski, *Gegel' v Rossii* (Paris, 1939), 209; and S. Bulga-kov, "Dushevnaia drama Gertsena," *Ot marksizma k idealizmu: Sbornik statei (1896–1903)* (St. Petersburg, 1903), 161–94. See also W. Wiedemaier, "Herzen and the Existential World View: A New Approach to an Old Debate," *Slavic Review* (Winter 1981): 557–69.

77. On this polemic, see *TAS*, chap. 6.

78. *SS*, 16:135–36.

79. Ibid, 11:72, 10:128.

80. Ibid., 16:137.

81. *OS*, 74; *SS*, 11:246.

82. *OS*, 35.

83. Ibid., 36.

84. Ibid., 75.

85. *SS*, 1:20.

86. Ibid., 18:364.

87. Ibid., 13:363.

89. Letter to *The Bell*, 1 December 1858.

90. *SS*, 14:317–27.

91. Ibid., 10:118.

92. See especially the fourth Letter of "Kontsy i nachala," and the articles "Robert Owen," "Pis'ma k puteshestvenniku," "Molodaia i star-aia Rossiia," "Nas uprekaiut."

93. *SS*, 19:184.

94. Ibid., 20:59–60.

95. Ibid., 10:320.

96. Ibid., 16:160.

97. Ibid., 10:320.

CHAPTER THREE
Herzen and Proudhon: Two Radical Ironists

1. Thomas Mann, *Reflections of a Non-Political Man*, trans. W. D. Morris (New York, 1983), 419.

2. R. Rorty, *Contingency, Irony and Solidarity* (Cambridge, 1989).

3. See I. Berlin, "Two Concepts of Liberty," in *Four Essays on Liberty* (Oxford and New York, 1969), 118–72.

4. Rorty, *Contingency*, 89.

5. See, for example, E. Acton, *Alexander Herzen and the Role of the Intellectual Revolutionary* (Cambridge, 1979); M. Partridge, ed., *Alexander Herzen and European Culture* (Nottingham. 1984); Zimmerman, *Midpassage*. Soviet publications include *Gertsen i zapad. Literaturnoe nasledstvo*, vol. 96 (Moscow, 1985); see the earlier volumes of *Literaturnoe nasledstvo* (7–8, 39–40, 60–62) also devoted to Herzen and his circle. See also the richly detailed commentaries in the thirty-volume Soviet edition of Herzen's works.

6. I. Berlin, "Herzen and Bakunin on Liberty," *Russian Thinkers*, 83.

7. Malia, *Herzen*; Zimmerman, *Midpassage*, 228.

8. Malia, *Herzen*, 117.

9. Vincent, *Proudhon*, 121–26.

10. See R. Labry, *Herzen et Proudhon* (Paris, 1928); M. Mervaud, "Herzen et Proudhon," *Cahiers du monde russe et soviétique* 12 (1971): 1–2, 110–88. Mervaud's study draws on correspondence among Herzen, Proudhon, and their associates (which was not available to Labry) to support his thesis that the ideological and tactical differences between them were greater than Labry believed.

11. *SS*, 24:217.

12. Labry, *Herzen et Proudhon*, 13. See Malia's discussion of the origins of Herzen's anarchism: *Herzen*, 362–64.

13. See, for example, Malia, *Herzen*, 323–24.

14. Mervaud, *Cahiers*, 135, 134, 137, 142. Mervaud's partisan approach, which relies heavily on the interpretations of Soviet scholars, has a broader polemical aim: to uphold Lenin's view of Herzen as a precursor of Russian social democracy against the view of "reactionary" critics that Herzen came to believe reform to be preferable to revolution.

15. Even a study devoted to Herzen's thought during the years of his closest association with Proudhon scarcely alludes to this material, quoting instead Mervaud's conclusions to support the view that Herzen was in no sense a disciple of Proudhon. Zimmerman, *Midpassage*, 114.

16. Ibid.

17. PJP, *Les confessions d'un révolutionnaire pour servir à l'histoire de la Révolution de février*, in *Oeuvres complètes de P.-J. Proudhon*, 15 vols. (Paris, 1923–59), 341–42 (all further references to Proudhon's works are to this edition, unless otherwise stated).

18. AH to Emma Herwegh, 27 November 1849, *SS*, 23:207.

19. *SS*, 7:298, 295. The quotation is from the opening lines of Pushkin's *Motsart i Sal'eri*: "Vse govoriat: net pravdy na zemle, / No pravdy net i vyshe."

20. *SS*, 2:388, 253, 370, 390, 273–74, 217, 394–95.

21. See, for example, Zimmerman, *Midpassage*, 140.

22. AH to N.P. Ogaryov, 11–26 February 1841. *SS*, 22:100.

23. Ibid., 2:98.

24. On Herzen's liberalism, see Berlin, "Herzen and Bakunin," 83–113.

25. *SS*, 29:148. For his view of the importance of Schiller's *Letters*, see ibid., 2:114, 298.

26. AH to N. Kh. Ketcher, 27 April 1844. *SS*, 22:183.

27. PJP to A. M. Ackermann, 25 May 1842. *Correspondence de P.-J. Proudhon*, ed. J.-A. Langlois (Paris, 1875), 2:47.

28. PJP to Marx, 17 May 1846. Ibid., 198–99.

29. PJP, *Système des contradictions économiques ou philosophie de la misère*, 1:392, 395.

30. Ibid., 2:174, 1:100, 85. PJP, *Idée générale de la révolution au dix-neuvième siècle*, 159.

31. For a summary of what he calls the philosophical nonsense of Proudhon's *Loi sérielle*, see Vincent, *Proudhon*, 84–85. On its tenuous relationship to Hegel's dialectic, see P. Haubtmann, *Proudhon, Marx et la pensée allemande* (Grenoble, 1981), 123–37.

32. PJP, *Contradictions*, 2:396, 397; *Qu'est-ce que la propriété?* 324–47.

33. *Contradictions*, 1:394, 396, 256, 368, 2:410.

34. *De la justice dans la révolution et dans l'Eglise*, 4:493; *Qu'est-ce que la propriété?* 311–12, 327.

35. On Schiller's concept of moral grace, see above, chap. 2.

36. *Qu'est-ce que la propriété?*, 342.

37. P. Haubtmann, *La philosophie sociale de P.-J. Proudhon* (Grenoble, 1980), 128. See his analysis of the *Cours d'économie* and the *Philosophie du progrès*.

38. *De la justice*, 1:423.

39. See Friedrich Engels, "Herrn Eugen Dührings Umwalzung der Wissenschaft," Karl Marx, Friedrich Engels, *Werke*, Institut für Marxismus-Leninismus beim ZK der SED (Berlin, 1962), 20:265, 262, 285.

40. *Philosophie du progrès*, 50–51. *Contradictions*, 2:397. On Proudhon's pragmatic attitude to forms of association, see Vincent, *Proudhon*, 196–200.

41. *Contradictions*, 1:86. See his summary of his argument on property in *Confessions*, 179–80.

42. *Contradictions*, 1:368; "Toast à la révolution," *Confessions*, 399.

43. *Contradictions*, 1:397. Proudhon's principal discussion of religion

is in *De la création de l'ordre dans l'humanité ou principes d'organisation politique,* and vol. 1 of *Contradictions,* prologue and final chapter.

44. Vincent points to a philosophical confusion in Proudhon's conception of God, whom he seems alternately to represent as an anthropological projection of humanity and as an ontologically distinct entity (*Proudhon,* 106). A more detailed and balanced analysis of the strengths and weaknesses of Proudhon's antitheism is to be found in Haubtmann, *Proudhon, Marx,* 138–61. Haubtmann concludes that Proudhon's antitheism was the "despairing affirmation" of a believer; Vincent argues that he ultimately resolved his religious doubts by rejecting religion.

45. Rorty, *Contingency,* 25.

46. PJP, *Contradictions,* 2:174, 409.

47. Ibid., 1:394.

48. See *SS,* 10:184, 11:398, 18:314, 23:175.

49. Ibid., 5:175–76.

50. PJP, *Confessions,* 351.

51. *SS,* 5:62; Proudhon, *De la célébration du dimanche,* 61.

52. *SS,* 19:91, 11:70, 19:184.

53. AH, draft letter to PJP, 27 August 1849. *SS,* 23:175–76.

54. PJP to AH, 15 September 1849. Mervaud, *Cahiers,* 152.

55. PJP to AH, 23 July 1855. Ibid., 172, 173.

56. Ibid.

57. AH to PJP, 24–31 July 1855. *SS,* 25:283.

58. *SS,* 20:589.

59. Ibid., 9:23.

60. Ibid., 13:172, 10:189.

61. For more discussion of this aspect of *From the Other Shore,* see my chapters "Herzen versus Schopenhauer" and "Irony and Utopia in Herzen and Dostoevsky" in *TAS.*

62. *OS,* 136, 138, 153, 120, 51–52.

63. Ibid., 31.

64. For Herzen's detailed discussion of this point, see above, 146–51.

65. *OS,* 32.

66. See Wiedemaier, "Herzen and the Existential World View," 557–69; Zimmerman, *Midpassage,*161.

67. *OS,* 132.

68. *SS,* 20:578, 593; *OS,* 33, 74.

69. *OS,* 67.

70. Quoted by D. C. Muecke, *The Compass of Irony* (London, 1969), 208.

71. *SS,* 11:246–47.

72. *OS*, 147.

73. Mann, *Reflections*, 11, 14.

74. Muecke, *Compass*, 129.

75. Rorty, *Contingency*, xvi.

76. Mann, *Reflections*, 422.

77. *SS*, 16:160.

78. Rorty, *Contingency*, 91.

79. R. Stites, *Revolutionary Dreams: Utopian Vision and Experimental Life in the Russian Revolution* (New York and Oxford, 1989), 9.

80. *SS*, 7:117.

CHAPTER FOUR
A European Nanny: Herzen and Mill on Liberty

1. On Chicherin's polemics with Herzen, see *TAS*, 224–26.

2. *SS*, 11:480.

3. See the portrayal of Herzen as a utopian in Malia, *Herzen*. For a view of Herzen as pessimist, see Wiedemaier, "Herzen and Nietzsche."

4. *SS*, 2:298. On Hampshire's assessment, see chap. 2, n. 4.

5. *SS*, 4:130.

6. JSM, *Autobiography*; ed. J. M. Robson (London, 1989), 96, 115.

7. *AE*, 53.

8. JSM, *Autobiography*, 118.

9. JSM to Thomas Carlyle, 12 January 1834. *Collected Works of John Stuart Mill*, 33 vols. (Toronto, 1963), 12:207–08. Mill warns against confounding the "two very different ideas" of contentment and happiness (an essential component of happiness being a sense of dignity), slightly changing his ground to defend moral strenuousness on the basis of utilitarianism's "Greatest Happiness Principle": "If it may possibly be doubted whether a noble character is always the happier for its nobleness, there can be no doubt that it makes other people happier, and that the world in general is immensely a gainer by it. Utilitarianism, therefore, could only attain its end by the general cultivation of nobleness of character." "Utilitarianism," *Essential Works of John Stuart Mill* (New York, 1971), 197, 199.

10. JSM, *Autobiography*, 118.

11. References to Schiller in Mill's correspondence concern only the dramas.

12. J. M. Robson, *The Improvement of Mankind: The Social and Political Thought of John Stuart Mill* (London, 1968), 129.

13. See JSM, "Utilitarianism," 221, 214ff. See also *Autobiography*, 118ff,

and his *Inaugural Address at St Andrews* (1867). Here he argues that while the two most important parts of education are the intellectual and the moral, the third part, the aesthetic, involving the education of the feelings and the cultivation of the beautiful (and primarily, of beauty of character), is also essential. Mill emphasizes the ethical value of poetry in presenting models of beautiful conduct. The man who has learned to appreciate beauty will try to realize it in his own life, "will keep before himself a type of perfect beauty in human character, to light his attempts at self-culture." He goes so far as to say that there is truth in Goethe's remark that the Beautiful is greater than the Good, for it includes the Good and adds perfection to it. Compare Schiller's distinction between moral dignity and moral grace: above, 49–51. Like Schiller, Mill holds that a person who has developed a habit of virtue should not be regarded as any less virtuous than one for whom a virtuous act is an act of self-renunciation. Again like Schiller (and Herzen) he resists the dualistic concept of the psyche implied in a rigid distinction between egoistic and altruistic acts: he argues that the curbing of inclinations for the end of promoting the general good should be seen not as the submission of the senses to norms set by reason, but as part of the process of reciprocal ordering of drives in the interests of inner harmony: "As much compression as is necessary to prevent the stronger specimens of human nature from encroaching on the rights of others, cannot be dispensed with; but for this there is ample compensation even in the point of view of human development. The means of development which the individual loses by being prevented from gratifying his inclinations to the injury of others, are chiefly obtained at the expense of the development of other people. And even to himself there is a full equivalent in the better development of the social part of his nature, rendered possible by the restraint put upon the selfish part. To be held to rigid rules of justice for the sake of others, develops the feelings and capacities which have the good of others for their object" (*On Liberty: with, The Subjection of Women, and Chapters on Socialism,* ed. Stefan Collini [Cambridge, 1989], 63).

14. JSM, "Utilitarianism," 205, 226, 219.

15. *AE,* 47.

16. JSM, *On Liberty,* 11.

17. On the early critics of *On Liberty,* see J. Rees, *John Stuart Mill's On Liberty* (Oxford, 1985), chap. 3.

18. JSM, *On Liberty,* 8, 61–62.

19. *AE,* 43.

20. JSM, *On Liberty,* 17.

21. See above, n. 13.

22. JSM, *On Liberty*, 62–63.

23. Ibid., 13.

24. See, for example, G. Himmelfarb, *On Liberty and Liberalism: The Case of John Stuart Mill* (New York, 1974), 106ff. See J. Rees's refutation of the idea that Mill assumed the existence of some private sphere in which the individual's actions would have no effect on others: *John Stuart Mill's On Liberty*, chap. 5.

25. "May it not be the fact that mankind, who after all are made up of single human beings, obtain a greater sum of happiness when each pursues his own, under the rules and conditions required by the good of the rest, than when each makes the good of the rest his only object, and allows himself no personal pleasures not indispensable to the preservation of his faculties?" ("Auguste Comte and Positivism," *Works*, 10: 337).

26. JSM, *On Liberty*, 115.

27. See above, 56–57.

28. Ibid., 16, 58, 13.

29. See JSM, *Autobiography*, 191; see also his summary of Humboldt's thesis in *On Liberty*, 58.

30. Wilhelm von Humboldt, *The Limits of State Action*, ed. by J. W. Burrow (Cambridge, 1969); Editor's Introduction, xlii.

31. J. G. Merquior, *Liberalism Old and New* (Boston, 1991), 4.

32. *AE*, 23.

33. Burrow, *Humboldt*, xlii.

34. I. Berlin, "John Stuart Mill and the Ends of Life," *Four Essays on Liberty*, 192.

35. See above, 22ff.

36. JSM, *Autobiography*, 139.

37. See ibid., 129–30: "If I am asked what system of political philosophy I substituted for that which, as a philosophy, I had abandoned, I answer, no system: only a conviction, that the true system was something much more complex and many sided than I had previously had any idea of, and that its office was to supply, not a set of model institutions, but principles from which the institutions suitable to any given circumstances might be deduced."

38. *AE*, 19.

39. JSM, *Works*, 10:270. See his comments on Comte's *Système de Politique Positive*—"The completest system of spiritual and temporal despotism, which ever yet emanated from a human brain, unless possibly that of Ignatius Loyola"—in *Autobiography*, 162–64. In the words of

J. Robson, "Comte is a scientific humanist; Mill, a humanist using science" (*Mill*, 103).

40. JSM, *Autobigraphy*, 141.

41. *SS*, 6:110; JSM, *Autobiography*, 136, 133.

42. JSM, *Autobiography*, 175. By socialism Mill meant principally the theories and experiments in cooperation (of Etienne Cabet, Charles Fourier, the Saint-Simonians and Owen) that Marx called utopian. See W. Thomas's comments on this "strange avowal," and Mill's revision of his *Principles: Mill* (Oxford, New York, 1985), 86–90. Mill goes on to explain, "While we repudiated with the greatest energy that tyranny of society over the individual which most socialistic systems are supposed to involve, we yet looked forward to a time when society will no longer be divided into the idle and the industrious; when the rule that they who do not work shall not eat, will be applied not to paupers only, but impartially to all; when the division of the produce of labour, instead of depending, as in so great a degree as it does now, on the accident of birth, will be made by concert, on an acknowledged principle of justice; and when it will no longer either be, or be thought to be, impossible for human beings to exert themselves strenuously in procuring benefits which are not to be exclusively their own, but to be shared with the society they belong to. The social problem of the future we considered to be, how to unite the greatest individual liberty of action, with a common ownership in the raw material of the globe, and an equal participation of all in the benefits of combined labour. We had not the presumption to suppose that we could already foresee by what precise form of institutions these objects could most effectually be attained, or at how near or how distant a period they would become practicable" (*Autobiography*, 175–76).

43. JSM, *On Liberty*, 57; see Robson, *Mill*, 183–84.

44. JSM, *Principles of Political Economy, Works*, 3:804.

45. JSM, *Autobiography*, 133.

46. *OS*, 114.

47. JSM, *Autobiography*, 176; "Allison's History of the French Revolution," *Works*, 20:118.

48. PJP, *Système des contradictions*, 396. There are close parallels between Proudhon's concept of liberty and those of Mill and Herzen. But whereas Herzen highly valued Proudhon's thought, Mill believed him guilty of the folly against which he warns in his *Autobiography*. He describes him as a "mischievous influence" in the aftermath of 1848; he later concluded that Proudhon had harmed the cause of progress by arousing fear in society (*Works*, 3:1027, 17:1609–10).

49. JSM, *On Liberty*, 64.

50. *SS*, 11:246, 13:363.

51. *AE*, 19.

52. Humboldt, *The Limits of State Action*, xiv.

53. JSM, *Autobiography*, 25.

54. Ibid., 124, 127.

55. Ibid., 226.

56. For a critical survey of this discussion, see Rees, *Mill*, chap. 4.

57. See ibid., 107. For a study that focuses on Mill's sense of the many-sidedness of truth, see Berlin, "Mill."

58. Berlin, "Mill," 189. Many critics have commented on Mill's confusing (and confused) mixing of absolutist and instrumentalist arguments in defense of the values of liberty and diversity; as Rees comments (*Mill*, 77), if we ask whether Mill believed in liberty as a means to progress and happiness or as a good in itself, "the answer must be that he believed both . . . for him the ideas of happiness and progress were thoroughly infused with his conception of a freely choosing human agent."

59. See Berlin's discussion of these ambiguities ("Mill," 189–90). He points to the weakness of Mill's defense in *On Liberty* of free discussion on the grounds that the truth, unless contested, would become dogma; if the truth were demonstrable, invention of false propositions would not be needed to preserve our understanding of it. Berlin suggests that it is in order to conceal the extent of his skepticism from himself that Mill uses bad arguments to support his belief that in the domain of values there are no final truths not corrigible by experience.

Another reason may be that Mill (like Darwin) was reluctant to spell out in all their clarity ideas that would be shocking to his contemporaries. See his comment in his *Autobiography* (174) that at the height of his reaction against Benthamism he was "much more indulgent to the common opinions of society and the world, and more willing to be content with seconding the superficial improvement which had begun to take place in those common opinions, than became one whose convictions, on so many points, differ fundamentally from them. I was much more inclined, than I can now approve, to put in abeyance the more decidedly heretical part of my opinions."

60. F. M. Dostoevskii, *Polnoe sobranie sochinenii*, 30 vols. (Leningrad, 1972–88), 5:116.

61. See above, 97.

62. See, for example, Robson, *Mill*, 200. He stresses that Mill is not praising eccentricity or liberty as ends in themselves, but rather as es-

sential means to the goal of discovering truth. But see Rees's refutation of this view in the form in which Maurice Cowling propounds it. He demonstrates that Mill repeatedly makes it clear that he values liberty, diversity, and originality for their own sake quite apart from their social utility *(Mill,* 125–36).

63. JSM, *Autobiography,* 189; *On Liberty,* 57, 72.

64. JSM to Gustave d'Eichthal, 8 October 1829. *Works,* 12:36.

65. SS, 6:46; JSM, *Autobiography,* 180.

66. SS, 10:187.

67. Ibid., 13:95.

68. Ibid., 6:74.

69. Ibid., 11:67, 68.

70. JSM, *Autobiography,* 174.

71. SS, 13:95.

72. Ibid., 11:68, 24:216.

73. Ibid., 11:74.

74. Ibid., 73, 69–70, 70–71.

75. Ibid., 73, 76.

76. Ibid., 18:96.

77. Ibid.

78. Ibid., 16:148.

79. Malia, *Herzen,* 358.

80. SS, 16:136.

81. Ibid., 11:227.

82. Ibid., 11:225, 231.

83. Ibid., 16:198.

CHAPTER FIVE
On the Origin of Species and From the Other Shore

1. *OS,* 39.

2. The description is V. V. Zenkovsky's: *A History of Russian Philosophy,* trans. G. Kline (London, 1953), 1:298. In common with many other critics, Zenkovsky equates this with a philosophy of despair, a "revolt against tarnished reality, . . . dictated by the last remnants of a religious consciousness which could have found peace . . . only in God" (ibid., 296).

3. S. J. Gould, *Wonderful Life,* 44.

4. J. Dewey, *The Influence of Darwin on Philosophy and Other Essays in Contemporary Thought* (New York, 1951), 2.

5. Ibid., 1.

6. Ibid., 13.

7. G. Himmelfarb, *Darwin and the Darwinian Revolution* (New York, 1968), 400.

8. CD to A. R. Wallace, 22 December 1857. *Life and Letters of Charles Darwin*, ed. Francis Darwin, 3 vols. (London, 1887), 2:109.

9. Ibid., 186.

10. Himmelfarb, *Darwin*, 283.

11. Ibid., 309.

12. CD, *On the Origin of Species* (Cambridge, Mass., 1964), 488, 489.

13. CD to C. Lyell, 11 October 1859. *Life*, 2:210. To Asa Gray, 8 May 1868. Ibid., 3:85.

14. "The Variation of Animals and Plants": quoted in ibid., 1:309.

15. CD, *Origin*, 322; see also *Life*, 84–85.

16. CD, *origin*, 314, 73.

17. CD, *The Origin of Species by Means of Natural Selection, or the Preservation of Favoured Races in the Struggle for Life*, 6th ed. (London, 1872), 163. This was one of the passages added to this expanded edition of the *Origin*.

18. CD, *Notebooks on the Transmutation of Species: Bulletin of the British Museum (Natural History), Historical Series*, vol. 2, no. 2 (London, 1960), 50.

19. CD, *The Descent of Man and Selection in Relation to Sex*, 2 vols. (London, 1871), 1:186.

20. CD to F. Müller, 2 August 1871. *Life*, 3:150.

21. CD, *Descent*, 1:92.

22. CD, *Notebooks on Transmutation*, 4:136.

23. R. M. Young, *Darwin's Metaphor: Nature's Place in Victorian Culture* (Cambridge, 1985), 97.

24. CD, *Descent*, 1:152–53.

25. *Life*, 3:237.

26. Young, *Darwin's Metaphor*, 122.

27. *OS*, 69.

28. Ibid., 75–76.

29. Ibid., 114–15.

30. Ibid., 40–41.

31. Ibid., 41.

32. CD to Asa Gray, 22 May 1860. *Life*, 2:311–12. See the commentary on this exchange by Gould, *Wonderful Life*, 290.

33. *OS*, 34.

34. Ibid., 34, 38–39, 34.

35. Ibid., 108–10, 89–90.

36. Ibid., 33–34.

37. Ibid., 37, 38, 66.

38. Ibid., 140.

39. Ibid., 106, 140.

40. Ibid., 106, 107, 67, 107.

41. Ibid., 41, 37.

42. Quoted in F. E. and F. P. Manuel, *Utopian Thought in the Western World* (Cambridge, Mass., 1979), 679.

43. *SS*, 11:213.

44. Ibid., 224.

45. Ibid., 220–21.

46. Ibid., 221.

47. Himmelfarb, *Darwin*, 356.

48. *SS*, 11:218–19.

49. Ibid., 226, 227–28.

50. *OS*, 31.

51. *SS*, 11:231.

52. Ibid., 232.

53. AH to A. A. Herzen, 20 April 1860; 26 March 1869. *SS*, 27:41, 30:77.

54. *SS*, 14:283, 17:30.

55. Ibid., 11:224.

56. C. Lyell, *Principles of Geology*, 2 vols. (London, 1867–68), 1:492.

57. *SS*, 11:218.

58. Ibid., 245–46.

59. Himmelfarb, *Darwin*, 356.

60. *SS*, 19:131.

61. See Himmelfarb, *Darwin*, 388ff.

62. *OS*, 58, 50.

63. Gould, *Wonderful Life*, 258.

64. CD, *Life*, 1:313–14, 2:353, 1:309.

65. CD to Asa Gray, 22 May 1860. *Life*, 2:312.

66. *SS*, 11:246–47.

67. Ibid., 247.

68. *OS*, 67.

69. *SS*, 11:249.

70. Ibid., 250.

71. Ibid., 252, 253.

72. Ibid., 248, 252, 253.

73. AH to A. A. Herzen, 17–19 April 1869. *SS*, 30:87.

74. AH to I. S. Turgenev, 19 December 1860. *SS*, 27:122.

75. AH to A. A. Herzen, 1 December 1859. *SS*, 26:314.

76. *SS*, 1:22.

77. AH to N. P. Ogaryov, 22 February 1867. *SS*, 29:42.

78. *SS*, 18:281. AH to Ogaryov, 3 February 1867. *SS*, 29:26.

79. *SS*, 20:434–38.

80. AH to Ogaryov, 13 February 1867. *SS*, 29:33.

81. *SS*, 20:437–38.

82. Dewey, *The Influence of Darwin*, 13.

83. CD, *Life*, 2:378. See his description of the gradual weakening of his religious beliefs: ibid., 1:307–13.

84. Ibid., 1:308, 307, 2:304, 1:13.

85. Ibid., 1:307.

86. Ibid., 311.

87. *OS*, 147.

88. Gould, *Wonderful Life*, 50–51, 84.

89. Himmelfarb, *Darwin*, 380 ff.

90. Gould, *Wonderful Life*, 277ff.

91. T. Kuhn, *The Structure of Scientific Revolutions* (Chicago, 1962), 170.

92. CD, *Life*, 3:241.

93. *OS*, 140; *SS*, 13:363 (Chicherin criticized the phrase in a letter to the *Bell* of 1 December 1858). See Wiedemaier, "Herzen and Nietzsche," 177–88.

94. *OS*, 103.

CHAPTER SIX
"Dealing in Pluses": The Thought of Anton Chekhov

1. See *ACL*, 12.

2. Ibid., 109.

3. Ibid., 261.

4. Ibid., 218.

5. Ibid., 165.

6. Ibid., 107.

7. K. Korovin, "My Encounters with Chekhov," *Triquarterly* 28 (Fall 1973): 562.

8. *ACL*, 261. In 1888 Chekhov refused an invitation to join a movement to promote solidarity among young writers, predicting that such a trend would inevitably lead to "spying, suspiciousness and controls" (a prophecy realized when the Soviet Writers' Union voted unanimously to expel Akhmatova, Pasternak, and Solzhenitsyn): "Solidarity and the like

I can understand on the stock exchange, in politics, in religious affairs (sects), etc., but solidarity among young writers is impossible and unnecessary. We can't all think and feel in the same way. We have different goals or no goals at all; we know one another slightly or not at all. As a result there's nothing to which solidarity can firmly attach itself. And is it necessary? No. To help a colleague, to respect his person and his work, to refrain from gossiping about him and envying him, lying to him and acting hypocritical toward him, all this requires that one be not so much a young writer as simply a human being. Let us be ordinary people, let us treat everyone alike and there won't be any need for artificially blown-up solidarity" (*ACL*, 99).

9. Ibid., 250. Chekhov loathed the crudely aggressive style in which literary polemics had been conducted in Russia since the 1860s, observing that the writing of the radical critic Dmitry Pisarev "reeks of the malicious, captious public prosecutor" (ibid., 220).

10. Ibid., 176.

11. Ibid., 390, 341.

12. Ibid., 265.

13. Ibid., 378.

14. R. Gilman, *Chekhov's Plays: An Opening into Eternity* (New Haven, 1995). See Ferguson's essay in R. L. Jackson, ed., *Chekhov: A Collection of Critical Essays* (Englewood Cliffs, N.J., 1967), 147–60. (Originally untitled: reprinted from *The Idea of a Writer* [Princeton, 1949], 161–77.)

15. Gilman, *Chekhov's Plays*, 146, 194.

16. AC, *Tri sestry*, act 3.

17. Gilman, *Chekhov's Plays*, 63.

18. AC, *Vishnyovyi sad*, act 3.

19. "On the town with Rex Reed," *New York Observer*, 17 March 1997, 37.

20. Reminiscence of the director E. P. Karpov. *Chekhov i teatr. Pis'ma, fel'etony. Sovremenniki o Chekhove-dramaturge* (Moscow, 1961), 373.

21. Cited by Gilman, *Chekhov's Plays*, 203.

22. D. Rayfield, *Anton Chekhov: A Life* (London, 1997), xv.

23. *ACL*, 112.

24. L. Tolstoy to L. L. Tolstoy, 4 September 1895. *Polnoe sobranie sochinenii*, 90 vols. (Moscow, 1935–64), 68–69:158. In this letter to his son, he records an otherwise positive impression of Chekhov, whom he had recently met for the first time: "I liked him. He's very gifted, and he seems to be kind-hearted."

25. Karlinsky's introduction together with his extensive notes and

commentaries provides more insight into Chekhov's views than any existing biography.

26. *ACL,* 150, 117.

27. Ibid., 156.

28. AC, *Letters on the Short Story, the Drama, and other Literary Topics,* ed. L. Friedland (London, 1965), 293.

29. *ACL,* 121, 104, 226.

30. AC to A. N. Pleshcheev, 9 April 1889. AC, *Polnoe sobranie sochinenii i pisem,* 30 vols. (Moscow, 1974–83), *Pis'ma,* 3:186.

31. AC to A. S. Suvorin, 30 November 1891. Ibid., 4:307–08.

32. *ACL,* 145–46.

33. AC, draft of a letter to D. V. Grigorovich, 12 February 1887. *Polnoe sobranie [Pis'ma],* 2:360.

34. *ACL,* 226–27, 203, 139.

35. Ibid., 139, 159.

36. AC, *Diadia Vania,* act 1.

37. AC, "Step'," *Polnoe sobranie (Sochineniia),* 13:56.

38. Ibid., 46.

39. *ACL,* 92. Chekhov was unhappy with the work, however, feeling that he had produced something "rather odd and much too original . . . an encyclopedia of the steppe" (ibid., 91–92).

40. *OS,* 33, 39. As noted in chap. 1 above, one of Herzen's mouthpieces in this work is a doctor who recommends the natural sciences as a means of preparing the mind for the study of history and society: "A doctor lives in nature, in the world of facts and phenomena—he doesn't teach, he learns: he seeks not revenge, but the alleviation of pain. When he sees suffering, when he sees defects, he looks for the reason, for the causal connection; then he looks for remedies within this same world of facts. If there are none, he shrugs his shoulders sadly, is distressed by his ignorance, and doesn't think of punishment or retribution and he doesn't condemn" (ibid., 102–03).

41. *ACL,* 50–51. Nikolai Chekhov, a talented musician and artist, studied at the Moscow School of Painting, Sculpture, and Architecture, but he never completed his studies owing to alcoholism and what Karlinsky describes as "a fatal attraction for the Moscow equivalent of skid row" (*ACL,* 52); he died at thirty-one of tuberculosis aggravated by alcoholism.

42. Korovin, "My Encounters with Chekhov," 562; Chekhov, "Rasskaz neizvestnogo cheloveka," *Polnoe sobranie (Sochineniia),* 14:271.

43. AC to A. S. Suvorin, 30 August 1891. *Polnoe sobranie (Pis'ma),* 4:267; *ACL,* 62.

44. *ACL*, 66.

45. AC to L. S. Mizinova, 27 March 1894. *Polnoe sobranie (Pis'ma)*, 5: 281; cited by Gilman, *Chekhov's Plays*, 137.

46. *ACL*, 191–92.

47. AC, "Rasskaz neizvestnogo cheloveka," *Polnoe sobranie (Sochineniia)*, 14:183.

48. Ibid., 168.

49. AC, "Tri goda," ibid., 9:75–76.

50. AC to L. S. Mizinova, 21 September 1898. *Polnoe sobranie (Pis'ma)*, 7:274.

51. *ACL*, 474.

52. Ibid., 475.

53. L. Shestov, *Chekhov and Other Essays*, ed. S. Monas (Ann Arbor, 1966), 4–5.

54. AC to Suvorin, 25 February 1895. *Polnoe Sobranie (Pis'ma)*, 6:29.

55. F. Nietzsche, *Gesammelte Werke* (Munich, 1920–29), 16:9. On reading Chekhov's story "The Lady with the Dog," Tolstoy commented in his diary, "This all comes from Nietzsche. People who have not formed a clear cut world view that distinguishes good from evil." L. N. Tolstoi, *Sobranie sochinenii*, 30 vols. (Moscow, 1960–65), 20:124.

56. *ACL*, 61.

57. AC, "Tri goda," 80.

58. *ACL*, 368.

59. Ibid., 80–81.

60. V. Feider, *A. P. Chekhov, Literaturnyi byt i tvorchestvo po memuarnym materialam* (Leningrad, 1928), 160.

61. AC, "Ionich," *Polnoe sobranie (Sochineniia)*, 10:40.

62. AC, "Step'," 64. The ancient servant Firs in *The Cherry Orchard* speaks of the happy times before the "great disaster" (the liberation of the serfs in 1861), when masters and servants all knew their place: "Now you can't make head or tail of anything" (act 2). Chekhov's own view of the relation of the Russian present to the recent past is expressed in a letter of 1899 to the writer I. L. Leontiev (Shcheglov): "It has always seemed to me that you are unfair in your treatment of contemporary life . . . I'm far from being enthusiastic about modern times, but one must be objective. . . . If the present is unpleasant, the past was simply abominable." *Polnoe sobranie (Pis'ma)*, 8:32.

63. AC, *Chaika*, act 4.

64. *ACL*, 122.

65. AC," Rasskaz neizvestnogo cheloveka," 191, 213.

CHAPTER SEVEN
The Flesh of Time: Mikhail Bakhtin

1. C. Emerson, *The First Hundred Years of Mikhail Bakhtin* (Princeton, 1997). As will become evident, this chapter is greatly indebted to Emerson's book.

2. V. L. Makhlin, "Nasledie M. M. Bakhtina v kontekste zapadnogo postmodernizma," eds. L. A. Gogotishvili and P. S. Gurevich, *M. M. Bakhtin kak filosof* (Moscow, 1992), 209–10.

3. G. S. Morson and C. Emerson, *Mikhail Bakhtin: Creation of a Prosaics* (Stanford, 1990), 23–32.

4. MB, *Problemy poetiki Dostoevskogo* (Moscow, 1979), 314.

5. Like earlier Russian moralists Bakhtin is an object of reverence among many Russian intellectuals as an ethical mentor: Georgii Gachev, one of the group who discovered him in the 1960s, relates that he became for them "something like a living church." Emerson, *Bakhtin*, 50.

6. MB, *The Dialogic Imagination*, ed. M. Holquist, trans. C. Emerson and M. Holquist (Austin, 1981), 354, 293, 357, 410; MB, *Problemy*, 193.

7. MB, *Problemy*, 126, 141.

8. Ibid., 141, 193, 195.

9. For a survey of criticism on these themes, see Emerson, *Bakhtin*, chaps. 3, 4. She notes that at the Bakhtin Centennial Conference nobody, neither Russians nor non-Russians, devoted a paper to Bakhtin on Dostoevsky (134).

10. See ibid., 94–96.

11. See Terry Eagleton's interpretation of Bakhtinian carnival as "a political weapon against ruling-class idealism's paranoid fear of the flesh" ("Bakhtin, Schopenhauer, Kundera," eds. K. Hirschkop and D. Shepherd, *Bakhtin and Cultural Theory* [Manchester, 1989], 180); and see Holquist's view that Bakhtin introduces a "kink" into traditional Marxist categories which has the potential for renewing socialist thought. Holquist argues that such critics as Eagleton and Fredric Jameson have demonstrated convincingly that Bakhtin "can serve as an armoury of conceptual weapons that will advance the cause of Leftist social analysis" (R. Barsky and M. Holquist, eds., *Bakhtin and Otherness: Discours social/Social Discourse*, vol. 3, nos. 1–2 [1990]). In contrast, the Soviet scholar Viktor Shklovsky accused Bakhtin in 1970 of not defining the political targets of carnival laughter sufficiently precisely. See Emerson, *Bakhtin*, 104–05.

12. MB, *Rabelais and His World*, trans. H. Iswolsky (Cambridge, Mass., 1968), 94.

13. MB, *Problemy*, 155, 184, 168–69.

14. Cited by J. Frank, "Lunacharsky was impressed," *London Review of Books*, 19 February 1998, 20.

15. Caryl Emerson argues that carnival for Bakhtin "is simply a name given to that moment of enablement—inevitably transitory—during which the self feels itself to be an agent in the world, that moment when a human being no longer feels helpless, nor prays, nor begs" (*Bakhtin*, 103).

16. From the stenographic transcription of Bakhtin's dissertation defense (cited in ibid., 95).

17. See the discussion of such parallels in V. Liapunov's notes to MB, *Toward a Philosophy of the Act*, trans. and annotated by V. Liapunov, ed. M. Holquist and V. Liapunov (Austin, 1993).

18. Herzen's name occurs very rarely in the context of discussions of Bakhtin. Two exceptions are Morson and Emerson, who mention Herzen as a representative of the tradition of Russian anti-ideological thinkers to which they believe Bakhtin belongs (*Mikhail Bakhtin*, 23); and K. G. Isupov, who points to (but does not discuss) a resemblance between Bakhtin's and Herzen's approaches to ethics as moral creativity. "Ot estetiki zhizni k estetike istorii (Traditsii russkoi filosofii u M. M. Bakhtina)," *M. M. Bakhtin kak filosof*, 70.

19. MB, *Rabelais*, 59; *SS*, 13:190.

20. *SS*, 5:89.

21. MB, *Problemy*, 191.

22. See above, chap. 2.

23. MB, *Problemy*, 191; *Rabelais*, 95, 122–23.

24. MB, *Rabelais*, 94.

25. MB, *Philosophy of the Act*, 50–51.

26. M. Holquist, ed., *The Dialogic Imagination: Four Essays by M. M. Bakhtin*, trans. C. Emerson and M. Holquist (Austin, 1981), 85.

27. MB, *Philosophy of the Act*, 6, 40, 41, 52.

28. *SS*, 11:248, 252.

29. MB, *Philosophy of the Act*, 27, 37; *Speech Genres and Other Late Essays*, trans. V. McGee, ed. C. Emerson and M. Holquist (Austin, 1986), 139.

30. MB, *Philosophy of the Act*, 19.

31. Ibid., 20, 53, 30–31.

32. Ibid., 31.

33. *OS*, 38, 24.

34. MB, *Art and Answerability: Early Philosophical Essays*, ed. M. Holquist and V. Liapunov, trans. and annotated by V. Liapunov (Austin, 1990), 2.

35. MB, *Philosophy of the Act,* 54.

36. K. Clark, M. Holquist, *Mikhail Bakhtin* (Cambridge, Mass., 1984), 64.

37. See Morson's and Emerson's discussion of the significance of this concept in Bakhtin's theory of the novel form (*Mikhail Bakhtin,* chap. 8), and their own use of the term "prosaics" to characterize Bakhtin's thought (ibid., 15–36).

38. MB, *The Dialogic Imagination,* 331, 250, 84.

39. See Clark and Holquist, *Bakhtin,* 66–67.

40. MB, *The Dialogic Imagination,* 327.

41. Ibid., 84.

42. MB, *Speech Genres,* 28.

43. Cited in Emerson, *Bakhtin,* 96.

44. *SS,* 19:191.

45. MB, *The Dialogic Imagination,* 37.

46. MB, *Art and Answerability,* 22–27; *Speech Genres,* 141.

47. MB, *Art and Answerability,* 87.

48. Ibid., 88, 103.

49. MB, *Speech Genres,* 7.

50. MB, *Rabelais,* 472.

51. Morson and Emerson, *Bakhtin,* 470. The authors observe that "Bakhtin presumes no absolute conflict between an organism and its surroundings, just as he presumes no conflict in principle between self and society" (ibid.).

52. T. Todorov, "I, Thou, Russia," *Times Literary Supplement,* 13 March 1998, 7.

53. See Emerson, *Bakhtin,* 169–71.

54. Ibid., 71.

55. See ibid., 276n13.

56. The texts in question—P. Medvedev's *The Formal Method in Literary Scholarship,* V. Voloshinov's *Freudianism: A Critical Sketch,* and *Marxism and the Philosophy of Language* (a work on semiotics), as well as a number of articles by Voloshinov and Medvedev—are all avowedly Marxist and at odds with Bakhtin's fundamental oppositon to "theoretism." On the controversy over their authorship and the reasons for the practice of attributing these works to Bakhtin, see Morson and Emerson, *Bakhtin,* 100–19. In my view their analysis demonstrates conclusively that Bakhtin was not the author of the disputed works.

57. See G. Gachev's view, based on acquaintance with Bakhtin in the 1960s: "In Bakhtin's understanding of sobornost . . . everyone gazes not upward, toward heaven, nor forward, at the priest or the altar, but at

one another, realizing the kenosis of God, on the low horizontal level that is our own." Emerson, *Bakhtin*, 158–59. On religious interpretations of his concept of carnival, see ibid., 172–79. See also Emerson, "Russian Orthodoxy and the Early Bakhtin," *Religion and Literature* 22, no. 2–3 (1990): 109–31. She describes Bakhtin's religion as "a very uncertain entity" (113).

58. MB, *Art and Answerability*, 128. Bakhtin defines faith as "need and hope . . . non-self-contentment and . . . possibility" (ibid, 144).

59. G. L. Tul'chinskii, "Dvazhdy 'otstavshii' M. Bakhtin: postupochnost' i inoratsional'nost' bytiia," *M. M. Bakhtin i filosofskaia kul'tura XX veka. Problemy bakhtinologii*, part 1 (St. Petersburg, 1991), 59.

60. Cited by Emerson, *Bakhtin*, 112.

61. MB, *Speech Genres*, 160. See Emerson's Afterword on the prospects for Bakhtin's "inonauka": *Bakhtin*, 264ff.

62. *SS*, 14:107.

63. F. Nietzsche, *Werke in Drei Bänden*, ed. K. Schlechta (Munich, 1954–56), 1:9.

64. *SS*, 20:345, 16:27.

65. MB, *Philosophy of the Act*, 64.

66. MB, *Speech Genres*, 155 (from notes made in 1970–71).

67. MB, *Art and Answerability*, 2.

68. Ibid., 1.

69. AC to A. S. Suvorin, 27 December 1889. *Polnoe sobranie (Pis'ma)*, 3:309.

CONCLUSION:
A New-Style Russian Idea

1. See, for example, the summaries of the proceedings of the 1993 conference on Russian philosophy and of the round table on the "Russian mentality," in *VF*, 1994, no. 1:25–52, 54–71.

2. N. A. Kosolapov, "Integrativnaia ideologiia dlia Rossii: intellektual'nyi i politicheskii vyzov," *VF*, 1994, no. 1:24.

3. A. A. Ermilov, "O mnimoi oshibke russkoi filosofii," *Veche. Al'manakh russkoi filosofii i kul'tury*. No. 4, 1995:184–85.

4. See S. Khoruzhii, cited in round table on Russian mentality, *VF*, 1994, no. 1:44.

5. G. L. Tul'chinskii, "Rossiiskii potentsial svobody," *VF*, 1997, no. 3: 16–30.

6. V. I. Mil'don, "Russkaia ideia v kontse XX-ogo veka," *VF*, 1996, no. 3:53.

7. Round Table on Russian Mentality, 51.

8. A. P. Ogurtsov, ibid., 52.

9. V. F. Ovchinnikov, "O poniatii istoricheskogo tipa filosofii," *VF*, 1996, no. 10:173–75.

10. A. F. Zotov, "Sushchestvuet li mirovaia filosofiia?" *VF*, 1997, no. 4:21–30.

11. G. L. Tul'chinskii, "Ob odnoi oshibke russkoi filosofii," *VF*, 1995, no. 3:83.

12. A. Walicki, "Po povodu 'russkoi idei' v russkoi filosofii," 71.

13. G. L. Tul'chinskii, "Rossiiskii potentsial svobody," 23.

14. Mil'don, "Russkaia ideia," 55.

15. Tul'chinskii, "Rossiiskii potentsial svobody," 27.

16. J. Frank, "Lunacharsky was impressed," *London Review of Books*, 19 February 1998, 20.

17. C. Emerson cites the observations of Russian participants in the Moscow Centennial Conference that the primary divide between Bakhtin scholars had ceased to be "Russia versus the West." An intellectual spectrum stretching from traditional philology to postmodernist approaches could be found in both. *Bakhtin*, 27–28.

18. The first two of Isaiah Berlin's essays on Herzen appeared in 1955 and 1956 (see the bibliographical note in Berlin, *Russian Thinkers*, ix–x). Simon Karlinsky (whose edition of Chekhov's letters was published in 1973) describes teaching courses on Chekhov at American universities in the second half of the 1960s as a particularly rewarding experience "because during those years the intellectual life of the Western world was gradually catching up with many of Chekhov's insights and preoccupations which his contemporaries had chosen to overlook." *ACL*, 28.

19. E. Zamiatin, "Chekhov," *Sochineniia*, 4 vols. (Munich, 1970–88), 4:156.

20. Berlin, *Russian Thinkers*, 83.

21. *SS*, 12:112.

22. Ibid., 7:326.

Index

Смотреть на конец, а не на самое
дело—величайшая ошибка.

[To look at the end, and not at the action itself, is the greatest of
errors.]
—A. I. Herzen